Equality and Freedom in Education

Equality and Freedom in Education

A Comparative Study

Edited by BRIAN HOLMES

Professor of Comparative Education,
University of London Institute of Education

London
GEORGE ALLEN & UNWIN
Boston   Sydney

George Allen & Unwin (Publishers) Ltd,
40 Museum Street, London WC1A 1LU, UK

George Allen & Unwin (Publishers) Ltd,
Park Lane, Hemel Hempstead, Herts HP2 4TE, UK

Allen & Unwin, Inc.,
Fifty Cross Street, Winchester, Mass 01890, USA

George Allen & Unwin Australia Pty Ltd,
8 Napier Street, North Sydney, NSW 2060, Australia

First published in 1985
Second impression 1987

British Library Cataloguing in Publication Data

   Equality and freedom in education.——
1. Educational equalization
I. Holmes, Brian
370.19'5   LC213
ISBN 0-04-370137-X
ISBN 0-04-370153-1 Pbk

Library of Congress Cataloging in Publication Data
Main entry under title:
   Equality and freedom in education.
Includes bibliographies and index.
Contents: Introduction – Education in England and
Wales / Crispin Jones – Education in France / Martin
McLean – [etc.]
1. Education and state – Addresses, essays, lectures.
2. Educational equalization – Addresses, essays, lectures.
3. Comparative education – Addresses, essays, lectures.
I. Holmes, Brian. II. Title. III. Series.
LC75.E68 1984   370   84-6431
ISBN 0-04-370137-X (alk. paper)
ISBN 0-04-370153-1 (pbk.: alk. paper)

Set in 10 on 11 point Plantin by Columns of Reading
and printed in Great Britain by Billing and Sons Ltd, Worcester

Contents

Preface

This volume has been loosely organized round the problems associated with the equalization of opportunity, access, provision and outcomes in education and the retention of what many of us believe to be a basic right – namely, the right of parents to educate their children in accordance with their wishes.

The dilemma finds somewhat different expression in each of the national systems described in this volume – England and Wales, France, the USA, the USSR, China and Japan. Each author has consequently approached the theme for his or her own perspective and in the light of events which have shaped the evolution of school systems since 1945 in these countries. To systematize the information the taxonomy adopted by the International Bureau of Education in Geneva has been used in each chapter.

Each author writes on the basis of an expert knowledge of the system concerned. All of them are members of the Department of Comparative Education in the University of London Institute of Education. The majority of them are members of staff – Professor Holmes, Mr Jones, Dr McLean, Dr Turner and Mr Tomiak. Pauline Chan was, at the time of writing, a doctoral student researching aspects of education in the People's Republic of China.

The intention is to provide a readable, authoritative account of education in some major countries for interested lay people and students of comparative education.

BRIAN HOLMES

Introduction
Equality and Freedom in Education

BRIAN HOLMES

The surrender of Germany and Japan in 1945 heralded a new era in the evolution of education. The victory of the allies raised aspirations throughout the world and immediately after the war emphasis was placed on the provision of education as a basic human right. Indeed, through the work of the Committee of Allied Ministries of Education in Britain, chaired by R. A. Butler, European governments in exile were preparing the ground for new initiatives in education. Some of these were already in train before the Second World War had ended. In England and Wales the 1944 Education Act was based on the belief that the three stages of education, primary, secondary and further, should be open to all regardless of the ability of parents to pay. A committee of French educationists in Algiers formulated proposals to extend secondary education to all. In the USA returning GIs initiated a boom in university enrolments. Policy in the USSR had been geared, virtually from the Revolution, to equalizing access to schools but postwar hopes were delayed by massive war losses.

The hopes entertained by individual spokespersons to equalize opportunities and accepted by national governments found expression in international declarations, notably the United Nations Declaration of Universal Rights. Along with the right of free speech and the right to work, the Declaration included the right of every child to primary education and the right of those who could benefit to attend secondary schools and institutions of higher education. The restriction placed on access to secondary and higher education reflected views advanced at the end of the eighteenth century by French and American revolutionary leaders. Indeed, while in the Declaration of Independence the Americans claimed that all men are created equal, so giving prominence to the notion of social and political equality, the slogan of the French revolutionaries – 'Liberté, égalité, fraternité' – also made liberty an inalienable right.

1

In this volume the difficulties of increasing equality of access, provision, and indeed outcomes in education, while retaining the freedom of individual parents to have their children educated in accordance with their wishes, are examined in national educational systems which have received worldwide attention in their own right and have influenced the evolution of schooling throughout the world. Traditional Chinese practices were copied particularly during the nineteenth century by Europeans; and English, French, American and Soviet models have been copied by many newly independent nations since 1945.

In the post-1945 world each national government, and the educationists who debate and help to formulate policy, faced the dilemma in the light of national traditions and political climates. Nineteenth-century European national systems of education were elitist. They were legitimized by political, psychological and epistemological theories derived from Plato's *Republic*. For Plato most individuals inherited the qualities of their parents. They were consequently innately unequal and should fit into niches appropriate to their skills. Some, the philosopher kings, were capable of acquiring knowledge of permanent ideas which would ensure that they would be wise and rule justly by preventing degenerating change. Other members of society would have their appointed role to play as auxiliaries and craftsmen in a stable society.

Translated into European educational policies and practice Plato's views justified a liberal education for the potential leaders in appropriate subjects, for example, mathematics, music and the classical languages. For the rest, training which would enable individuals to fit efficiently into their occupational niche was all that was necessary. This frankly elitist system, perpetuated by selective secondary schools, small universities and vocational schools, survived with few modifications in most Western European countries until the end of the Second World War in spite of some radical innovations proposed by the French encyclopaedists.

In Plato's scheme, only a few individuals had the innate potential to benefit from a generous liberal education but Condorcet and Jefferson followed Pericles in accepting that all men possessed a measure of civic virtue or reason which if exploited through education would make it possible for all citizens to judge policies, although ony a few members of a democracy could formulate them. Thus throughout the nineteenth century and well into the twentieth century the education of the masses had a limited but important role to play. Equality before the law and equal political rights were fought for and won in most Western nations sooner and more successfully than the fight to overthrow belief in psychological inequalities which persists even today. Present debate turns on whether or not intelligence is determined at birth and to what extent it is a product of the environment.

Changes in US educational theories took place earlier than in Europe in spite of the fact that the negro slaves were not emancipated until after the Civil War and negro suffrage was legalized only during the period 1866–71. Women had to fight for their rights too. By 1918 they had been granted votes in some fifteen states and when the Nineteenth Amendment to the Constitution was ratified in 1920 by thirty-six states universal women's suffrage became the law of the land.

During the nineteenth century, however, for white males and increasingly white females greater equality of access to education paralleled but was ahead of trends in Europe. Common elementary schools, pioneered by Horace Mann in the 1840s, were set up throughout the country. Later high school enrolments shot up exponentially so that, in contrast to the Western European elite schools, by 1939 the high schools of America were for everyone and equality of access to high schools had been achieved in comprehensive neighbourhood schools. In theory the separate schools for blacks were equally good – in practice they were very inferior. Other inequalities remained. Facilities in the high schools for white youngsters depended on the economic circumstances of the communities who financed the schools. In short, inequality of high school provision was related to race and, as elsewhere, socio-economic position.

Inevitably, in comprehensive schools, relationships between the achievement of individual pupils and the socio-economic position of their parents were discovered. During the thirties a number of sociologists in the USA investigated these relationships and concluded that achievement, as measured by intelligence and other objective tests of attainment, was greatly influenced by social class. This proposition further undermined the traditional European justification for selective academic secondary schools and elitist universities on the basis of innate ability.

Psychological testing nevertheless became the vogue in the USA. Intelligence and objective attainment tests were standardized to ensure that on the basis of national samples around 25 per cent of those tested were categorized as above average, some 50 per cent were average and about 25 per cent were below average in their attainments. The testing movement and the use made of test results have ensured that while equality of opportunity has been realized in America to a considerable extent inequality of outcomes is expected and reinforced.

Soviet educationists and politicians also gave importance to equality of access to schools. After the 1917 Revolution Soviet leaders set out to remedy the failure of the Tsarist system to provide education for more than a tiny minority of the population. The Tsarist system was similar to, but less developed than, those in Western Europe. Indeed its founders Peter the Great and Catherine took over ideas from England and France. During the nineteenth century K. Ushinsky made comparative studies of European systems with the intention of improving the Russian schools. In the event the revolutionaries inherited in 1917 a Western European elitist system of education in which Russian was the medium of instruction despite the multiplicity of mother tongues spoken throughout the Russian Empire. Inequality of access to school was starkly apparent to the leaders of the USSR and throughout the period of Soviet reconstruction equality in education regardless of social position, mother tongue and place of residence has been an aim. Differential attainment has been regarded as due more to physiological and environmental influences than to innate ability. Soviet pedagogues, eschewing psychological testing to classify pupils for admission to elitist schools, have worked to eliminate illiteracy and to universalize primary, secondary and higher education.

Thus, informed by different ideological perspectives, American and Soviet educational policies had, prior to 1940, emphasized equality of access to schools. In practice the Americans had universalized high school education. In the Soviet Union for most children primary education lasted no more than four years, and the provision of general secondary and higher education was less extensive than in many Western European countries. Vocational training schools had, however, been developed along the lines of those found in Germany, the Netherlands and indeed several Western European nations.

China and Japan have a long history of elitist education. The mandarin system in China was designed to ensure that children of humble origin could be selected for training as scholar-officials in the imperial bureaucracy. Scholarship, largely confined to textual analyses of Confucian classics, was a prerequisite for appointment as an official. Knowledge, however restricted in scope, was prized for its practical administrative value. Influenced by Europe and America, the elitist system was not abandoned until the Communists came to power in 1949. Since then, against the resistance of traditional scholars and academics, claims to equalize access and provision have been pursued with vigour. Resistance by academics to policies proposed by the Chinese Communist Party and economic conditions have inhibited the realization of equality of opportunity.

In contrast, by 1940 Japan had equalized opportunity to a great extent. During the nineteenth century European influences had been resisted until the Meiji Restoration in 1868. Thereafter attempts had been made to modernize the country along Western lines. Modern industries were successfully established. Liberal democratic institutions were introduced but failed to take firm root. There was widespread resistance to proposed changes in the customs and habitual dress of the Japanese people. Formal institutions of education along European and North American lines were, however, introduced and developed extremely rapidly so that by 1940 Japan was one of the most literate countries in the world and possessed a system of education which compared favourably with those in Europe. Inequality in education was legitimized by a class system in which the *Samurai* performed leadership roles and were educated to do so. Merchants, and farmers, were members of less powerful and less well educated social classes.

Thus during the nineteenth century the growth of education was based on the view that, while all citizens should enjoy the same legal and political rights, not all of them were equally capable of benefiting from a truly liberal education. In practice inequalities of access were associated with social class, ethnic origin, sex and rural/urban differences. For example, it is difficult to ensure that children living in isolated rural areas have the same opportunities to attend school as their urban or small-town peers. It was, and is, easier to set up selective secondary schools and institutions of higher education in densely populated areas than to provide comprehensive facilities for children living in the rural areas. Boarding schools in France, the USSR and elsewhere have offered a partial solution, particularly at the second level of education.

Against governmental attempts to universalize primary education and to establish non-selective secondary schools should be weighed parental claims that their children should be educated in accordance with their wishes. In particular some parents, wanting schools to inculcate a particular set of religious beliefs, come into conflict with secular governments. To resolve this conflict national policies have differed. In general, a distinction has been drawn between the freedom individuals should enjoy to worship as they think fit and reluctance to provide public support for religious institutions. So fearful were the founders of the American Republic that church leaders would continue to dominate the political life of communities that they agreed in the First Amendment to the Constitution that freedom of conscience should be protected but institutionalized religion should not be promoted. A succession of supreme court decisions in the USA have effectively denied federal and state funds to Catholic schools. A somewhat similar formula informed French policies until reforms passed under the de Gaulle regime made it possible for the Catholic authorities to receive, under contract, public money to equip and staff their schools adequately.

Consequently in the parochial schools in the USA (and until fairly recently in the Catholic schools in France) facilities are frequently inferior to those in publicly maintained schools. Teacher salaries, and qualifications, are lower. Teachers of subjects like mathematics, physics and chemistry, who may command high salaries elsewhere, are in short supply. Church authorities cannot always replace old school buildings, provide good libraries, or equip their schools adequately. Consequently in retaining their right to choose for their children a particular kind of education Catholic parents (in particular) often pay a heavy price to achieve equality of provision, or have to be satisfied with less satisfactory facilities. In general, their freedom has been at the expense of equal educational provision.

In communist countries schools run by religious bodies are not permitted. The constitution of the USSR allows freedom of conscience but the authorities prohibit private schools. In Communist China the same policy is in operation. In these countries private parochial schools are not allowed to operate on the grounds that they would constitute a threat to the preparation of a 'new communist man'. There is no doubt that in pursuing this policy the communist authorities deny, to some groups of people at least, a freedom which they would like to enjoy and exercise.

In England and Wales a formula has been worked out which allows the Christian churches and the Jewish authorities to receive the costs of running their schools from public funds as well as a substantial proportion of their capital costs. As a result the voluntary schools in England and Wales match, in terms of staffing and equipment, the publicly maintained schools. In the 1980s pressure mounted from Islamic groups to be recognized under the 1944 Education Act as qualifying for public money to run schools for Muslim children. It remains to be seen (1984) whether the formula adopted in 1944 to reconcile the demands of equality and freedom in educational provision will be extended to members of the different religious groups who have settled in large numbers since 1945.

The right of parents to send their children to fee-paying private schools is challenged on social grounds in those countries where private schools enjoy a prestige which places their products at a distinct advantage in terms of getting a job or entering a prestige university. In the USA many commercial private schools, favoured by parents who have difficult children or who wish to circumvent the desegregation decisions of the Supreme Court which apply to all states, do not enjoy a particularly high status and although a relatively few long-established private schools like Groton, open to wealthy parents, confer on their pupils considerable advantages, they are too few in number to make attempts to abolish them the object of major campagins. Moreover, American commitment to *laissez-faire* capitalism makes it unlikely that such a campaign will develop. This is not the case in Britain, where the products of the public (independent private) schools enjoy distinct advantages in terms of access to power and professional occupations. Labour Party politicians have frequently suggested that when they come to power these prestige schools will be closed or brought into the system of publicly maintained schools. Opposition to such proposals is fierce and legitimized by appeals to the belief that parents should be free to choose how their children are educated.

The abolition of private fee-paying schools or schools meeting the specific needs of particular parental groups in a nation state may be regarded as a denial of basic right. Failure to subsidize such schools, while allowing them to operate, might be regarded as an acceptance of freedom of choice while denying the principle of equal provision. Where schools designed to meet the needs of any special group are prohibited, freedom of choice is not available. In none of the countries whose policies are analysed in the volume is there complete denial of parental choice.

Clearly a national commitment to equality in education is not always associated with an equally strong commitment to freedom of choice in education. Indeed, logically and in practice, far from being acceptable and reconcilable constituents of an overall pattern of educational aims, equality may be promoted only at the expense of liberty and conversely liberty may be safeguarded only at the expense of equality. It is through the application of general aims that the logical dilemma becomes obvious in practice.

Aims of Eduction

Reports submitted by member states to the International Bureau of Education (IBE) in Geneva make clear that, in most widely conceived terms, education is regarded as a universal human right and that certain aims of education have been widely adopted. These are that education should develop the all-round intellectual, moral, physical and aesthetic capabilities of individual children and that education should contribute to the improvement of society economically and, depending on circumstances, politically and socially. These aims are interpreted in different ways. So are the objectives derived directly from these aims. Today they include the expectation that not only should a first level of basic schooling be available to all children regardless of race, language, religion, sex, social class and place of residence, but that second level or secondary education and indeed higher education should be accessible to all regardless of their ability to benefit from traditional forms of academic studies. Practices, however, differ.

Thus these general aims and their derived objectives inform policies pursued in Britain, China, France, Japan, the USA and the USSR, although the explicit emphasis placed on either child-centred or society-centred policies and practice differs from one country to another. Indeed, during certain periods since 1945 debates about the relative merits of child- and society-centred aims have been fierce and as overt as the disagreements between egalitarians and those educationists who hold that freedom of choice in education should be protected. There is no doubt, however, from IBE reports that the stress on the equality of educational provision has increased everywhere and that the right to education now included access to schooling at all levels.

Since the Second World War circumstances have made the realization of education as a human right difficult. Parents, accepting the rhetoric of politicians and educationists, have pressed to have their children admitted to first-, second- and third-level institutions of education. The immediate postwar explosion of population increased the demand for places in primary or first-level schools during the early fifties and towards the end of the decade, for access to second-level or secondary education. The 1960s was a decade during which, faced with growing demands, universities and other institutions of higher learning expanded massively. Indeed, aspirations have been maintained and increased to include recent calls for an expansion of pre-school facilities and for adult or lifelong educational opportunities. However, birth-rates have fluctuated so that since 1945 the size of the age cohorts competing for places in schools and universities has varied. There has been a steady growth in the accumulated knowledge of mankind – particularly in the natural sciences – and the applications of scientific knowledge to industry and commerce have transformed the working life of millions of young people and adults. Fluctuations in economic prosperity have affected most countries, even those with governments, as in the USSR and China, committed until recently to developing their economies without depending on the resources of the capitalist world. The desire and ability of governments either directly or vicariously to finance the expansion of educational provision should be analysed in the light of aspirations, population trends, the growth of knowledge and worldwide economic booms and recessions.

Within this framework of aims, objectives and changing world circumstances, educational policies in Britain, China, France, Japan, the USA and the USSR can be seen as responses to problems faced by educationists. The problems are similar, and very general aims have been shared, but policy responses differ. Traditions, the climate of political opinion and economic circumstances all play their part in the formulation of policy responses.

The Administration of Education

For example, the extent to which the power to formulate, adopt and implement educational policies is concentrated in central or national organizations or is devolved varies greatly. In the USA the role of the federal government, though viewed with considerable and frequently violent distrust, has increased both in law and practice to equalize provision for blacks, but not for Roman Catholics, Hispanic-speaking children, and those with special needs. At the same time carefully allocated federal funds have been sanctioned to promote the education of 'gifted' children in the interest of national security. A gradual shift from support for vocational education towards a federal involvement in the national interest, in the equalization of education for all and the promotion of some aspects of it for the few has created anomalies.

In Britain the partnership between the national government and the local education authorities is designed to promote equality (without achieving it in *per capita* expenditure terms) and safeguards certain freedoms. The limited statutory powers of the national government have been the subject of considerable debate but the principle that national resources should be distributed across the country to equalize, as far as possible, expenditure on the education of children and the establishment of national salary scales for teachers suggest that the role of the central government is not as seriously questioned as it is in the USA. The power of the national government in the UK to influence other aspects of policy varies considerably. Since 1945 successive government have tried to reorganize or prevent the reorganization of second-level schools along comprehensive lines. Government has successfully influenced the supply of teachers in the face of changes in the number of school-age children. It has successfully, although indirectly, influenced university admission policies and fee structures. Modest and to some extent successful attempts have been made by government to modify public examinations. However, attempts by national agencies to modify university entrance examination requirements have largely failed.

It is clear that party politics in Britain increased the tension between educationists pressing for equality and those striving to retain freedom of educational choice. Members of the Labour Party, in and out of office, have argued in favour of equalizing access to schools and reducing school leaving examination requirements. A major principle of Conservative Party policy has been that parents should be free to choose for their children an education in accordance with their wishes, including the right to send children to private schools. Conservative governments have resisted the imposition of comprehensive schools on unwilling local education authorities. Members of both parties have overtly respected the rights of local authorities while, in government, increasing their own powers. Neither party has been prepared to challenge the right, sanctioned by tradition, of teachers in individual schools to devise their own curricula. On balance, in the name of equality, in Britain, as in the USA, the intervention of the national government in the administration of education has increased since 1945.

France, the USSR and Japan are countries with traditions of powerful central administrative agencies. In all three countries access to education is guaranteed but progress in the development of education in each differs and freedom of choice varies. In the USSR the freedom of parents to have their children educated in their mother tongue, granted in the Soviet constitution, is justified principally on the ground that such a policy guarantees equality of access, provision and outcome. Access to prestige institutions of higher education is nevertheless regulated by each institution and is very competitive. A similar situation exists in Japan, where upper-second-level and third-level education is open to all but competitive entrance examinations administered by individual universities favour certain children. Parents are anxious for their children and many can afford to have them coached for admission to a desired school. Centralized systems of administration equalize provision but allow access on merit. The Soviet Union and France are meritocracies of talent, Japan is a meritocracy of talent influenced by the ability and willingness of parents to pay for the education of their children.

Major sources of inequality, which only a powerful central authority can overcome, are the differences between urban and rural conditions. Boarding schools in Leningrad are designed to help rural children compete on equal terms with their urban peers for admission to university. Throughout the country boarding schools for children learning a trade serve a similar purpose. National policy in Japan has for many years been directed towards ensuring that the quality of teaching in rural schools and the performance of pupils in them equals those in urban schools. Historically in France second-level boarding schools were to ensure that village children enjoyed the same opportunities as those from the big cities although it must be said that in terms of prestige the most famous *lycées* are concentrated in Paris.

In China, after a period during which attempts were made to

consolidate power in the hands of the central government, more recently an aim of policy has been to decentralize control. This move is typical of many countries. The early emphasis on equality and the centralization of power is now matched by stated governmental desires to increase participation in the formulation, adoption and implementation of policy by granting to local authorities more responsibility for the running of schools. However, early postwar attempts in Japan to decentralize the administration of education and make it more democratic by reducing the powers of the Ministry of Education and increasing the powers of local authorities have been successfully resisted. Whether decentralized systems of educational administration are more or less democratic than centralized control is an open question. That decentralized control produces inequality in terms of provision seems undeniable.

In general local administration allows for participation by members of the community and historically primary schools have been run by local authorities. Academic secondary schools have been regarded, at least in France, and to some extent elsewhere, as national institutions which should be run by the central government. This principle does not apply in the USA or Britain although in both countries prestige private schools enjoy a national reputation and admit pupils from many parts of the country. In most countries the older high-status universities are regarded as national institutions; tradition legitimizes a degree of autonomy in their administration which is not acceptable at the earlier levels of education but the proliferation of universities and expanded enrolments have brought academic freedom and university autonomy into question.

Since 1945 debates about what should be the balance of power and responsibility between national, regional and local governments have been continuous. *De facto* centralization has been a response to demands for greater equality. Pressure to decentralize decision-making has been justified by appeals to preserve local autonomy and increase local participation. Nowhere has the debate been more obvious and acrimonious than in Japan, but in the USA and Britain initiatives taken by the federal and national governments have been regarded as potential threats to the rights, respectively, of individual states and the people of America and to the local authorities in Britain.

The assertion that since 1945 the *de facto* power of central governments has increased and that it has been legitimized by the rhetoric of equality of access and provision is worth careful consideration, but it is too simple. An examination of specific aspects of national policy reveals that in some cases national responsibility has been increased; in other aspects of policy responsibility has remained with local authorities or been devolved on to them.

Finance

Central to the achievement of equal provision are the arrangements made to finance education. Egalitarians expect national governments to finance schools. Libertarians demand that members of local communities should run schools. The British financial formula appears to meet the expectations of both groups. In the USA the states, with some exceptions, delegate powers to raise money to local school boards. Within each state attempts to equalize at a minimum level *per capita* expenditure on schooling are widespread. An increase in federal funds has been made for educational activities designed to promote economic well-being, guarantee defence and improve facilities in schools serving communities in which family incomes are extremely low. Even so, a high, though decreasing, percentage of the funds raised to finance schools comes in the USA from taxes raised by local school boards. It is the inability of local communities to raise enough money to make their schools equal to the best in the country that worries egalitarians. Traditional fears are that if the federal government provided more money across the board for school education it would seek to impose policies on reluctant states and local authorities.

In the so-called centralized systems of administration not all school funds come from the national government. In France private and municipal secondary schools are entitled to state subsidies making up to 80 per cent of running costs. In Japan the national government subsidizes prefectures, municipalities and private educational bodies and a local allocation tax is distributed to prefectures and municipalities to reduce financial inequalities. In the USSR education is financed by the state but considerable sums are made available for public education from the funds of industrial ministries, co-operatives, trade unions and other social organizations as well as collective and state farms. They may pay for equipment and teaching aids and finance the construction of pre-schools and boarding schools.

In no country is the financing of schools simple. Funds for education are raised nationally (and in some cases at the regional level too) and locally. Income, property and sales taxes are the most usual forms of taxation. Tuition fees and donations from industrialists, philanthropists and others add to the amount of money made available to the educational services. These funds are used to meet recurrent and capital costs. Funds to meet recurrent costs may be raised in one way, funds to meet capital costs in another, as for example in the USA. Universally, however, the item in a nation's educational budget which costs the most is payments to teachers. Consequently it is of some significance in a comparative study to examine the extent to which teachers are on national or local salary scales, what these are and how they are determined. At one end of a continuum all teachers in publicly maintained French schools are civil servants on a pay scale determined nationally in the light of qualifications and length of service. Depending on their position, teachers may receive salaries comparable to the highest-paid bureaucrats in the civil or armed services. This system ensures that schools everywhere have equally well paid and well qualified teachers although many teachers are in fact employed at lower salaries in positions for which they are not fully qualified.

In Britain nationally negotiated scales ensure that teachers receive similar salaries wherever they are employed. They are not civil servants, however, and relatively few of them, possibly only headteachers in large secondary schools, command a salary comparable to that of senior civil servants. Salaries are related to length of experience and positions of responsibility and only marginally to qualifications. The same can be said of the Soviet Union. Salary scales are negotiated nationally between the government and the Union of Scientific Workers, to which all teachers belong. In so far as schoolteachers are included with a great variety of others in these negotiations their salaries are relatively good. Differentials in Japan are considerable. They are based on qualifications (and period of training) and the type of school – primary, lower secondary and upper secondary – in which they teach.

National salary scales are unknown in the USA. Each local school board pays its teachers what it thinks it can afford, and what it thinks each teacher is worth. Annual contracts are drawn up on the basis of which a teacher is employed. Security of tenure is limited, in contrast to the situation in the other countries. Competition for good teachers and pressure from the American Federation of Teachers ensures some comparability within a state, but not necessarily between states. Salary increments are built into contracts on the basis of experience and qualifications. Nevertheless salaries differ greatly and, in spite of the fact that teachers have to satisfy state certification requirements, teachers are very mobile in search of higher salaries. They are unlikely to move from the north to the southern states but frequently move to the west to earn more money. Regional and local salary differentials related to qualifications are bound to promote, or sustain, inequalities. Centralized scales, which may include differentials based on the level of teaching, are more likely to distribute well qualified, ambitious and experienced teachers evenly throughout a national system.

Against the inequalities of provision arising from methods of financing should be weighed the uneven financial burdens placed on those who, in one form or another, provide the funds. Taxes on property are still used to raise money either directly, as in the USA, or indirectly, as in Britain, to finance schools. Property taxes give rise to inequalities of provision. For example, industrialists in the USA may object to paying high educational taxes on their property if they do not benefit their own children directly. Since many well paid employees may live outside the school district in which a factory or firm is located this frequently occurs. At the same time taxes on domestic property in crowded industrial areas may raise relatively small amounts of money while the schools cater for a large number of children. Enormous discrepancies in funding based on property taxes exist between neighbouring school districts and state equalizing subsidies can only prevent them from being even greater.

Income is now a more obvious source of wealth and taxes on it constitute a substantial proportion of the money spent on schools. Income taxes are usually national, may be provincial and are rarely raised locally. National income tax levels are determined nationally and since a relatively small percentage of the population benefits directly from schools at any one time levels of taxation depend on the willingness of members of the electorate to accept them. High expenditure on education may become a party political issue and a good deal of persuasion may be needed before elderly and middle-aged well paid taxpayers are willing to pay high taxes to support the education of other parents' children.

Non-specified taxes disguise, more than a direct educational tax, the contribution income tax payers are expected to make to maintain schools throughout the country. Wealthy parents, paying property or educational taxes directly to support the schools attended by their own children, are frequently willing to tax themselves highly to ensure that these schools are good. They may at the same time demand the right to participate fully in policy decisions. The high quality of provision in wealthy districts in the USA reflects the importance given by parents to education and the view that those who pay for a service should help to determine what is offered. Thus relationships between consumers (parents) and producers (teachers) are close in locally financed systems. They may even be democratic but, in the absence of powerful central mechanisms to equalize provision, local finance gives rise to inequalities. On the other hand research is needed to show, more precisely in comparative terms, how the burden of financing education is distributed.

Wealth, for example, is now concentrated in the new industrial areas although not necessarily in the inner parts of the older cities, so that the fund-raising capacities of people who live in urban areas vary greatly. Moreover, teachers, along with many other well trained people, in general prefer to work in towns and contribute to the urban drift. In many countries, in order to equalize provision, special incentives are offered to keep teachers in or attract them to rural schools. Free accommodation and salary increments are among the inducements. In centralized systems it may be possible to assign young teachers to rural schools – a policy followed in France, the USSR and China. Salary scales and the power of central government to assign teachers to particular schools determine to a considerable extent whether facilities in schools are equal in urban and rural areas.

The Structure and Organisation of Schools

Undoubtedly since 1945 egalitarians have concentrated their attention on inequalities associated with traditional, and consequently elitist, features of school organization. They press for equal access to first-, second- and third-level institutions and demand in particular that access to second-level schools should not be based on academic achievement or socio-economic position. Access to universities should, they claim, be more 'open' and pre-school and lifelong educational provision should be available for every parent and adult.

Europeans, who for the most part had prior to 1940 established systems of universal primary schooling, concentrated after the war on the reorganization of second-level schools along comprehensive lines. They had at least two models – the American and Soviet – from which to choose. The nineteenth-century American common elementary school lasting eight years for children in a neighbourhood followed by a four-year high school has now been replaced in many areas by a 6–3–3–4 pattern (primary, junior high, senior high, college) of schooling. Four-year degree courses in liberal arts colleges, teachers' colleges and universities have become the norm. It is a mass system of education.

Policy in the Soviet Union since 1917 has been to create a common school. Progress, retarded by economic conditions and the devastation of the Second World War, means that ten years of education has been effectively achieved in the larger cities if not in the small villages. In the past many pupils left school after seven – now eight – years of general instruction to attend specialized vocational schools. Recent experiments have been carried out to allow some choice after eight years of compulsory education by offering in selected schools enriched courses for pupils intending to enter higher education. In spite of such experiments the Soviet model, which comes nearer and nearer to achievement, is the unified ten-year school which serves children living in a particular neighbourhood.

In the event, Japan copied successfully the US 6–3–3–4 model and introduced almost overnight nine years of compulsory schooling. Policy in Communist China was very much influenced after 1949 by Soviet policies. Lack of industrial development and resistance from traditional Chinese scholars help to explain the slow progress made in China to extend primary and secondary education to all children.

In Western Europe the reform of secondary education to improve equality of access took various forms. Scandinavian comprehensive schools of nine years' duration are similar in structure to those in the USSR. French plans – which were debated endlessly and rejected frequently by the French parliament during the 1950s – were first designed to introduce a common lower secondary school and then to create a period of orientation lasting two years. The difficulties of placing pupils in different schools with an orientation cycle were considerable. Nevertheless the creation of a common lower secondary stage in which a two-year observation cycle is followed up by a two-year period of guidance prior to differentiated upper secondary schools has continued to inform policy since the de Gaulle reforms.

In England and Wales the first comprehensive schools enrolled children from the age of eleven to eighteen. This original model adopted by the London County Council still exists but after Department of Education and Science circular 10/65, in which local authorities were invited to submit plans to reform secondary schooling along comprehensive lines on the basis of one of six models, several types of comprehensive schools have been adopted. While the pressure to 'go comprehensive' exerted by Labour governments has been reduced by Conservative administrations, nevertheless a majority of pupils now (1984) attend comprehensive schools and only a small number of selective grammar schools remain. Plans to reintroduce them emerge from time to time.

In spite of the high hopes of those expecting that comprehensive schools would equalize access and provision there is evidence in England and Wales to suggest that such schools have not been the expected panacea. Doubtless the presence of secondary schools run by the Catholic authorities has not helped to make all secondary comprehensive schools equally popular or acceptable to parents. The private and particularly the independent public schools which charge high fees have encouraged parents dissatisfied with the publicly maintained system to opt out and create an enlarged system of selective secondary schools.

The speed and completeness with which systems in Western Europe became comprehensive or remained selective do not explain the degree to which, in the 1960s, the universities and other institutions of higher education expanded. The first comprehensive secondary schools were established later in France and the Federal Republic of Germany than in England and Wales, but enrolments in the French and German universities grew far more than in England. Moreoever, in no country is there much evidence to show that comprehensive secondary schools radically altered the social class composition of the universities – particularly in the prestige faculties and departments. Equality of access to secondary schools may have been achieved through the introduction of comprehensive schools; equality of provision and equality of outcomes clearly depend on a number of other features of the school systems and the societies they serve. In particular curricular policies have a significant role to play.

Curricula

If access to schooling is a measure of equality of opportunity, what curricula are offered to pupils is a measure of equality of provision. Traditional views about innate psychological differences in intelligence and ability were used to justify different curricula in different types of schools. Prior to 1945 except in the USA a small proportion of young people received an education which prepared them for the universities, the professions of law, medicine, the church (except in the USSR) and teaching. A restricted curriculum similar to the medieval seven liberal arts, legitimized by Aristotle, typified the content of English grammar schools. Specialization in appropriate academic subjects continues to inform general curricula in English schools. I describe this as an 'essentialist' curriculum because it is based on the view that through a few essential subjects (or disciplines, for Paul Hirst), or by a selection from high culture, a sound general education can be provided.

Towards the end of the eighteenth century French encyclopaedists argued that all knowledge, rather than a few essential subjects, should be taught in schools. In practice this theory was accepted in Europe and meant that a wide range of subjects including mathematics, classical languages, the pure sciences, modern languages, history and geography, music, art and design are included in the general curriculum in continental European schools. Soviet educators, supported by the authority of Lenin, retain their faith in an encyclopaedic curriculum in which all the socio-economic and historical experiences of mankind are included. The polytechnical principle, central to Soviet curriculum theory, is not intended to change or reduce the content of education but to interpret it in a Marxist way.

Against these two subject-centred theories might be contrasted US curriculum theory which emerged out of discussions among the pragmatists. In theory, at least, progressive educationists led by John

Dewey abandoned subject-based curricula and suggested that the content of education should be selected to illuminate the problems young people are likely to meet when they left school.

The retention of subject-based curricula under conditions of expansion and reorganization suggests that they are more difficult to change than school structures. Perhaps this is because, while party politicians influenced changes in structure and organization in an attempt to promote equality of opportunity and access, teachers have almost exclusive control over the content of education, how it should be taught and to whom it should be offered. The unwillingness of teachers to relinquish control has created problems everywhere. They continue to decide what is taught, even though curricula are laid down by national ministry of education officials. They continue to 'cool out' some pupils and encourage others to prepare for the next level of education and are confirmed in their attitudes by the evident failure of all pupils to reach the same levels of achievement in all subjects.

Compulsory national curricula may mean that not all pupils in the same type of school follow the same courses. In France curriculum differentiation increases as pupils go through second-level schools until at the upper stage distinctly different courses are offered in different types of school. Where differentiation takes place within schools inequality is legitimized on the basis of the assessment teachers make of pupil abilities. To equalize provision, core curricula have been developed to ensure, at least in the lower stage of second-stage education, that all pupils study the same subjects. Outside the core, optional subjects allow for differentiation on the advice of teachers. Great efforts are made in the USSR to provide a common compulsory curriculum throughout the first and second levels of education. Some pupils, to be sure, study a modern foreign language from the second grade rather than compulsorily from the fifth grade. Children are taught in one of many mother tongues in accordance with parental wishes. Teachers accept, nevertheless, that their task is to make it possible for all pupils to complete successfully the same course of subjects up to upper age of compulsory attendance. In the USSR, as in France and Japan, curriculum differentiation in the same or in different schools takes place at the upper stage of second-level education. Such differentiation is made on the basis of student attainments in prescribed subjects. It could be argued that to offer pupils different curricula after the age of compulsory attendance does not violate the principle of equality, and that the power of teachers to determine the content of education and distribute it in accordance with their judgement does not run contrary to the principle of liberty. Some educationists hold that since knowledge confers power teachers should not be in a position to decide on whom it should be conferred.

It may seem that there is more freedom of choice in English schools. Primary schoolteachers in individual schools can virtually teach what they like in a way they think fit. Secondary schoolteachers are still constrained by external examination requirements. Any number of subjects may be studied for the Ordinary Level General Certificate of Education and internally moderated Certificate of Secondary Education examinations may be taken. University entrance requirements allow for further specialization so that two, three or at most four related subjects are studied for the Advanced Level General Certificate of Education. Specialization in terms of subjects studied is more the result of decisions by teachers than the result of pupil choices. Pupils can easily be 'cooled out' of academic courses in comprehensive schools just as they were when they failed to get into the former academic grammar schools. Attempts by the Department of Education and Science to establish acceptable curriculum guidelines have failed. Even in the schools in one local education authority, pupils in different comprehensive schools need not follow the same curriculum. Idiosyncratic decisions made by headteachers and staff ensure extreme curricular inequalities. Teacher power effectively denies parents any real choice in what their children study.

Pragmatic curriculum theory implies that the content of education should be negotiated. The information pupils need to solve their problems should determine the content of education. Problems may be local, national or international and be located in the familial, economic, political, moral and leisure aspects of life. In the USA considerable attempts were made, particularly in the 1930s, by progressive educationists to devise curricula along these lines which would meet the needs of all children. Basically subject-centred courses have prevailed and many high school teachers accept the entrance requirements of high-status universities in organizing school curricula. Credits are required in the language arts, the natural sciences, mathematics and the social sciences. Options may be taken in addition, and there is in the USA a tradition that pupils may select freely from the options or electives on offer. Choice is available and indeed during the 1950s and in a report published in 1983, *A Nation at Risk*, criticism was made of the 'Mickey Mouse' smorgasbord of courses which were on offer in many American high schools. There is no doubt that in curricular terms US high schools emphasize freedom of choice at the expense of equality of provision and while teachers select and distribute knowledge their power to confer privileges on successful students is much less than in most countries.

The control teachers exercise over curricula in all countries, however, grants them enormous powers of patronage. Most teachers do not consider all pupils capable of studying the same subjects successfully and justify differentiated curricula in terms of ability to benefit. In achieving equality of opportunity and indeed equality of access to the second and third levels egalitarians have not yet convinced teachers that everyone is equally capable of achieving the same level of performance. Only a common compulsory curriculum for all pupils or students at any level of education ensures equality of provision. Only if all pupils achieve the same high standards in the subjects studied can it be said that equality of outcomes has been achieved. Even where this is seen as a major objective of compulsory education, as among teachers in the USSR, there remains a belief in the ability of some students to excel. General standards may, in short, be raised in the interests of equalizing outcomes but unless individuals are prevented from realizing their potential it is unlikely in the foreseeable future, that standards of achievement can be raised for all individuals to the level previously reached by a favoured few. The content of education is the rock on which progress in realizing equality in education has foundered.

Teacher Training

Faith in the ability of teachers to teach everybody anything, provided the right methods are used, has helped to disguise failures to achieve equality of outcomes. Failure on the part of pupils is, as has been stated, increasingly ascribed to their poor family background or low socio-economic position rather than to innate differences of intelligence or ability. Great attention has consequently been given since 1945 to the psychology of education and the sociology of education in the training of teachers in the belief that teachers who understand children in their social setting are better able to compensate those who come from disadvantaged homes. This faith in teachers may have been misplaced but it underlies policies to improve teaching quality since 1945. Unfortunately at the same time governments and educationists have been firmly committed to a policy of making sure that enough teachers are trained to maintain pupil–teacher ratios throughout their country at an acceptably low level. Emphasis on the quality of teachers is antithetical to an emphasis on teachers at any price. Although this latter judgement might be challenged there is evidence to suggest that the supply-and-demand equation has had a decisive influence on fluctuations in teacher-training policies.

Two policies have, however, been consistently adopted, namely that all teachers should be trained prior to their first appointment and that all of them should receive this initial training in institutions of higher education – preferably, at least in some countries, in universities. Implicit in this policy is the expectation that in future all teachers will be university graduates – or their equivalent. An 'all graduate' profession is an ambition which has been virtually achieved in the USA and towards the achievement of which considerable progress has been made in England and Wales. It has been central to policy in the USSR for many years, although secondary schools for teachers continue to train teachers for the first years of the ten-year school. Certification procedures in Japan vary with school level. As in the USA teachers may receive a certificate to teach all subjects in the elementary school, but are authorized to teach specified subjects in the lower and upper secondary schools. The pattern of courses is, indeed, rather similar to those in the USA. First-class certificates for teachers in upper secondary schools are granted only to teachers with masters' degrees.

In pursuit of graduate training for teachers courses have lengthened, except during periods of acute teacher shortage. Debate, particularly in the USA, has turned on the proper constituents of teacher-training programmes and the proportions each of them should occupy. The traditional status of a university degree as a licence to teach has been abandoned. Graduates who wish to teach in academic secondary schools are now expected to follow a course of initial training, although in England and Wales in shortage subjects they were until recently excused. A secondary school course with some advice on methods of teaching is no longer regarded as an adequate preparation for first and lower stage second-level teachers. Teachers entering institutions of further education in England and Wales are encouraged but not required to train. In-service training is either required, as in the USSR, necessary if full certification is to be obtained, as in the USA, or encouraged for promotion purposes, as in England and Wales.

Belief in knowledge of a teaching subject as the basis on which the expertise of teachers depends has been modified. In the USA and England and Wales great emphasis is placed on the need for primary schoolteachers to know their children and to understand the society in which they live. Knowing a subject remains an important qualification of the academic secondary schoolteacher but, and this has been a bone of contention, knowing the child and society through an introduction to psychology and sociology is still regarded by some educationists as desirable in the training of teachers for second-level schools in the USA and England and Wales. Most teacher trainers regarded professional studies and supervised teaching practice as necessary ingredients of a sound course of initial training. The proportion of time devoted to these aspects of training is debated, however.

The debates are conducted between university academics, teacher trainers and practising teachers. Traditions of academic freedom and autonomy protect educationists in universities from the direct influence of politicians, industrialists and parents. In the USA, it is true, state boards of education lay down certification requirements but these are negotiated largely by professors of education and state administrative officers, many of whom are the products of university schools of education. The autonomy enjoyed, vicariously, by those responsible for the training of teachers makes it difficult for public wishes to be articulated in ways which might bring about intended change. Debates about the adequacy of teacher training courses were both public and acrimonious in the USA during the 1950s and there is now a strongly supported movement to ensure by monitoring the training of teachers and their classroom performance that teachers are performing competently. The cult of efficiency is more obvious in the USA than elsewhere. Among other reasons for this is the extent to which the American education system has responded to demands for greater equality of opportunity by abandoning, to a considerable extent, the traditional European commitment to knowledge of subject matter as the basis of the teacher's authority. Criticism of teacher education has been less open and less vociferous in other countries because traditions have been less readily abandoned. There is, however, evidence in England and Wales that public demands that teachers should be held accountable are growing.

The abandonment of many traditional theories about psychological differences, non-negotiable knowledge and the nature of society has freed teachers, and those who train them, from the constraints which legitimized inequalities in education. The freedom teachers have had to respond to changes brought about in education to equalize opportunity and provision may well have increased inequalities or, at best, simply changed criteria of inequality without radically changing the groups of people in society who are collectively at a disadvantage. Teacher and teacher-trainer freedom may be antithetical to the realization of greater equality. Teacher power and teacher-trainer autonomy may seriously restrict the ability of the consumers to hold them accountable in democratic societies.

Universities – a Key to the Problem

In no institutions is the freedom of teachers more clearly exemplified than in the universities. Academic freedom and university autonomy were fought for and won in the early days of the European universities. Academic freedom implied that university teachers were free to choose whom they would teach, what they would teach, how they would teach it and how they would evaluate the performance of students. Students, by the same token, were free to study where they thought fit and under a 'master' of their choice. These traditions of freedom doubtless served a valuable purpose when universities were elitist institutions. The expansion of universities has created a situation in which such freedoms should be questioned. In short, the equalization of opportunity calls into question the legitimacy of university teachers' retaining their privileges. Attempts in China to regulate university affairs have failed to a large extent. Intense competition for places in prestige universities in Japan is the result of a *laissez-faire* approach to expansion and the retention by academics of their power to regulate admission on examination results. Evidently universities in Japan, while a large proportion of the age cohort attend them, are unequal in status and in the kind and level of courses they provide.

The domination exercised, institutionally, by universities and the power university academics possess place them in a position to maintain inequalities of access to the lower stages of educational systems and, in preserving their academic freedom, they restrict the power of those who wish to enter the system to make free choices or to negotiate the kind of curriculum they wish to follow.

At the same time civil liberties may best be protected by the articulate advocacy of university academics whose social function has been to offer in a non-partisan way constructive criticisms of society. More open access to universities has created in many countries a large growth of potential critics of society. The dangers of extraparliamentary political action mobilized by students were all too apparent in the late 1960s, during a period of student unrest and in some cases violence. The delicate balance between criticism and activism was disturbed and many lessons were learned. What has not been resolved, however, is how to restore the balance between the pursuit of equality in education and the maintenance of liberties which have been cherished, in spite of attacks, in many countries. The wisdom with which university academics exercise their power over education will influence the extent to which equality is promoted and liberty is preserved.

1

Education in England and Wales
A National System Locally Administered

CRISPIN JONES

It is a common mistake, usually made by the English, that the English educational system and the United Kingdom educational system are one and the same thing. This reflects the insularity of the system rather than its reality. Indeed, it is another manifestation of the general insularity of British society as a whole, perhaps best typified by the apocryphal newspaper headline 'Fog in Channel, Continent Isolated'. The 'British system' actually consists of five different systems, with many similarities it is true, but also with significant differences. So this chapter will be concentrating on the system in England and Wales and will not deal with the systems of Scotland, Northern Ireland, the Channel Islands and the Isle of Man. A fruitful starting point for such a study is an examination of the aims of the system.

Aims

A key legal document for understanding the aims of education in England and Wales is the Education Act of 1944, the Butler Act, brought in by the Conservative-dominated National Government that governed Britain during the Second World War. Accepted by all the major political parties, it is the cornerstone of much modern British education, despite a considerable amount of subsequent legislation down to, and including, the 1980 Education Act. Its very importance makes it the more surprising that the Act contains very little in the way of stated aims for the educational system. This vagueness typifies the incremental nature of much English education, for there has been comparatively little real public, as opposed to professional, debate about this issue, either then or subsequently. This statement must not be taken as meaning that there are no issues and that the education system operates in some sort of societal vacuum – far from it. Two broad strands of debate lie behind the 1944 Act and most subsequent discussion, both concerning the purpose of education in a modern industrialized society. The first is whether education should be child-centred or directed towards the needs, mainly economic, of the state. The second is the continual conflict between concepts of liberty and egalitarianism which has dominated British political life generally for a very long time, and educational thought from the inception of mass education early in the nineteenth century.[1] Responses to the first of these strands are visible in much current educational debate. Responses to the second are less obvious, but are certainly there and are perhaps more significant in understanding some of the complexities and confusions in the present educational system of England and Wales.

Having said this, what the 1944 Act actually says is both important and instructive in this area. The Act states that education should contribute towards 'the spiritual, moral, mental and physical development of the community'[2] without closely defining what any of these terms mean. Interestingly, the more famous statement of aims in the Act, that children should be given an education 'suitable to their age, ability and aptitudes',[3] actually comes from a portion of the Act referring to the obligations of *parents*. Within this broad framework, parental choice – the concept of liberty – is secured, provided that the education their children receive is 'efficient' and that it can be provided in an economic manner, a point to be taken up later. Although the Act says very little about the aims of education it does imply a great deal. The stress on choice and an education appropriate to age, ability and aptitudes suggests a child-centred approach to education that still continues to dominate the debate on educational aims. The vagueness of the societal aims of education was not seen then as the troublesome issue that it has since become. In previous Education Acts, particularly in the nineteenth century, the reverse had been true, and many of the institutional and other frameworks extant in 1944 tended, despite the Act, to perpetuate former aims, albeit in some cases unwittingly. Equally, the emphasis on liberty was to have important consequences, particularly in the areas of parental choice, denominational schools and the relationship between local education authorities (LEAs) and the central Ministry of Education. Yet many of the Act's supporters believed that it would lead to a more egalitarian society, unaware of the inherent tension between the two concepts of liberty and equality.

This lack of specificity has caused increased problems for the system as British society has evolved and changed in the thirty or so years since the Act was passed. A brief example will illustrate this. Since the passing of the Act, a major impact on British society, particularly in the large English conurbations, has been made by the immigration and settlement of significant numbers of people from the New Commonwealth, notably from the Caribbean and the Indian subcontinent. Ideas of the essential unity and homogeneity of English society which the 1944 Act took for granted are increasingly being questioned. In terms of the Act, what exactly, in England and Wales today, are the appropriate 'spiritual, moral, mental and physical' developments that the educational system should foster? In 1944 'spiritual' development broadly meant some form of induction into Christianity. (Judaism was tacitly acknowledged as being present but was considered as either insignificant or a peculiar and exceptional case!) This consensus no longer holds, especially in multi-faith inner-city schools, but no clear reformulation of this aim has been made, or, more important, generally accepted.

This seeming state of confusion should not be seen either as indicating a lack of interest in the subject or as evidence of unanimity of opinion on the part of the educational world. A continuous and lively debate amongst the professional educators has been going on from before 1944 about the relationship between the educational system and wider society. Occasionally, particularly when the economy seems to be in a state of crisis, the relationship is more publicly explored. The most recent occurrence of this public debate about the aims of education was the so-called Great Debate initiated by the then Prime Minister, James Callaghan, in 1976. In a speech at Ruskin College, Oxford, he raised the question of how the educational system should prepare children for effective participation in industrial life. The actual debate was in some respects a trivial one but the issues raised were of extreme importance. Significantly, much of the opposition to the Prime Minister's views came from the left of the political spectrum, who thought the debate marked a shift away from the child-centred aims they thought were enshrined in the 1944 Act. Others saw it as an attempt to strengthen the power of the central government. What is clear from the discussion that took place then and subsequently was that there was a widespread feeling that despite the resources that had been poured into education over the last thirty years society had not benefited to the extent that had been hoped for. The last phrase is of course a blanket one. The various interest groups party to the debate had very different views as to what constituted a benefit to society. So the schools were blamed for not producing an efficient workforce and also blamed for producing too docile a workforce, willingly embracing the degradation of working for capitalism. Where you stood on the debate to some extent reflected where you sat. More seriously, the debate reflected the fact that the conflict between liberty and equality had still to be tackled effectively. With little consensus within society at large on these issues, and with the legislation being unhelpful, the educational service was in an unfortunate position, appearing to be condemned by all the conflicting groups for having promised much but delivered little. Although it would be too dramatic to say that there had been a breakdown in confidence, it is not without significance that the various curricular, administrative and financial changes that have been initiated since the debate have as one of their aims a greater accountability of the educational system to the society that it serves. The details of these changes and the debates that informed them will be discussed in more detail later on in this chapter. Indeed, in discussing the general aims of education in England and Wales, this final point is of great significance. The painful readjustment to becoming a second-class nation without an empire and with a declining industrial base has meant a massive upheaval in British society over the last thirty years. The 1944 Act was an attempt to formulate a blueprint for education for a brave new world recovering from the horrors of a world war. The brave new world did not take the form anticipated and that, combined with the persistence of aims formulated in differing circumstances, had led to the feeling that education in England and Wales has, in some ways, lost its sense of purpose and direction.

Administration

The manner in which the system is administered is a good example of this persistence and confusion. As it stands, it is a monument to pragmatism. It works, in a somewhat creaking fashion, and most of the constituent parts have little relish for major changes. It is often described as a national system locally administered, but this statement disguises the fact that it is an administrative system based on territoriality and boundary maintenance. Under the 1944 Act the old Board of Education was transformed into a new Ministry of Education, now the Department of Education and Science (DES), headed by the Secretary of State for Education, who is a member of the Cabinet. Originally the Minister's duty, according to the Act, was to:

promote the education of the people of England and Wales[4] and the progressive development of institutions devoted to that purpose, and to secure the effective execution by local authorities, under his control and direction, of the national policy for providing a varied and comprehensive education service in every area. (Section 1)

This section gave far more power ('under his control and direction') to the designated minister than is generally recognized and there were powerful attempts to delete or alter these words when the Bill was passing through Parliament. In defending the phrase Mr Butler claimed that it would not destroy the old partnership with local authorities but would enable the central authority to give a strong lead. Events have shown that the opponents' fears and Butler's hopes were equally unfounded. Local authorities have considerable control still and the DES is hardly renowned for its strong leadership of the system. As partners to the DES are just over a hundred local education authorities. These are the local administrators of the educational system, again set up in the present form principally by the 1944 Act. Local education authorities were traditionally run as separate empires within the local authority structure, but the introduction of corporate management to local authorities in the late 1960s, coupled with the reorganization into larger units of many local authorities at the same time, reduced their autonomy. Now the education department of a local authority has to compete for funds with other departments through the corporate structure. Despite these changes within the local authority structure, much of the debate about the administration of education lies in this dual structure. At its crudest, the debate is a simple party political one, particularly when the LEA is controlled by a political party that is in opposition to the existing national government. It is more than this, however, as this duality expresses in concrete form the differing aims of liberty and equality in the educational system. These somewhat oppositional positions between the DES and the LEAs produce a fine balance and it is important to examine this in more detail if some of the educational issues of the last thirty years are to be understood. The DES, and in particular the Secretary of State for Education, have overall responsibility for the system. Actual control, although theoretically in the hands of the Secretary of State, in practice lies with the LEAs as it did to a large measure before the 1944 Act. The powers that the minister had under the Act do, however, enable the central authority to put considerable pressure upon the LEAs. This can be shown by the way the DES administers the capital expenditure side of the educational finance programme. This would appear to be a straightforward process but it can be used as a powerful inducement to LEAs to follow directions given from the centre. For example, in the continuing debate about the comprehensive reorganization of secondary schools, money can be given by the DES for the building of new comprehensive schools or alterations to existing non-comprehensive schools to help them become comprehensive. At the same time, money can be withheld from LEAs whose building programmes maintain a selective secondary system. This policy was used, not too effectively, it must be admitted, to help implement a DES circular, 10/65, on comprehensive reorganization. The circular requested LEAs to submit plans for comprehensive reorganization if they were not already comprehensive. Implicit in the request was that non-compliance would affect the capital grants that LEAs received from the DES. However, submitting plans and actual reorganization are two very different things. A few determined local authorities managed to delay matters in such a way that capital grants could not rightfully be withheld while their selective systems flourished. Their hope, realized, was that delay until a change in national government took place would mean no major change would have to be undergone.

A less partisan example of this financial power is the issue of roofs over heads. There is an urgent need for a rebuilding programme in many of the declining inner-city areas; at the same time money is needed for new schools in areas where the population is expanding. Limited financial resources have meant that both needs cannot be met. So which should have priority? It only appears a non-party-political issue. Rebuilding in the inner cities supports LEAs of one political party rather than another and the reverse often holds true in the demographically expanding areas, such as East Anglia. So changes in national government often precede changes in building policies.

In other areas too, the Secretary of State for Education can influence policy at the LEA level. The training, supply, registration and regional allocation of teachers is handled by the DES. Salaries, although negotiated between the local authorities and the teacher unions through the Burnham Committee, are finally approved by Parliament on the recommendation of the Secretary of State for Education. This latter step has traditionally been seen as a formality, but this has become less apparent in recent years, particularly if central government economic planning contains an incomes policy element. A less well known power is that the Minister of Education approves, but does not draw up, the short lists for the appointment of chief education officers. Another power, better known now than in the past, is the position of the Secretary of State for Education over school closures. Under the 1944 Act, final approval lies with the Secretary of State. In the past, with fewer school closures, this was not a major concern, but increasingly it is becoming one. It is, incidentally, a power which it seems the Minister would gladly relinquish, as the 1980 Education Act indicates. The power of the DES and the

Secretary of State for Education in other areas is there, albeit less clearly defined. As the person .responsible for national standards in education, the Secretary of State has powers directly to intervene in an LEA if he or she believes that LEA is acting 'unreasonably'. What exactly unreasonable behaviour entails is more difficult to establish and legal opinion is that it would be most difficult to establish in the courts. Indeed in a legal case in 1978 (the Thameside decision) the judiciary upheld a complaint by the local authority against the Secretary of State who claimed that he had been acting within the powers given him by the 1944 Act. The courts ruled that the powers were not there as had been claimed by the Secretary of State.

It is an interesting speculation that there is likely to be a move towards spelling out in greater detail the exact nature of some of these supervisory powers during the next few years. This would, however, go against a long tradition of executive rather than legislative clarification of administrative issues which runs right through government in Britain. Given this desire for flexibility, or fudging, depending on your point of view, it is not surprising that, where legislation is more specific, problems also arise. The 1944 Act also required education to be organized in three stages, namely, primary, secondary and further education. LEAs which attempted to change this pattern ran into trouble until the law was changed. The famous example of this was in the West Riding where middle schools were proposed, cutting across primary and secondary stages.

In general, though, the last few years have seen determined, if not successful, moves by the DES to have a greater say both in the way the schooling system is organized and also in what is taught within the schools. Responsibility for the curriculum lies, according to the 1944 Act, with the local education authorities and has traditionally been jealously guarded by them with the active support of the teacher unions. But recent moves to establish a common core curriculum by the DES, coupled with the establishment of a national monitoring service to examine educational standards, the Assessment of Performance Unit (APU), would indicate some modest success for the DES. In a similar manner, Her Majesty's Inspectorate (HMI), a centrally appointed body of experienced educators, has been taking a more active role in the public debates about current educational issues. The assisted places scheme is yet another attempt by central government to maintain academic standards, though more cynical people might prefer to regard it as a device for ensuring the continuation of subsidized academic education for the middle classes. This scheme, introduced in 1981, to a large extent replaces the system of direct-grant funding that was abolished by a previous Labour administration. The stated aim is to identify intellectually able children and place them in private or public schools. The implication is that these schools will develop these children's talents to the full, whereas state schools would not. This is also a good example of policy attempting to tackle the problem of liberty versus egalitarianism, with the DES, with some LEA support, advocating the primacy of the libertarian case. Many of the major administrative decisions about schooling, however, are taken at the local level by the LEAs. They are a world apart from the DES and the interdepartmental squabbles of central government.[5] Nowhere is this better shown than in London. The DES is across the road from the headquarters of the Inner London Education Authority (ILEA), the largest local education authority. However, the road that separates the two buidings is, in metaphorical terms, several miles wide. There is communication, of course, but far less than might be expected. This is considered desirable by both parties, if not in public, then in private.

The LEAs in England and Wales administer in one form or another some 28,000 schools. (There are about 3,000 schools that are independent or private, the most famous of which being the prestigious 'public' (i.e. private) schools like Eton, Harrow, Winchester and Rugby.) Most LEA-administered schools are 'maintained' schools, that is they are both established and maintained by the LEA. In addition there is a significant number of denominational or parochial schools, called 'voluntary' schools, which have a variety of arrangements with the local LEAs. These voluntary schools, and there are some 9,000 of them, were usually established by either the Church of England or the Roman Catholic Church. Many of them are primary schools and many of them, although not most, are in the central areas of large cities, reflecting their historical origins as evangelical educational centres for the urban poor. Under the 1944 Act a variety of control options were offered to the voluntary organizations, ranging from near total control to near total independence. In practical terms, the great majority now accept both recurrent and capital financial aid from the LEAs and/or DES, while retaining authority over certain key staff appointments. There are complicated variations in the degree of financial aid and control but clarifying the issues involved would probably create more problems. The reason for this is that the financial arrangement, called 'dual control', was a masterly compromise in that none of the parties to it was satisfied by it but all recognized that little better could be expected. Freedom of choice on religious grounds was confirmed while its potentially divisive nature was ignored. Declining school rolls coupled with the popularity of voluntary schools has caused the issue slowly to float to the surface again, as the maintained sector complains of unfair and unjust competition. Couple this issue with the one mentioned earlier, the multi-faith nature of our society, and it can be seen that the question of dual control is likely, again, to be an important educational issue. What is clear is that most of the voluntary schools could not survive removal of state funding. But no government could survive such a drastic measure either.

Worrying about voluntary schools is only a tiny part of an LEA's responsibility. They decide on the size and organization of schools, including their governance; in effect this also means that they control individual recruitment of staff. Political influence over this is usually considered minimal, but there are significant regional variations, best revealed in advertisements for posts which expressly prohibit canvassing. The major decisions about size, organization and staffing are important. However, in the day-to-day bureaucratic running of a local education authority decisions are constantly being made that directly affect the quality of education that is provided. For example, allocation of funding to older pupils rather than younger pupils tends to benefit one group in the community as opposed to another. Money for textbooks varies enormously from one LEA to another as well. The number of part-time teachers, in-service provision and the various educational support systems are all subject to considerable local variation with consequent effect on the education provided.

The unbridled consequences of such local control, coupled with local financing, would be a very unequal education system. This is not the case. There is regional variation but comparatively few major inequalities as a consequence. Such inequalities as there are, for instance in differing pupil–teacher ratios, money spent on textbooks, etc., are not greatly significant in terms of explaining differential outcomes of the system. The socio-economic status of the area of the LEA is of much greater significance. For example, the Inner London Education Authority is one of the highest-spending education authorities yet its educational outcomes, as measured by examination results, are poor compared with much of the rest of the country. This reflects as much as anything the fact that the authority covers the classic inner-city area of central London. Regional variations, particularly between the north and south, are again more a reflection of the socio-economic standing of the areas concerned than simply a reflection of differential financing of the school system. That this is so is partly due to the regulatory influence of the DES but also to the way in which the educational service is financed, so that financial inequalities between rich and poor LEAs are partially remedied by central government intervention. These financial matters deserve closer examination.

Finance

Education in England and Wales is not only compulsory, it is free if you use the state system. There is an interesting debate on the value of providing free and compulsory education but in general the concept is seldom questioned. State education is of course not free. It is just that it is not paid for directly. All taxpaying citizens and institutions pay for education through national taxes, usually income-based, and local property taxes or rates. As it is a local system, most educational expenditure is controlled locally even it if is collected centrally and then disbursed to the local authorities. Central government at the DES level is comparatively unimportant in financial terms. Its capital programmes and other educational expenditures amounted to only about 14 per cent of the total budget of £8,551 million in the financial year 1979–80.[6] The local authorities distribute but do not necessarily collect the rest. The high local authority element is paid for out of local property taxes (the rates) and the rate support grant (RSG) provided by central government. The actual amount raised by local authorities through the rates is only about 40 per cent of their total expenditure, the rest being RSG. The purpose of the RSG is to ensure a minimal standard of provision throughout the country. This means that more affluent authorities may, if they wish, spend more on education than other authorities who have less revenue coming from the rates.

The yearly rate support grant is fixed as a result of protracted wrangling and dealing between the interested parties. The subsequent agreement is then justified by various indicators of need. On the surface these indicators gave an air of impartiality to the exercise although in some respects the revised system, introduced in 1981, is more open. The old RSG was also based on the system of matching grants, so that those local authorities who had to spend more, especially those in declining areas, were given more money, again on the 60:40 ratio. This was felt by some to lead to profligacy, hence the introduction of block grants, controlled from the centre. The effect of this will be greater control over spending but this in some respects is more illusion than reality. By far the vast majority of education's financing is extremely difficult to change. For example, teachers' salaries have to be paid; the only debate is the rate of pay and that is often known in advance of the financial year. With so much of the money committed, free money for experimentation and innovation is extremely marginal, being about 2 per cent of total educational expenditure. From this 2 per cent nearly all intervention strategies are funded, such as the Educational Priority Areas experiment of the late 1960s. The sums of money involved in these projects may seem enormous but in relation to the problems they are meant to help solve they are very small.

Curiously, the DES has little direct relationship with the rate support grant system, as the grant covers the whole range of local authority services. This lack of direct control over money is because other agencies of central government such as the Department of the Environment, the Treasury and the Home Office actually give out the funds. The implications of this are quite serious, because no central monitoring of local authority *educational* expenditure is really made. Consequently, attempts by the DES to ensure that certain elements in the rate support grant are earmarked for special educational purposes, such as the provision of in-service training, have not been very successful. If they were the funding agency, they would have this control, but such a change would very likely be fiercely opposed by the local authorities, whatever their political inclinations were, as well as by other central government departments.

What is very important about the rate support grant is not so much how it is organized as how much of it there is. The crude 60 per cent central government rate support grant and 40 per cent local authority rates figures mentioned earlier are just indicative of the balance of funds between the two parties. The exact split, whether it be 60 per cent, 61 per cent or 62 per cent, is critical because of the vast sums of money involved. Equally important is the way in which the money is balanced between the large urban authorities and what is loosely called the shires – the less urban, more suburban and rural authorities. This balance is made on political grounds as much as anything, although this would be vigorously denied by all parties concerned in negotiations; unless your side loses out, that is.

When all these negotiations are finished, the local authorities have a sum of money which is used by them to provide for all their local services, of which education is only a part. Consequently a further level of negotiation between departments takes place, but this time at local authority level. Most of the money is already spoken for so the debate is about the most marginal activities. In education, for example, claims for more money could be made for curriculum development work, or meeting the special educational needs of specific groups, such as ethnic minorities. Such sums of money are comparatively small and it is because of this marginality that other sources of funding have been evolved by central government to deal with specific educational issues.

Four examples of this additional funding would be monies available under Section 11 of the Local Government Act of 1966, the Urban Programme and its continuation, Partnership, the EEC Social Fund and money from the Department of Employment through the

Manpower Services Commission. The third one, although based in the Common Market administration, is administered in Britain by the Department of Employment, so in many practical respects it is a central government fund.

All four of these supplementary fundings address themselves to the egalitarian issue of disadvantage, not exclusively in its educational sense. Again, the money usually goes from central government to local authorities, who give out the money and decide who is to get it. In practice much of the money that has gone to education under these schemes has gone to two major areas, namely the education of immigrants and the education of young people in the declining centres of cities. A glance at the demographic profile of the inner cities shows that often the two groups coincide. Examination of these schemes is very revealing in that it shows how the education service has responded to these two important problem areas.

Section 11 of the Local Government Act (1966) was patched into the Act as a response to a rise in racial tension within the cities. The Act authorized the Home Office to refund to local authorities 50 per cent (later raised to 75 per cent) of the salaries of staff whose work helped meet the special needs of 'immigrants', the local authorities providing the rest. Any local authority with a 'substantial' number of immigrants could claim the money; 'substantial' was later defined as being 2 per cent or more of the local authority's population. Although local authorities provide a wide range of services that deal with such groups, most of the money was in respect of teachers. The actual sums of money are comparatively small in terms of the total education budget, but the commitment under the Act is, unusually, an open-ended one. The result of this is that in some local authorities as many as two teachers in each comprehensive school could be funded out of this money, while in other authorities in the early years of the scheme, at least, very little was claimed, although there may have been significant numbers of 'immigrant' children.

For example, in 1973 Derby was claiming over £22 per head of immigrant population while Harrow was claiming only 40 pence per head. Differential take up is one problem – obviously one that the financial departments of central government are not too disturbed about; another is exactly who is supposed to benefit from the money and what form this benefit takes. When the Act was passed an immigrant could be easily defined. Since then immigration has declined and the group for whom the money was intended, the ethnic minorities originating from the New Commonwealth, no longer are 'immigrant' in the official Home Office definition, many of the children now being British born. The solution to this problem is yet another example of muddling through. Local authorities no longer have really accurate statistics of their population in terms of cultural groupings, so extrapolations are made from the data collected in the 1971 Census to get an approximate (and it really is approximate by 1984) idea of the scale of provision required. The distinction between 'immigrants' who have an entitlement to the financial aid provided by this Act and minority ethnic group members, many of whom do not, being no longer 'immigrant', is blurred and merged together. This suits the local authorities and central government, who fear that renewed public debate about this issue would bring about its ending. This links in with the other issue, namely what form of special help do the people paid for under this Act actually provide? The answer is that nobody really knows, including many of the people funded by the Act; for they do not know that their salary is thus paid. To give an example, a large authority may have claimed several hundreds of thousands of pounds to pay the salaries of teachers, under Section 11, who will deal with the special needs of such children. The money gained is used to lower the pupil–teacher ratio in the schools on the unjustified assumption that this will help the education of these children. Ignoring the belief that the lowering of pupil–teacher ratios axiomatically improves educational opportunities for the moment, these extra teachers may not know that they are being employed out of this money. Until recently, there was no check by the Home Office, who have not the staff, by the DES, who say it is not their concern as it is not money disbursed by them, or by the local authority, who long ago learnt not to look a gift horse in the mouth. It serves a useful purpose, however, in that something can be seen to be being done about a controversial issue. The effectiveness or otherwise of this something is another matter. It also demonstrates the action that is likely to arise from failure to resolve the equality versus liberty dilemma.

The Urban Programme is another significant if marginal addition to educational finance. In 1968, a then prominent MP, Enoch Powell, made a widely reported speech on the condition of the inner cities of England, in which he forecast that current *laissez-faire* immigration policies meant that the centres of cities were becoming alien to the British way of life and that violence and 'rivers of blood' would inevitably follow. The Urban Programme was announced shortly afterwards by the Home Secretary. Under this, money was to be made available to projects that dealt with the issue of deprivation in the inner city, again on a 75 per cent central, 25 per cent local authority basis. Preference was to be given to projects designed to meet the needs of ethnic minorities. Education authorities claimed money under the programme for a wide variety of purposes, mainly in the area of out-of-school provision. Some curriculum development work was also funded. The problems that arose are, in retrospect, obvious. Short-term fundings mean real problems of continuation and, second, the level of thought that went into applications seems to be concentrated on getting one's hand in the till and worrying about how to spend the money later. A thin scattering of rather expensive buildings within the inner city are a not inappropriate memorial to the programme. Its continuation, the so-called inner city partnership scheme, is an attempt to make the programme more coherent and effective. Perhaps its main virtue is a commonplace one, maintaining some educational gilding on what has become a rather shabby structure.

The EEC Social Fund is a sort of European Urban Programme. It is likely to be an important future source of funds for certain aspects of educational innovation, particularly with respect to urban education and the education of migrants. At present much of the fund money that comes to Britain, via the Department of Employment, is claimed by central government in respect of the payments it is making under Section 11 and parts of its Urban/Partnership programmes. This is not exactly in the spirit of the fund's objective, which is to support innovation rather than existing practice, but the government is within its legal rights in so doing.

A fourth and increasingly important source of funding comes again, not from the DES but from the Department of Employment, through its Manpower Services Commission (MSC). Directed at the 16–19 age group, the MSC monies are used to fund a rapidly proliferating number of schemes to help with the education and training of young people unable to obtain access to the job market. Initially reasonably successful, in that young people on the courses often did find work after completion of their course, they are now increasingly being seen as a safety net to cushion the effects of widespread youth unemployment by giving them short courses with a general education and vocational slant. Little evaluation of their efficacy has yet been made but they do keep down the unemployment statistics; one hope is that when the economy revives the young people will be better prepared for entering employment. More recent experience of these schemes indicates that this originally marginal activity is rapidly becoming very important, not only at the level of further education, but also in the secondary schools. It suggests that the government, with or without the co-operation of the DES or the LEAs, is keen to tackle the whole question of vocational education in a more determined manner than before. However the massive and rapid expansion of these schemes has been generally criticized as being badly co-ordinated and ineffective. What is interesting is that the debate on vocational education and training has, for almost the first time in British educational history come to the forefront of educational debate.

As was mentioned earlier, all these sources of money are mainly directed at two key educational issues, namely multicultural and urban education. But there are other areas of non-mainstream financial provision which are also worth mentioning.

The first of these is the way finance is channelled towards the voluntary and independent sectors. As was mentioned earlier, there is a variety of financial arrangements respecting voluntary schools. The LEA will provide recurrent expenditure, (salaries, etc.), but in addition will help out on the capital expenditure side, so that up to 80 per cent of approved expenditure on capital requirements can be claimed back.

Aid to the independent sector, another of these areas, is always controversial. After the 1944 Act, a significant number of old-established grammar schools did not fully integrate into the LEA based and financed system. The schools were funded directly from the DES, hence their name – direct grant schools. Many, like Manchester Grammar School, had national reputations. In 1973, this grant was stopped and the schools had the option of either becoming independent schools or joining in with the local LEA, usually under a comprehensive form of organization. Many chose to go independent, although in 1980 the Assisted Places Scheme, mentioned above, attempted to restore the principle of the direct grant schools, although the funding is pupil-based rather than school-based.

This new scheme is about the only direct way that schools outside the state sector can get public funds. Such funding as they do get is more a negative funding, in that many educational establishments have privileged tax positions, many of the older foundations, particularly the public schools, being registered in law as charities. Many parents of children in private sector schools complain that in financial terms they are severely penalized by the tax system for sending their children to fee-paying schools. Fees are paid, usually, out of tax-paid income and as normal taxpayers they also contribute towards the state education system. It is unlikely that much will be done about this in the near future. The reason is that parents' rights over education have been maintained in the face of considerable opposition from people who see private education as socially divisive and perpetuating inequality. To give such parents tax concessions as well would produce little political return and very likely the reverse.

The funding of higher education is a separate issue. Non-university higher education is funded on a pool basis. This means that local authorities contribute to a central pool an amount proportionate to the number of students from their area attending higher educational institutions. Each LEA takes from the pool an amount proportionate to the facilities that it provides in this area. It is a system that prevents areas like London subsidizing higher education for other areas and seems an unusually fair system.

At university level, the picture changes. Being institutions ruled by royal charter, universities are technically independent of the DES. Over the last few decades the rapid expansion of all higher education, including university education, has meant that this independence is under increasing review, particularly over the issue of finance. Three-quarters of current expenditure and nearly all capital expenditure comes from grants given out by the University Grants Committee (UGC), a quasi-autonomous non-governmental organization (Quango), which although independent of the DES has its membership appointed by the Secretary of State for Education. Universities have been slow to realize the implications of this almost total reliance on central government for financing. During the 1980s this lack of foresight is likely to cause much pain and distress to them, a point to be taken up later.

The financing of the English and Welsh education system is thus a very complex matter, frequently changing. Because of this, many people involved in education do not pay a great deal of attention to it, until it actually affects them. During the 1960s and most of the 1970s, there was a feeling that the admitted shortcomings in the system could be readily solved either with more money or alternative methods of funding, or both. This did not really happen and education's demands for more money are no longer axiomatically regarded as above discussion. This is likely to make the next decade a painful one for British education, as critical evaluation of practices becomes more dominant. Control of the purse strings will likely fall more and more into the hands of central government and the consequent power of local authorities is likely to decline. Again the conflicting claims of equality and liberty will have to be assessed, although resolution is unlikely. One major debate which is likely to forward this debate is the one about the appropriate structure and organization that education should take in England and Wales. This debate deserves closer examination.

Organization and Structure

Many teachers in schools in England and Wales would claim that their better primary schools can be amongst the best in the world. If they were then asked about secondary schools it is likely that there would be silence or an argument. The reasons for this are complex but relate in part to a crucial debate that has been going on since long before the

war. The debate is in two parts. The first is how equality of
educational opportunity should be measured and described; the
second is about what is the appropriate educational structure which
will help bring about this desirable state of affairs. It has been a bitter
and acrimonious dispute and is by no means settled. Perhaps one
reason for this long-drawn-out battle is that the debate has
concentrated on the second point, the appropriate structure, rather
than on the first part, namely, what exactly is this equality of
educational opportunity that is being looked for. In crude terms this
has meant that the debate has concentrated on one issue – the
comprehensive reorganization of secondary schools. In one corner, the
educational ideologues, extremists and progressives; in the other
corner, another group who can equally fairly be described as
ideologues, extremists or progressives depending on your point of
view. The debate is partly about the clash between the drive for a
schooling system that will produce equality and the equal desire to
maintain freedom of choice both within and outside the state
educational system. At another level it expresses, in an educational
form, the debate about the nature of British society that has
dominated much postwar political thinking. In practice, this more
serious debate has been obscured by the discussions on structure, and
it is by no means settled. However, much of the debate on the subject
does bring images of Tweedledum and Tweedledee into mind. This is
not the only issue in connection with the organization and structure of
education. There are debates over private education, nursery
education, primary education, special education and the whole range
of further and higher education. Many of these debates take place
within the closed world of education and seldom raise public passions
as much as the first issue mentioned. Higher education will be looked
at later, but before returning to the issue of secondary reorganization
it would be useful to briefly review these other features of the system,
to help make clearer the overall framework of education. As Figure
1.1 shows, the organization of education falls into a fairly typical
pattern if the broad outline is examined. There is some state nursery
provision for the under-5s but it is on a much less widespread basis
than in many other countries in Western Europe. Consequently, it is
not compulsory, whereas primary education, from the age 5 to 11, is.
Primary schools are often further divided into infant schools, taking
children from 5 to 7, and junior schools, from 7 to 11. There are also a
small number of middle schools of an alternative pattern, taking
children from either 8 to 12 or 9 to 13, the former being classified
administratively as primary schools, the latter as secondary. Secondary
schools present a bewildering variety of types, reflecting the structural
and organizational changes that have occurred over the last few years.

Figure 1.1 Structure of the education system in the United Kingdom

Age	3 4 5 6 7 8 9 10 11 12 13 14 15 16 17 18 19 20 21 22 23 24
Level	I II III IV
Stage	1 2 3 4 5 6
Compulsory	
School type	Infant Primary Junior — Grammar and comprehensive; Middle — Comprehensive; Secondary modern — Further education colleges; (a) Nursery schools (b) Nursery classes

Education preceding the first level

Examinations:
(a) General Certificate of Education ordinary level or Certificate of Secondary Education at end of stage 3
(b) General Certificate of Education advanced level at end of stage 4

Colleges of education
Polytechnics
Higher educ. inst.

Universities
Under-graduate | Post-graduate

Source: B. Holmes, *International Yearbook of Education*, Vol. 32 (Paris: IBE/UNESCO, 1980), p. 212.

After the 1944 Act, the predominant structure was what was called the 'tripartite system', consisting of grammar schools, technical schools and secondary modern schools. Children were assessed as to which form of school would be most appropriate for their needs by a selection test, commonly called the eleven-plus examination. In theory, nobody failed, as the idea was to place the child in the school best suited for his or her needs. In practice, it was widely regarded as a pass/fail examination with passing leading to entrance to the prestigious academic grammar school. Although there was supposed to be parity of esteem between the various types of school this never really existed. Success in the system meant going to a grammar school, or, to a lesser extent, one of the few technical schools. Going to the 'secondary modern' was seen as a type of failure.

The debate over equality of opportunity took as one of its starting points this difference. It was claimed that it was impossible to assess children fairly at 11 and that the very act of selection was socially divisive, biased as it appeared to be towards middle-class children and against working-class children. Against this it was argued that the grammar schools had provided a ladder for social mobility for a large number of working-class children and that the schools themselves were an efficient provider of the potential high-level manpower that it was claimed Britain needed so desperately in the postwar period.

The debate became polarized quite quickly, particularly as the two major political parties quickly took up opposing positions on the issue, with the Conservative Party wishing to retain grammar schools and the Labour Party wishing to abolish them and bring in comprehensive schools to replace both them and the technical and modern schools. The argument was also about the freedom of parents to choose the school type they wanted for their own children. The counter-argument was that few children in fact had a choice, being allocated to secondary modern schools.

Despite this polarization the move towards comprehensive schools progressed steadily during the 1960s and 1970s. The debate brought out into the open the divide between what local and central government wanted, as under the 1944 Act it was the local authorities' respon-sibility. This is well illustrated by the reaction to the DES circular 10/65 mentioned above, where those authorities who wished to retain grammar schools delayed submitting plans or submitted plans which could not be implemented in the hope that their delay would take them to a general election, a Conservative victory, and a halt to compulsory reorganization. As was mentioned earlier, this is in fact what happened, and alternating central government having led to a series of DES circulars encouraging reorganization followed by their cancellation. The latest stage in this debate was the Conservative Education Act of 1979 which repealed those sections of the Labour Education Act of 1976 making comprehensive reorganization compulsory. Despite these political wranglings, some 86 per cent of children in England and more than 90 per cent of children in Wales now go to comprehensive schools.

So for the majority of children the pattern is now that they go to some form of secondary comprehensive school. Most are 11–18 schools, but there is a wide variety of other age-range schools. In areas where there are middle schools, children may start at 12, 13 or even 14. Some schools transfer their children at 16 to sixth-form colleges, and this 11–16 pattern until recently looked likely to become a dominant pattern in future years. This is due to a variety of causes, the decline in viable numbers in many sixth forms being a major one. This also reflects an increasing debate about the nature of 16–19 provision, and a desire to integrate more closely secondary and further education. The entrenched interests in both types of institution make this a difficult area to attempt rationalization in, but there are signs, particularly in the larger metropolitan areas, that separate 16+ institutions are likely to become the norm during the 1980s. However, current thinking in the DES favours the retention of sixth forms within schools so that forecasting future trends has become more problematic.

Curriculum

To return to the point made at the beginning of this chapter, the debate about secondary reorganization has concentrated on its structure more than on a detailed analysis of what specific purposes and ends were to be achieved. Nowhere is this more clearly shown than in the debate about the curriculum. For putting all children into similar schools has not answered the real question, namely, how and what they should be taught when they actually enter their comprehensive classrooms.

On the how question, the debate has been principally about the internal organization of the school. Should children be taught in groups of similar ability or in groups of mixed ability or some combination of both? Again, what started as a debate about teaching methods within the educational world has become overtly politicized with those arguing for streaming, banding or setting on one side and those supporting mixed ability groupings on the other. In some ways the debate parallels the one about school organization. What research evidence there is has suggested that mixed ability teaching requires a greater degree of organizational and other skills than more traditional methods. As a consequence, to paraphrase, when it is good it is very very good and when it is bad it is awful. The debate continues, but within many secondary schools the various forms of internal organization are to be found, uneasily, co-existing.

Within this framework the majority of children take a five-year course leading either to the General Certificate of Education (GCE) Ordinary Level Examination (O level) or the Certificate of Secondary Education (CSE). Ordinary level is a subject-based examination, as is the CSE, in that a child can pass in any number of subjects, from one to ten, with the average being about five. The more able students attempt O level, the theory being that it should cater for the top 25 per cent of the ability range, while the next 50 per cent attempt the CSE. The top grade at the CSE, Grade 1, is accepted as being the equivalent to an O level pass in that subject. In practice, children who wish to go on to higher education, like universities or polytechnics, will take their O level examinations, usually in from five to eight subjects, before studying for another two years to take their GCE Advanced Level examinations in two, three or four specialized areas. (In 1984 it was announced that a common form of examination at 16+ would replace the separate GCE O level and CSE. This reform, after some twenty years of acrimonious debate, will combine the existing two examinations into one.) Two typical combinations would be English, history and geography, a humanities-based grouping, and maths, physics and chemistry, a science-based grouping. The standards are very high and as a consequence only a small percentage of children sit for this examination. The CSE is seen mainly as a school-leaving examination and, although many children with good grades in the CSE may go on to further education, many do not, using them as qualifications in the job market that they enter at 16. However a significant number of children, particularly in the large conurbations, still leave school without any formal qualification. Such children are finding it increasingly difficult to find employment, due mainly to the absolute decline of unskilled jobs in the British economy.

The examinations will be returned to later on. Both these and the forms of internal organization discussed previously are part of the debate about how a comprehensive education should be delivered. The other important aspect of this issue, the 'what' question, is mainly a question about the curriculum. This area has once again become the subject of a lively debate within education.

The only subject that children have to be taught by law in schools in England and Wales is religious education; that is written into the 1944 Education Act. Everything else is at the discretion of the local education authorities, for they hold the legal responsibility for the curriculum. In practice this responsibility is delegated to the governing body and headteacher of the school, and in turn this means, for the day-to-day organizing, that it is the heads, with or without their staffs, who made decisions about the subjects taught, the balance between subjects and the actual content in each subject area.

Having said that, it must be admitted that discussion and debate about the curriculum in schools in England and Wales is neither very sustained nor particularly analytical. If you went into a school and asked to see the curriculum, you would probably be shown the timetable. This is, however, what appears to be rather than what actually is the case. The curriculum is saturated with covert theory and a somewhat insular theory at that. In a comparative analysis essentialism comes out as the peculiarly British approach to the curriculum. It dominates curriculum theory in the higher levels of the secondary school and the universities and, until comparatively recently, deeply influenced the curriculum at all levels. What change there has been is seen mainly in primary schools, a process accelerated by the abolition of the eleven-plus selection examination. At this level, the influence of Dewey, mediated by his British supporters, has become increasingly powerful, to the point that the curriculum in the lower classes in the secondary school has also changed over the last fifteen years, Here child-centred learning, problem-solving and other associated ideas, in theory at least, underpin the curriculum.

To see this curriculum working at its best in a good primary school is a most exciting experience for a visitor. Purposeful activity, a wide variety of tasks being done at the same time and a genuine air of excitement persuade many such visitors that they are seeing primary education at its very best. Done badly, as can also be seen, it verges on the maleducative. As one would expect, however, much primary education is still comparatively traditional, despite the dominating rhetoric of progressivism.

In secondary schools the picture is more confused. At the theoretical level there has been a considerable literature, often associated with people like Paul Hirst, Denis Lawton, and Malcolm Skilbeck.[7] Although various schools of thought have appeared to arise, most of what is written seems firmly ethnocentric and placed in this tradition of essentialism. For example, there has been a long and continuing debate along the theme of which subjects are of most worth. This insularity, shown for instance is the almost complete dearth of reference to other curriculum traditions except perhaps that of the United States, has meant that the curriculum in most secondary schools has changed very slowly over the last few decades. There have been changes of emphasis, it is true, the decline of Classics and the growth of the upper-school option system being two examples, but in many cases the curriculum offered in secondary schools is similar to the curriculum offered in such schools some thirty years ago.

What this means is that in a typical secondary school the majority of students will follow a common curriculum for the first three years, followed by a small common core plus a wide range of option subjects in the fourth and fifth years, often considered preparation years for the O level and CSE examinations. What goes into this curriculum will vary from school to school as is the English way, incidentally making pupil transfer a disorienting experience for the many children who do change schools, but the subjects on the timetable will look similar. Thus, a typical lower-school curriculum would contain English, maths, science, a modern language, history, geography, religious education (RE), physical education (PE), games, some craft work and art. In many schools, a humanities course may well take the place of some of these separate subjects, particularly history and geography. In the fourth year, most children will continue with maths, English, games, PE and RE as core subjects, and choose from a wide variety of options for the rest of their curriculum. The option systems attempt hopefully to ensure the continuation of science and modern language teaching but this does not always happen. Often what occurs is a subtle form of streaming, with the more able children doing the higher-status options and the less able the low-status ones. In one secondary school in a large conurbation this could mean that two children follow a core of English, maths, social studies (including

RE), games and PE with the first child doing French, physics, chemistry and biology as option subjects and the other child doing catering, tailoring, woodwork and child development. The latter child could hardly be said to be doing a broadly based curriculum.

This last list of options introduces another theme and that is the *ad hoc* way in which new subject areas have been introduced into the curriculum. These have often been introduced because a teacher had an interest in an area rather than as a result of careful thought about the curriculum. Another mode of introduction has been a result of a hasty reaction to some expression of educational need by central government. The introduction of microprocessors and computer technology bids fair to being a disaster because of this. Every school will have one but who will work with them? Certainly there are not enough teachers with the requisite skills, especially in the primary sector.

More recently there have been attempts to have a more systematic approach to the curriculum. The first stage in this was the setting up of the Schools Council in 1964 as a national agency for curriculum development. The Council was set up in part to preempt efforts at that time being made by the DES to set up a national curriculum agency of its own. Opposition, mainly from the teacher unions at this extension of central control over the curriculum, led to the Schools Council being dominated not by the DES but by teacher representatives. Thus the Council, intended to herald a new initiative in national curriculum design, merely institutionalized the existing state of affairs, namely that teachers, and especially headteachers, controlled the curriculum.

Despite a plethora of curriculum projects over the fifteen or so years after 1964, the general opinion is that the Schools Council has had little effect on curriculum practice. It has made some innovations in the field of curriculum materials, it is true, but usually within the traditional curriculum framework. In one other key area, that of examinations, its record has also been patchy.

This rich variety of public examinations – GCE, O and A level, CSE and the experimental extension of the CSE, the Certificate of Extended Education (CEE) – is seen by many people as unnecessary and inefficient. Attempts to merge the examinations have been constant. Proposal after proposal has come from the Schools Council but all have been opposed and consequently dropped. A major reason for the lack of agreement is the question of who will control the new unified examination. Traditionally the universities controlled the GCE examination and the teachers themselves the CSE examination. Neither side wishes to lose control of any new examinations, the more so as the teachers only gained their controlled examination, the CSE, in 1965 after many years of struggle. At some point, rationalization of the existing system will have to come but few people now believe that the Schools Council will be the agency to bring this about, even in its new truncated form (its authority was considerably reduced by its forced contraction in 1982). However, as was indicated earlier, in 1984 the decision was finally made that O level and CSE would be merged.

Although the impact of the Schools Council has not been as great as had been hoped for, particularly by the DES, the quest for a national curriculum policy has gone on. The major recent thrust has stemmed from the so called Great Debate, mentioned earlier. From this base a new initiative was taken by the DES, attempting to establish criteria for a curriculum common to all schools. A series of surveys and discussion papers led to proposals for a national curricular framework in 1981. Considering the amount of consultation, the results verge on the banal. The set of curricular aims is a ragbag of worthy generalities lacking sufficient clarity to be operationalized. The actual proposals about subjects are clearer, suggesting a common curriculum for all schools based around English, maths, a foreign language, science, religious education and physical education, to be taught throughout a child's school career. In addition, subjects that help prepare children for working life should be stressed. Such a curriculum should be drawn up by each school, including the aims of such a curriculum, and continuous evaluation of results against these aims should be practised. On the surface, this seems little more than a modest codification of existing practice, but within it is the start of an attempt to re-establish the control of the centre over the curriculum that was relinquished in the mid-twenties. (At that time, control was relinquished to the LEAs due to fears that any incoming Labour government would use such power for doctrinaire reasons.)

To see this whole exercise as comparatively unimportant is incorrect, however. The desire for more accountability in schools, the first tentative steps for which were taken in the 1980 Education Act, and the increased mobility of the population do indicate a desire for a common curriculum and one that is more readily evaluated by the public at large. As for the needs of the world of work, current employment trends and the permanent loss of many traditional unskilled jobs pose daunting tasks for the curriculum. It is to this most difficult task that the curriculum planners, at all levels in the system, will now have to address themselves, as a matter of urgency.

The employment position, the increasing stability of the teaching force and the decline in school numbers are all likely to mean that the current debate about the curriculum will be maintained through-out the 1980s. New issues such as urbanization, the multicultural nature of British society and a growing awareness of gender as an educational issue will help to make the curriculum issue more complex and, probably, more controversial. It is to be hoped that concentration on a centralized or decentralized ordering of the curriculum will not become so vigorous a debate that these other issues will not be given the attention that they deserve. The prognosis, however, is that British schools in the 1990s will very likely be similar institutions to those around today and that the curriculum will also appear very similar.

Higher Education

The same is equally likely to be true of the system of higher education in this country. A traditional starting point for looking at this sector of the education system is Oxbridge, the ancient universities of Oxford and Cambridge. A visitor to an Oxbridge college, wondering at the beauty of the lawns in one college, asked a passing gardener how such perfection was achieved. 'Well you rakes it, then you rolls it, then you mows it. And you do that for three hundred years.' This apocryphal story sums up the calm assurance with which the universities of Oxford and Cambridge regard the rest of the world. These two universities have occupied a predominant role both in academic life and in society generally for a very long time indeed and see themselves as being at the apex of the British educational system. Whether this position is merited in another matter. The last thirty years have seen an unprecedented expansion of higher education in Britain and although Oxbridge has been a model for some of this, notably in some of the new cathedral city universities, in many other ways it has been removed, or removed itself, from the debates that have accompanied this expansion.

In 1939 there were 17 universities in England and Wales with some 50,000 full-time students. By 1979 there were 35 universities with over 200,000 full-time students. Most of this growth has occurred in the period sice 1966, following the earlier publication of a government inquiry into higher education, the Robbins Report. This report was the spur for a staggering expansion due partly to the alleged need for more high-level manpower, but also to meet the rising aspirations of the population at large, as more children wanted to go on to higher education rather than join the job market at 17 or 18 years of age. This expansion was not confined to the universities, as will be discussed later on, but it is interesting to see what effect it has had on the universities, particularly in respect of the training of teachers.

Most British universities follow a similar pattern. Most subjects and disciplines are taught at most universities. Being autonomous institutions, funded through the University Grants Committe (UGC), they have each individually controlled their own destinies. This means that many of them contain small and, it is generally accepted, uneconomic departments and that if there are any societal needs for certain types of graduates the universities may, or may not, take notice of these requirements. The fact that many of the university teachers have tenure, an almost unbreakable contract, has meant that many have thought of themselves as almost being removed from the constraints that affect other areas of education. This attitude, which must have appeared at times to central government to be arrogant and intransigent, was successfully maintained throughout the sixties and seventies but has received a severe jolt in the eighties. This is because central government has both reduced the amount of money available to the UGC and has ceased subsidizing foreign students, of whom there are a great many in the universities. Just as the earlier expansion was uncoordinated, so the contraction is likely to be. Their autonomy, leading to reluctance to close small uneconomic departments or merge them with other similar departments in other universities, and the tenure of university teachers in their posts mean that any economies suggested have been fiercely resisted. However, as the UGC no longer has the money, reality will at some point have to be recognized. This will make this decade a fascinating one to observe.

Although the universities are moving into a critical period of change and development, their actual methods of operation remain much the same as they have been over the last thirty years, if not longer. The actual pattern of work within the universities is broadly similar in all institutions. The courses are usually highly specialized three-year courses, leading to a bachelor's degree. In 1978/9 about two-fifths were reading science and technology, a fifth arts subjects such as English and modern languages, a fifth social sciences, with the remaining fifth being scattered over a wide range of subjects, with medicine, dentistry and education being perhaps the most significant. The course of study is usually intensive, with a high completion rate. This is mainly because the competition to get on is comparatively high, but is also a reflection on the amount of personal supervision that undergraduate students get.

Much of the growth in higher education was not in the university sector, however. The new polytechnics have taken on much of this rapid expansion in numbers. Polytechnics are comparatively new institutions, set up, like the new universities, in the period since 1966, often as developments of existing institutions, especially the old colleges of advanced technology. The aim behind their establishment was to strengthen the technological side of higher education, being institutions with close links with business and industry and running courses to provide the skilled manpower that these sectors of the economy were demanding. Other factors behind their establishment were, first, the belief that more local control (they are not centrally funded) would lead to a greater sensitivity towards local and national needs compared with the universities, and, second, and perhaps this is a more cynical reflection, to ensure that the university sector was neither diluted nor forced to make changes in line with the changing manpower needs of a modern industrial society.

This binary system has theoretical parity of esteem built into it, rather like that originally hoped for in the old grammar school/modern school division. This hope has proved an illusion, as few people are in much doubt as to the relatively greater prestige of the universities when compared with the polytechnics, despite the fact that they are both degree-granting institutions. This fact is illustrated by the manner in which many polytechnics have attempted to become similar institutions to universities. Arts faculties, social science faculties and an increasing bias towards 'pure' research as opposed to applied research indicate this. But again, like the universities, a harsher economic climate may well force such institutions to move back towards the more practically based type of work which they were set up to undertake.

Teacher Education

Most students leave the university after gaining their bachelor's degree, although there is an increasing trend for students to go on to do further work. Much of this is at master's degree or doctoral level, although there is an increasing number of shorter one-year courses leading to a specific professional qualification. The most important of these is the one-year Postgraduate Certificate in Education (PGCE), the essential qualification now for new graduates who wish to teach. (Until recently possession of a degree alone was sufficient qualification for teaching in the state sector.) As the teaching service is shrinking at the moment, mainly due to demographic and economic factors, it is likely that the PGCE will become an increasingly important route into teaching for the next decade, a significant change from the previous pattern.

The other major traditional path for people wishing to become teachers was the teacher training college, or college of education as it later became. Initially offering two-year courses, these were upgraded to three-year courses and finally to four-year courses, leading to a bachelor in education degree. The move towards an all-graduate teaching profession, though a worthy enough aim in itself, has not taken place without problems. The extension of courses did not always go hand in hand with an upgrading of their content, and the idea that the B.Ed. degree would have a status equal to any other first degree, although recognized in theory, has never really been accepted in fact. These failings were highlighted in the seventies, when after a period of too rapid expansion in the sixties the teacher training sector went into decline, principally due to forecasts of future needs which showed a marked falling off in demand for new teachers in the 1980s. Most colleges of education ceased to exist as such during this period. A few merged with nearby universities, more with polytechnics or with other tertiary institutions, forming colleges or institutes of higher education. The majority of teacher training takes place in these institutions, but the problems of gaining acceptance of the currency of a B.Ed. degree is likely to remain, particularly during a period of overproduction of teachers.

Conclusion

To sum up. Although Oxford and Cambridge will continue to prosper and go their own way, it is likely that the rest of the higher education system will go through a dramatic readjustment period in the next decade. The decline in demand for teachers will force a further contraction in the area of teacher education, although this may, to a limited extent, be compensated for by an increase in in-service provision. To predict the future is extremely difficult in this area, but institutions of higher education are likely to be very different, at least on the surface, by the end of the century.

Now that the United Kingdom is within the European Community much of the insularity that has been apparent within the system may slowly change. However, if this ever happens, it is likely to be a very slow process. The one feature that is very clear in the present system is the persistence of attitudes, institutions and organizational arrangements despite efforts to change the system. At the beginning of this chapter two strands of debate that inform this persistence were mentioned. Of these two, perhaps the most important is the continuing tension between the demands of egalitarianism and liberty. The consequences of this tension have been indicated. It makes the system of England and Wales a fascinating one, and from which much can be learnt.

Notes: Chapter 1

1 Marxist and neo-Marxist writers would probably see the conflict in different terms.

A useful and stimulating analysis along such lines is to be found in Birmingham
Centre for Contemporary Cultural Studies, *Unpopular Education: Schooling and
Social Democracy in England since 1944* (London: Hutchinson, 1981).
2   The Education Act (1944), Part 11.7.
3   ibid., Part 11.36. A good introduction to this Act and subsequent legislation is in
H. C. Dent, *The Education Act, 1944* (London: University of London Press, 1944;
12th edn 1968). Extracts from this Act and other educational documents can be
found in J. S. Maclure, *Educational Documents: England and Wales 1816 to the
Present Day* (London: Methuen, 1965; 4th edn 1979).
4   Responsibility for education in Wales at central government level rests with the
Secretary of State for Wales, although the DES often takes education in Wales into
its remit.
5   Observers of central government initiatives to help inner-city areas, such as the
Urban Programme, have noted that the greatest difficulty is in getting central
government departments to co-operate with one another. What was initially seen as
a problem, i.e. the articulation of central with local government, was much less of a
problem in reality.
6   DES, *The Educational System of England and Wales* (London: HMSO, 1983), pp.
70–1.
7   See, for example, R. Hooper (ed.), The *Curriculum: Context, Design and Development*
(Edinburgh: Oliver & Boyd/Open University Press, 1971); J. Reynolds and M.
Skilbeck, *Culture and the Classroom* (London: Open Books, 1976); D. Lawton,
Politics of the Curriculum (London: Routledge & Kegan Paul, 1980); M. Golby, J.
Greenwald and R. West (eds), *Curriculum Design*, (London: Croom Helm/Open
University Press, 1975).

Further Reading

The Auld Report, *Report of Enquiry into William Tyndale Junior and Infants
Schools* (London: ILEA, 1976).
H. C. Barnard, *A History of English Education from 1760* (London: University
of London Press, 1969).
G. Baron and D. A. Howell, *The Government and Management of Schools*,
(London, Athlone Press, 1974).
R. Bell and N. Grant, *Patterns of Education in the British Isles* (London: Allen
& Unwin, 1977).
R. E. Bell, G. Fowler, K. Little, *Education in Great Britain and Ireland*
(London: Open University Press, 1973).
The Crowther Report, *15–18* (London: HMSO, 1959).
DES, *Education in Schools*: *A Consultative Document* (Green Paper), ref. 6869
(London: HMSO, 1977).
DES, *Aspects of Secondary Education in England* (London: HMSO, 1979).
DES, *Local Authority Arrangements for the Curriculum* (London: HMSO,
1979).
DES, *A View of the Curriculum* (London: HMSO, 1980).
DES, *Annual Report, 1980* (London: HMSO, 1981).
M. Galton, B. Simon and P. Cross, *Inside the Primary Classroom* (London:
Routledge & Kegan Paul, 1980).
A. H. Halsey, *Educational Priority, Volume 1* (London: HMSO, 1972).
HMI, *Curriculum 11–16*, (London: DES, 1977).

W. R. Jones, *Bilingualism in Welsh Education* (Cardiff: University of Wales Press, 1966).

M. Kogan, *The Politics of Educational Change* (London: Fontana, 1978).

D. Lawton, *Class, Culture and the Curriculum* (London: Routledge & Kegan Paul, 1975).

E. Midwinter, *Patterns of Community Education* (London: Ward Lock, 1973).

The Newsom Report, *Half Our Future* (London: HMSO, 1963).

The Plowden Report, *Children and their Primary Schools* (London: HMSO, 1967).

The Robbins Report, *The Committee on Higher Education* (London: HMSO, 1963).

The Rampton Report, *West Indian Children in our Schools* (London: HMSO, 1981).

M. L. Rutter *et al.*, *Fifteen Thousand Hours: Secondary Schools and their Effects on Children* (London: Open Books, 1971).

M. Skilbeck and A. Harris, *Culture, Ideology and Knowledge* (Open University Course E 203) (Milton Keynes: Open University Press, 1976).

B. Simon and W. Taylor (eds), *Education in the Eighties* (London: Batsford, 1981).

W. Taylor, *Research and Reform in Teacher Education* (Windsor: National Foundation for Educational Research, 1978).

J. Tierney (ed.), *Race, Migration and Schooling* (London: Holt, Rinehart & Winston, 1982).

J. F. Watts (ed.), *The Countesthorpe Experience* (London: Allen & Unwin, 1977).

J. P. White, *Towards a Compulsory Curriculum* (London: Routledge & Kegan Paul, 1973).

P. Willis, *Learning to Labour* (London: Saxon House, 1977).

Organizational and Statistical Appendix

England and Wales

Agencies of Administration

NATIONAL

Statutory Parliament. Secretary of State in charge of Department of Education and Science (DES) (Secretary of State is member of Government and in the Cabinet).

Advisory 1 Her Majesty's Inspectorate (based at DES).
          2 Schools Council (advises on curriculum and examinations. Being restructured).
          3 Assessment of Performance Unit (monitors standards in education; based at DES).
          4 Council for National Academic Awards (controls degree courses, principally those organized outside the universities).
          5 Various national advisory councils on educational matters, for example teacher training and supply.
          6 Economic Science Research Council, a research body funding educational research.

REGIONAL

Statutory —

Advisory —

LOCAL

Local educational authorities, responsible to elected local authority administration. An exception is the Inner London Educational Authority, which is semi-autonomous from consistuent local authorities.

Statutory Local authority inspectors or advisers. Individual school governing bodies.

Advisory —

The Structure and Organization of the Educational System

Age	Level and stage	Types of institution	Number of institutions	Enrolments
	Adult Education	Part-time vocational and recreational courses, some to O and A level.	6,345	1,708,200
	Level 4	Universities 2 years for master's degrees, 3 years + for doctorate.	35	45,000
22		Polytechnics full and part-time	30	260,000 (Figures include level 3 members)
	Level 3 Stage 2	Degree-awarding institutions: universities, polytechnics, colleges of education, colleges of higher education. Bachelor degrees lasting 3–4 years (mostly full-time). Further education and technical colleges and Stage 2 institutions minus universities. Vocationally biased. Courses lasting 2–4 years.	Colleges of higher education and education, etc.: 597	229,000 (excluding polys and universities)
17+	Stage 1	Also sixth-form colleges		

continued

Age	Level and stage	Types of institution	Number of institutions	Enrolments
16	Level 2	Secondary schools (grammar, comprehensive and some middle schools). Courses leading to GCE O level and CSE at age 16 and A level at age 18. (Also private or 'public' schools leading to GCE exams.)	4,680 (plus 2,347 registered independent schools at Levels 1 and 2)	3,318,00
11	Level 1	Primary schools (infant 5–8, junior 8–11 and first and middle schools in some LEAs). (Also some private preparatory schools – age 8–12/13).	21,442	3,850,000
5	Pre-school	Nursery schools (including nursery classes attached to infant or first schools) (Unregistered playgroups or playschools, kindergartens, etc., exist, as well as childminders.)	596	409,000
3				

Compulsory education (spanning ages 16 to 5)

The Progress of Pupils through the School System

Age and admission and transfer procedures

Pre-school 3–5 *Nursery school* (Sometimes nursery classes in first-level school.) Application by parents. School admits. Not compulsory.

First level 5–11 *Primary school (some middle)* Application by parents. School admits. Special eduational provision for some groups – physically handicapped, educationally subnormal (from 8) – may be recommended by the authorities. Compulsory.

Second level

Stage 1 11–16 *Secondary school* Application by parents. Local education authority admits, in most cases taking parents' wishes into account (e.g. ILEA, 1982, 90% of parents had children put in first choice). Under Education Act 1980 parents have right of appeal. Compulsory to 16.

In areas where selection is still practised selection tests will be taken by children wishing to go to academic selective schools.

Entry to public school (at 13) is by application by parents. School admits, usually on the basis of Common Entrance Exam.

Stage 2 Entry to sixth forms, sixth form colleges, colleges of further education, or after 16, to work.

Third level

Stage 1 16–19 *Further Education College* Student applies. College admits. Entrance requirements vary, often based on school leaving qualifications.

Stage 2 18–21+ *Polytechnics, Colleges of Education, etc.* Student applies. Institution accepts on basis of grades in public examinations (CGE).

Universities Student applies to central clearing house (UCCA). University departments select on basis of public exam results. Also scholarship examinations, especially at Oxbridge.

Fourth level 21+ *Postgraduate Work* (usually at universities) Student applies. University department selects on basis of first degree.

Curricula

Pre-School Supervised play. Emphasis on language, art and music. Social training and preparation for formal schooling.

First level *Primary* (infant, junior, some middle schools)

Stage 1 *Infant* religious knowledge (statutory obligation), language, maths, nature study, art, music, drama, physical education, games. (Each school decides curriculum but most contain most of these elements.) Some topic work.

Stage 2 *Junior and middle* As Stage 1, with possible addition of some science and a first foreign language, usually French. Also

	history and geography, often based on topic work. Private (preparatory) schools will also do Latin.
Second level	*Secondary* (Mainly comprehensive with some grammar schools. Also private sector, most prestigious being 'public' schools.)
Stage 1 Years 1–3 (usually)	Religious knowledge (statutory obligation), English, maths, science (sometimes separated into physics, biology, chemistry), history, geography (sometimes combined in integrated studies or humanities), art, music, craft, PE, games, first foreign language (usually French, German, Spanish). Classics (Latin and Greek), mainly in private sector.
Stage 2 Years 4–5/6	Religious knowledge (statutory obligation). Usual format is core (English, maths, social studies) plus four options, either carried on from Stage 1 or new, e.g. sociology, second foreign language; leading to public examinations (GCE or CSE).
Years 6–8	Usually advanced study for GCE A level in three or four subject areas.
Third level Stage 1 age 16–19+	*Further Education* Usually vocationally oriented courses with academic courses similar to Stage 2 of second level.
Stage 2	*Higher Education* (1) Vocationally biased courses leading to near or below degree-level qualification. (2) University first degree – usually honours – specializing in one subject area.
Fourth level	Higher degrees – master's and doctorates in universities. Also higher professional training – e.g. medicine, law.

Teacher Education and Training

Type of Institution	Qualification awarded	Level of school in which teacher can teach
University	(i) Postgraduate Certificate in Education (PGCE).	All – usually work in secondary schools.
	(ii) Diplomas and Certificates in Education – in-service qualification.	—
	(iii) BA (Ed.), B.Ed. – usually upgrading of basic qualification to graduate status.	—
	(iv) MA (usually taught course for 1 year full-time, 2 years part-time. Academic qualification.	(Non-mandatory qualification for work in teacher education)
	(v) Research degrees in education at master's (M.Phil.) and Doctorate (PhD) level.	—
Polytechnic	Mainly (i)–(iii), but some do research level work.	As universities.
Colleges of Higher Education/ Colleges of Education	(i) PGCE (cf. (i) above)	All – usually work in primary schools.
	(ii) B.Ed.	
	(iii) Diplomas and Certificates in education.	—

UNESCO Statistical Information: United Kingdom

UNESCO date of entry: 20 Feb. 1946
Surface area (km²): 244,046
Population 1980 (millions): 55·95
Persons/km² 1980: 229
Rural population (%) 1980: 9·2
Births per 1,000 pop. 1980: 13·5
Deaths per 1,000 pop. 1980: 8·9
Infant deaths per 1,000 live births 1977: 14
Life expect. at birth 1979: 73 years
Pop. growth rate (% p.a.) 1975–80: −0·1

Est. illiteracy rate 15+ (%) 1980
  M: 0·5 F: 0·5 MF: 0·5
National currency: Pound sterling
National currency per US $ 1980: 0·4193
GNP per capita in US $ 1979: 6,320
GNP per capita real growth rate
  (% per annum) 1960–79: 2·2
% agriculture in GDP 1978: 2
% industry in GDP 1978: 36
  of which manufacturing: 25

Data Series	1975	1977	1978	1979
Education				
Education Preceding First Level				
1 pupils enrolled	388,309	324,369	333,009	—
2 of which female (%)	49	49	49	—
3 teaching staff	—	—	—	—
4 of which female (%)	—	—	—	—
Education at First Level				
5 duration (years)[a]	6	6	6	6
6 official age range[a]	5–10	5–10	5–10	5–10
7 gross enrolment ratio (%)	105	105	105	—
8 pupils enrolled	5,725,167	5,495,784	5,326,864	—
9 of which female (%)	49	49	49	—

10 teaching staff[b]	285,786	275,564	275,020	—
11 of which female (%)[b]	81	78	78	—
12 pupils repeaters (%)	—	—	—	—
13 pupil/teacher ratio[b]	21	21	20	—
Education at Second Level				
14 duration gen. educ. (years)[a]	7	7	7	7
15 official age range gen. educ.[a]	11–17	11–17	11–17	11–17
16 gross enrolment ratio (%)	83	83	83	—
17 pupils enrolled	5,154,371	5,344,922	5,380,774	—
18 of which female (%)	49	49	49	—
19 teaching staff	—	—	—	—
20 of which female	—	—	—	—
21 pupils repeaters gen. ed. (%)	—	—	—	—
Education at Third Level[c]				
22 students per 100,000 inhabit.	1,308	1,356	—	—
23 students enrolled	732,947	760,085	788,186	—
24 of which female (%)	36	36	36	—
25 students scient./tech. fields (%)	37	36	42	—
26 foreign students	49,032	58,563	59,625	—
27 teaching staff	—	—	—	—
Public Expenditure on Education				
28 total in nat. currency (000,000)	7,020	—	—	—
29 of which current expend. (000,000)	6,292	—	—	—
30 total as (%) of GNP	6·7	—	—	—
31 current expendit. as % current government expenditure	—	—	—	—

continued

Data Series	1975	1977	1978	1979
Science and Technology				
32 stock of university graduates per million inhabitants	—	—	—	—
33 stock of persons with complete second educ. per million inh.	—	—	—	—
34 scientists and engineers in R&D per million inh.[d]	1,419	—	—	—
35 technicians in R&D per million inh.[d]	1,356	—	—	—
36 expend. on R&D as % of GNP[e]	2.1	—	—	—
Culture and Communication				
37 book titles published	35,526	36,196	38,641	41,864
38 circulation daily newspapers per 1,000 inh.	388	410	424	—
39 consumption (kg) newsprint per 1,000 inh.	22,359	22,778	23,723	24,872
40 consumption (kg) printing and writing paper per 1,000 inhab.	25,338	27,841	30,281	31,794
41 cinema seats per 1,000 inh.	15·7	13·7	13·2	12·9
42 radio receivers per 1,000 inh.[f]	698	716	906	931
43 TV receivers per 1,000 inh.[f]	361	390	—	394
44 volumes in public libraries per 1,000 inhabitants	—	—	—	—

Notes:
[a] The educational structure allows for other alternatives.
[b] Including education preceding the first level.
[c] Including students at the Open University.
[d] Not including the higher eduction sector.
[e] Not including social sciences and humanities.
[f] Licences.

Source: Statistical Digest 1981 (Paris: UNESCO, 1981).

2

Education in France
Traditions of Liberty in a Centralized System

MARTIN McLEAN

Several analyses of French politics and society have emphasized the contrast between abrupt revolutionary changes and strong forces of continuity. France has experienced dramatic revolutions, as under Louis XIV, Napoleon I and de Gaulle. Many institutions and attitudes have survived these radical changes. De Tocqueville showed how the administrative institutions of the *ancien régime* persisted through and beyond the 1789 Revolution. Karl Marx's famous statement that men make their own history but are at the same time constrained by circumstances inherited from the past is found in an essay on the 1848 Revolution and its aftermath.

This concept of cultural lag can be applied to the study of French education. Since 1945, official statements have stressed that education is a human right and a means to develop the potential of each individual. The way that education is organized and the dominant views of what knowledge should be transmitted continue to emphasize hierarchy and uniformity. The interaction between new aims and historical practices provides a central theme for the study of contemporary education in France.

Aims

One recent statement of the aims of education is contained in the 1975 Law known as the Haby Reform. Five major aims can be identified:

1 Every child has the right to schooling. It is free and compulsory between the ages of 6 and 16. It is the foundation for lifelong education.
2 Schooling fosters the development of the child. The state guarantees respect for the personality of the child.

63

3 The family has an important role in education.
4 There should be equality of opportunity which should make it possible for everyone, according to his ability, to have access to different types or levels of schooling.
5 Schooling allows the child to acquire a culture. It prepares him for working life. It allows him to exercise his responsibility as a man and citizen.

The first four groups of aims focus on individual rights, whether these are rights of access to education, respect for the individual personality, recognition of the family, or equal chances to participate in the selective and competitive aspects of the schooling process. The last set of aims has a society or national-needs orientation. They are concerned with the cultural, economic and political development of the nation as a whole.

A tension between the individualist and collectivist strands in French educational ideologies can be traced to the conflicts inherent in the first and last concepts of the revolutionary slogan 'Liberty, equality and fraternity'. Generally the revolutions from 1789 to the students' uprising of 1968 have initially stressed liberty. The weight of tradition has tended to emphasize fraternity in the intervening periods.

Yet French history is not purely cyclical. Since 1945, the individual has been given greater prominence in official statements on educational aims. The parameters of individual rights contained in the 1975 Law have expanded both since the 1789 Revolution and since 1945. The extent of change can be gauged by a comparison between the 1975 Law and two classic statements of educational purposes: Condorcet's report to the Legislative Assembly of 1792 and the 1947 Langevin-Wallon Plan. Particular attention can be given to the conception of the right to education, equality of opportunity, the development of the individual and the rights of the family contained in each statement of aims.

Condorcet had proposed that the state should provide universal free education to achieve the ideals of liberty and equality. Individuals should know their rights and be aware of their duties. To have access to the knowledge and ideas transmitted by school was to gain individual liberation. For all future citizens to have an education was a guarantee of political equality and democracy. This conception of universal education as the basis of a democratic state of autonomous individuals who were equal before the law and in their rights to participate in the political process has been fundamental to the French belief in education since the 1789 Revolution. In the event, duties rather than rights were emphasized.

Condorcet assumed that universal free education could be provided only for children between the ages of 6 and 10. This was understandable as in 1792 France was a rural society without a tradition of widespread education. It was not until Ferry's laws in the 1880s that free universal and compulsory schooling for children aged between 7 and 13 became a reality. It was only after the First World War that there was influential support for the idea of universal free secondary education and this programme did not receive wide endorsement and official support until the 1947 Langevin-Wallon Plan. Significantly, the 1947 plan, like the Ferry laws, came after a major war, when the re-establishment of democratic government gave an impetus to the democratization of education.

The Langevin-Wallon Commission report proposed that education should be available for all children between the ages of 3 and 18, even though the lower limit to compulsion was to remain at 6. By 1975, concepts of individual rights had changed sufficiently for the link between educational opportunities and childhood to be challenged. Schooling was only compulsory for ten years but education was to be permanent in the sense that it would be available for citizens at every age, virtually from the cradle to the grave.

Condorcet had proposed that selection to secondary education should be on the basis of merit in the sense of Carnot's phrase that a career should be 'open to talents'. Only a small minority would go on to post-primary education so that the selective principle was meritocratic rather than egalitarian. This apparent contradiction with the ideal of equality could be reconciled by reference to the principle of the common good. Those chosen for higher-level education should use the knowledge and skills they so acquired to contribute to the social, political and economic progress of the country as a whole from which all citizens would benefit. Condorcet's support of a human rights justification for the universal provision of primary education co-existed with his belief that selection was necessary in the interests of communal development.

After 1945, equality of opportunity acquired a different meaning in major statements of aims. The emphasis moved away from society's needs towards the rights of individuals. The Langevin-Wallon Report put forward the principle of justice as the first consideration. Each individual would have the right to stay in the selection contest for as long as possible even though in the long run and in the interests of society leaders should be selected out and educated in accordance with their talents. The same type of formulation is found in the 1975 Law where the emphasis was placed upon the opportunities open to each individual rather than the duties placed upon the selected elite.

Thus, in spite of the emphasis placed on rights, in both the

Langevin-Wallon Report and the 1975 Law there is an admission that pupils will have different futures and that the education system will provide different types of courses. The principle of selection is not denied and the emphasis is placed upon opportunity as much as on equality. But the rationale for selection in 1947 and in 1975 was the differing aptitudes and personalities of children which require different types of education rather than the needs of society for a talented elite. While this aim, in one interpretation, may be seen to be society-centred, in that the recognition of the process of differentiation between children in the education system may be linked to social and economic differentiation within an industrial society, the formulation of the aim and its overt purpose lay stress on releasing the capacities and potential of individual children.

The other two individualist aims of 1975 found little expression before 1945 in official statements. Though the idea that education should be concerned with the unique personality of each individual had been given expression in the eighteenth century by Rousseau, it did not receive significant official endorsement until 1947. The Langevin-Wallon Report drew upon child psychology to emphasize a need to respect the individual personality of each child. The rationale had become wider by 1975 when it was stated very firmly that the state respected the individuality of the child and this commitment was linked to a recognition that the state should not usurp the rights of the family in educational matters. After the 1968 student risings, education at every level from pre-school to university began to be regarded by significant groups of people as an activity in which the recipients and participants – pupils, teachers, parents – had a right to consultation and decision. A centralized state monopoly in educational decisions – which had been accepted since the 1880s – was more vigorously challenged prior to and after 1968. The 1975 Law recognized the legitimacy of those demands.

The three society-centred aims of 1975 have a much older lineage. The idea that one national culture should be transmitted to all children was supported by Condorcet, who like the eighteenth-century encyclopaedists believed that one body of knowledge could be organized which would benefit both the individual and society. There developed the concept of a *culture générale* of rational, humane and scientific knowledge, the possession of which by as many citizens as possible would both liberate the individual from the narrowness of working life and create a fraternity among the whole population.

The transmission of a *culture générale* as a central aim of education received as enthusiastic and emphatic support in the Langevin-Wallon Plan as it did in Condorcet's report. By 1975 there had been a slight retreat. Reference was made to the acquisition of *a* culture rather than *the* culture and *the culture générale* of the Langevin-Wallon Report. There was some concession to the idea that some children and some communities might have different cultural needs.

The aim of giving training to pupils in the exercise of their responsibilities as men and citizens has been less prominent in official statements in recent years. However, it may be argued that it is still central in French education. Historically it has been very significant. After 1789 mass loyalty was important to defeat the adherents of the *ancien régime* and its foreign supporters. The political aim was important when universal compulsory education was introduced in the 1880s. Ferry's educational reforms were designed partly to revive France militarily after her defeat by Prussia in 1871 and partly to strengthen the newly established Third Republic against its internal monarchist and clerical opponents. Again after 1945, a high priority was given to reasserting the political cohesion of France after five years' rule by a puppet government during the German occupation.

The economic aim of 1975 was consistent with some of the basic ideas of Condorcet but also had a particular meaning in the context of economic changes since the late 1950s. Condorcet had argued that higher levels of education should prepare a professional elite which would lead overall national development. Mass education appeared to have no specifically economic aim presumably because there was little that education could do to make the children of peasants more productive when they inherited their parents' farms. The Langevin-Wallon Report was more concerned to adjust the social consequences of industrialization through education rather than to stimulate further economic change.

The 1975 injunction that education should prepare children for working life can be seen in the context of the transformation of France from an agricultural society into one of the most advanced industrial countries in the world. Since the end of the Second World War, but particularly after the accession of the Gaullist government in 1958, a manpower planning approach has influenced the establishment of educational priorities. Comprehensive economic plans produced by government, which are designed to intensify the development of a high technology economy, have attempted to link the provision of courses in the education system to projected manpower needs. The growing importance of 'individual rights' justifications for education in the period since 1945 has been tempered by the priority given to an economic society-centred aim.

Government statements of educational aims frequently appear contradictory. The individual rights aims of the 1975 Law do not fit easily with its society-centred aims. The imprecision of the statement of aims often represents an attempt to mask these contradictions. The vagueness of general aims is frustrating for the educational practitioner. But this lack of clarity is the crucial starting point for analysis of educational systems. The imprecision indicates areas of possible conflict within the system which may then be explored further.

Two kinds of approach may be taken to the investigation of conflicts in general aims. Some aims may be seen as reactions to recent political, social and economic changes. Others may reflect older traditions. Cultural lag may be demonstrated within a statement of general aims. The other approach starts from the assumption that governments include particular aims in their statements to meet the demands of influential groups of people. New aims are included when particular groups of people change their views or new groups become politically important. Older aims survive because they have powerful supporters. The two approaches are not incompatible. Groups change their views or new groups become important in response to social, economic and political changes. Older traditions may survive because groups committed to them are powerful enough to defend them successfully.

The industrialization and urbanization of France, especially since 1945, may be associated with the increasing emphasis on individualistic aims of education. A complex, socially and economically differentiated urban society is more likely to produce demands for individual rights than more homogeneous rural communities in which hierarchical social and power relationships are legitimized by tradition and close personal relationships. On the other hand, industrialization is also likely to bring pressures that the education system be geared to prepare more sophisticated and specialist workers.

The 1975 Law was introduced by a centre-conservative government which had strong links with industrialist interests and a commitment to continuing the state capitalist revolution which had taken off after the Gaullist victory of 1958. This Law was also an attempt to appease centre-left parties. These parties had been influenced by teacher unions, parent organizations and student groups, most of which had pressed for a more libertarian approach to educational matters, especially since the student risings of 1968.

Governments cannot implement educational reforms simply on the basis of overt support at party political level. Successful reform involves changing institutions and the behaviour patterns of the people who operate them. The forces of tradition are most likely to be entrenched in those institutions where the power, privileges, stability and ease of mind of professionals are often threatened by radical changes. Sometimes these professionals can impress their views upon government sufficiently for their attitudes to be incorporated in statements of aims. This may lie behind some of the conflicts in the 1975 statement of aims.

The statements of individualistic general educational aims in 1975 may have reflected social and economic changes and new party political aims. The institutions of education in France in 1975 – including the administration, educational structures and curriculum – and the attitudes of those working in them were more collectivist. These institutions (and the attitudes of people who run them) are likely to change more slowly than stated aims and can provide important constraints on the achievement of educational reforms. The interaction of individualist aims and collectivist institutions can now be explored more fully.

Administration

The French system of educational administration is typified usually as highly centralized. It is seen to stress hierarchy, authority and uniformity. If this is true then the administrative system is a major constraint on the attainment of individualistic general aims. Such a hypothesis needs to be explored carefully to discover whether the French system is totally inimicable to the recognition of diversity and whether any changes have been effected which bring greater harmony between general aims and administrative practices.

Four levels of educational administration can be identified for purposes of comparative analysis – national, regional, local and institutional (school). In France, national administration is centred on the Ministry of Education, whose personnel transmit orders and advice to the other levels. General principles are contained in laws, such as that of 1975, which originate in the Ministry of Education and the Cabinet but which require the approval of the National Assembly. General regulations which implement laws are promulgated through decrees which are issued by the Ministry of Education but which also require the signature of the President and the Prime Minister. The interpretation of aspects of general regulations is dealt with through ordinances, *arrêtés*, circulars and instructions which do not require formal approval from any agency outside the Ministry of Education. All these instruments of government are disseminated by publication in the weekly *Bulletin officiel de l'éducation nationale*.

The powers of the Ministry are very considerable. It decides where schools are to be opened and closed, how much money will be available to each region and the principles by which it will be spent by each school, how many teachers will be allocated to each region and how much the teachers will be paid. The Ministry also decides what subjects will be taught in each grade of schooling for how many hours each week and the general outlines of the syllabus for each subject. It also administers external examinations and validates the major educational qualifications. It recommends textbooks and other teaching materials and draws attention to certain pedagogical methods. Ministry inspectors supervise upper secondary institutions, a legacy of the Napoleonic creation of a corps of bureaucrats and *lycées* as national secondary schools.

The Ministry of Education does not initiate all national level decisions. As in most countries, the global sum of money to be spent on education needs the approval of the President, the Cabinet and the Ministry of Finance. In France, the initiative in deciding the resources to be available for each level and type of education is taken by an interministerial committee. The Ministry of Finance also gives approval for detailed items of educational expenditure.

The regional unit of administration is the *académie*. It is headed by the *recteur* who is appointed by the Ministry of Education and is responsible solely to it. His major role is to ensure that ministry instructions are implemented. He supervises the allocation of staff to primary and lower secondary schools. The twenty-six *académies* are groupings of *départements*, which are the units of general regional and local government. Each of the ninety-five *départements* in France has an *inspecteur d'académie* who is responsible to the *recteur* of the *académie* in which his *département* lies. The *inspecteur d'académie* exercises surveillance over lower secondary schools to be sure that they comply with objectives produced by the Ministry and the *recteur*. He is the chairman of the council of each lower secondary school. He heads a team of local inspectors who supervise primary schools at department level. He has delegated powers of financial control but is required to report to the *préfet*, who is the general administrative head of the *département*, and to liaise with him on matters concerning the provision and finance of primary schools.

Académie officials are agents of the Ministry of Education and they execute national policies. They are the main implementers of those national decisions in relation to primary and lower secondary schools. It is at *académie* level that the allocation of individual teachers to individual schools is decided and it is the *académie* inspector who is the powerful executor of ministerial objectives with whom teachers and parents or their representatives will have contact. Though there is a national source of authority, this power is experienced at regional level by those involved in schools.

The unit of general local government in France is the *commune*. There are around 38,000 *communes*; some are large towns, but most of them have less than 500 inhabitants so in practice *communes* are grouped together for educational purposes. The *commune* has a locally elected municipal council and *maire*. The municipal council has responsibilities but few powers. It provides the building, maintenance and non-pedagogical services of primary and junior secondary schools but has little or no influence on teaching matters.

At school level, there is a head of administration who is responsible for the implementation of directives from higher authorities, the allocation of the school budget and the return to these authorities of estimates of future school enrolments and teachers required. His deputy oversees the day-to-day running of the school in matters of the timetable, provision of substitute teachers and pupil discipline. There is no strong tradition of school autonomy in educational decision-making.

Not all schools in France are fully controlled by the Ministry of Education. About 16 per cent of pupils are in private schools, mainly religious and Catholic, which are found at both primary and secondary level. After the conflicts between church and government in the late nineteenth and early twentieth centuries, these schools were largely outside the influence of the state. They had to receive a licence from the *préfet* but the conditions were not related to their educational effectiveness. Since 1959 those private schools accepting state financial aid had to employ qualified teachers. Contracts were introduced whereby private schools accepting state assistance would adhere to state programmes and timetables according to the judgement of *académie* inspectors. State intervention in private education has increased but is still limited. Not all private schools accept state aid and with it state surveillance.

Three types of judgements have been made about highly centralized systems of educational administration. First it is claimed that they ensure a more balanced and egalitarian distribution of resources than a decentralized system. Second, it is argued that central agencies are overloaded and tend to be slow and cumbersome in implementing changes that have been adopted. Linked to this is the argument that Ministries of Education tend to be overdepartmentalized and that there is little co-ordination between various sectors of the educational system. Third, it is claimed that centralization is associated with lack of consultation, especially of the interests of the teachers, parents and pupils involved in education. If these judgements are valid in relation to France, then the system of educational administration may facilitate the achievement of the aim of equality but discourage rapid change and frustrate the recognition of the right to individual diversity.

It is certainly possible that centralized administration in France does achieve a more balanced distribution of resources, particularly of money and teachers. In the Ministry of Education, a school map is maintained so that the relationship between population movement and school provision can be constantly reviewed and adjusted. The same procedures are followed at *académie* level. The supply of teachers is regulated by the Ministry and by each *académie*. There should be no serious teacher shortages in particular geographical areas where all state school teachers are Ministry employees and may be sent to any school in their region. Regulations exist to ensure that teachers of a particular grade teach the same number of hours to classes of approximately the same size.

Some children in some areas may need extra educational resources to compensate for socio-economic disadvantage. Historically such children have been found mainly in remoter rural areas but in recent years the children from certain urban areas – particularly from immigrant families – have suffered disadvantage. Action to compensate for such disadvantage is a matter for political decision and is affected more by the outcome of political debates than by the effectiveness of administrative action, which is geared to uniformity of treatment rather than positive discrimination.

Informal pressures at local level may partially frustrate intentions to achieve greater equality. Teachers may be allocated initially to certain areas but they can apply for transfers, which means that the more experienced and best teachers are likely to be concentrated in those parts of France where the majority of teachers would like to live. The distribution of resources can be affected by the lobbying of local bureaucrats or national politicians by pressure groups. Studies of urban renewal programmes suggest that government aid is likely to be allocated disproportionately to areas which are politically marginal and capable of being swung to support the political party in power in elections rather than to areas which have greater need on socio-economic criteria but which are not politically marginal.

The claim that powerful central administrations tend to be cumbersome may have had some validity some years ago since the Ministry of Education was divided into directorates, each of which was responsible for a different sector of the education system – primary, secondary, technical, higher, youth and sports – and there was little co-ordination between these agencies. Similarly the ministry was overloaded with work so that decisions on local matters could be slow in being effected.

Recent reforms have gone some way to meet such criticisms. In 1974 branches of the ministry were reorganized. The directorate of planning and co-ordination is concerned with the establishment of priorities between plans for all sectors of the system. Large-scale reform plans can be put into effect more quickly and smoothly.

There has been criticism that the introduction of new management techniques has meant that a new type of professional administrator is employed often without any direct previous experience of education.

This argument assumes, somewhat debatably, that a professional administrator, who is advised by educationists, is less qualified to make educational administrative decisions than an administrator who has had long experience in the school system. But it is possible that educational aims which stress diversity receive less attention when they are not easily reconcilable with administrative efficiency.

After 1970 the Minister of Education, Olivier Guichard, tried to give greater power to the *académie* administrations so that they could respond more effectively to local needs without constant reference to Paris. Such a reform would meet the criticism that the central ministry is too rigid and unresponsive. It should be noted, however, that such a reform is informal. Whether *académies* exercise greater local initiative depends on the way that central and regional administrations behave rather than on the formal structure of the administration. A centralized administration is equally capable of encouraging or stifling local initiative depending on how central administrators view their relations with local officials.

The claim that a centralized system engages in less consultation with those concerned with and affected by educational policy is clearly not true in relation to France. What is significant is that consultation takes place in a different way in a centralized system from one that is decentralized. At each level of educational administration in France, consultative bodies are established. The most senior and oldest of these bodies is the *Conseil Supérieur de l'Éducation Nationale*, which was created by Napoleon. This body originally included educational administrators and teachers but its composition has been widened to include representatives of other ministries and of associations of parents, students, employers, and trade unions. There are also committees at national level which advise on specialist matters like the curriculum and examinations and consist mainly of teachers, administrators and academics.

Similar consultative councils and committees exist at *académie* level while in the *commune* the municipal council is an elected body. In 1969 school administration councils were established which include educational administrators, employer and trade union representatives and elected representatives of teachers, non-teaching staff, parents and, in secondary schools, pupils. These councils must meet at least once a term though their deliberations are confined wholly to internal school matters.

These councils at each level are purely advisory. They have no statutory or executive powers. At the highest levels there is a majority of officials. Outside representatives are chosen by the ministry though, in relation to well organized groups such as teacher unions or parent associations, it is difficult for the ministry to choose any other than the nominees of the most important teacher or parent group.

The major criticism of this system is not the lack of consultation but the centralization of the mechanisms of consultation. The school councils have little influence and representatives of their views are rarely heard at the higher levels. Interest groups organize themselves at national level and it is the national representatives of these groups who are consulted.

The organization of teachers, parents and pupils at national level encourages fissiparous movements among each group. The teacher unions representing different grades of teachers are split not only in terms of their occupational interests but also often in political ideology. There are several national parent unions and often rivalry between them, especially between those committed to private education and those who are militantly in favour of state schools.

It is also argued that the officials can exploit divisions between the various interest groups and can exploit the political inexperience and lack of expert knowledge of parent and pupil organizations to ensure that advisory bodies reach conclusions which are acceptable to the administrators.

Influence is brought to bear on the administration by agencies outside the formal network of advisory councils. While the law courts exert little influence, the political parties represented in the National Assembly are important. Governments are influenced by the attitudes of political parties to particular educational issues especially when the survival or the re-election of the government in power depends on the ability to win continued political support. Educational interest groups such as teachers and parent associations are linked to political parties and each political party has an educational spokesman.

Yet again, the influence of political parties is strongest at national level. Local political influence interests are rarely consulted except where a local political change of support is likely to have a significant impact on a national election.

Distinctions ought to be drawn between debates about, on the one hand, wider educational issues such as the principles of access to schooling and the articulation of various levels of schooling and, on the other, specialist curriculum issues. In the first area, many groups participate openly in the debates and influence decisions. In the latter, discussion is more closed and is confined to educational specialists. In matters of detailed implementation of general principles in regard to particular schools and areas, the professional administrators are rarely challenged very effectively except where local groups are able to mobilize obstructive efforts.

Is the French system of educational administration capable of encouraging the attainment of individualistic aims of education? The system has become more open and flexible. But it is still highly centralized, authoritarian and hierarchical. It is relatively well adjusted to the achievement of equality of opportunity at national level. It is not in any way adapted particularly at the second and third levels of education to making varied responses to a local diversity of interests. Local institutions have still not developed in a powerful or effective way. Different interests are more widely represented at national level but even there laymen can be outmanoeuvred by an established corps of professional administrators.

Finance

The main issue in the finance of education are what methods of raising money and distributing it to schools best achieve equality of provision and attention to particular needs. It is sometimes argued that the French centralized system of raising and distributing financial resources leads to a more equal spread of these resources but is not always as adapted to meet special, especially localized, needs.

The structure of the system of finance should be described. Most expenditure on the French state school system comes from central government sources. The rest is provided by the communes. The central government pays all state school teachers' salaries, which account for 73 per cent of educational costs. It pays all the costs of education in upper secondary institutions. Communes pay for the building and running costs of primary and lower secondary schooling apart from teachers' salaries but they receive grants from central government which cover about 85 per cent of these costs.

There are several types of contract between private church schools and the government. Up till 1959 they received rather insubstantial state support based on individual needs. Since 1959 the majority of church schools receive the costs of teachers' salaries while others have all their running costs paid by government. In 1971 an arrangement was introduced whereby the latter system became standard (so the church authorities only had to meet capital costs). State-subsidized church schools are not allowed to charge fees to parents (except for boarding costs). Some private schools have remained totally independent. Thus a traditional emphasis on internal government financial responsibility has increased with the subsidies to communes and to private school authorities.

Generally, revenue is not raised by specific taxes for educational purposes. Central government revenue comes mainly from sales, income and company taxes while communes raise money through a variety of local taxes, often linked to the granting of licences for markets, etc. In neither case is the revenue raised for educational expenditure distinguished from funds intended for other purposes. The exception is the apprenticeship levy on employers which has existed since the 1919 Astier Law and is used exclusively to finance vocational training of young workers and school leavers in state-run apprenticeship centres and similar vocational training institutions. More recently employers have been required to finance educational leave for their employees.

Decisions on the proportions of educational expenditure to be allocated to various levels and types of education (pre-school, primary, secondary, higher, technical, general education) are made initially by the interministerial group responsible for producing the government economic plans. This overall distribution between types of education is decided therefore outside the Ministry of Education though with the ministry's involvement, in the light of the projected manpower requirements.

The decisions of the economic planning committee on educational expenditure are advisory. They can and often are changed by Cabinet decisions. The credits also have to be approved by the National Assembly. In general, overall educational expenditure is determined less by the Ministry of Education 'bidding' for funds which are then reduced in the Cabinet or by the Ministry of Finance and more by an interdepartmental economic planning exercise.

The Ministry of Education does decide how much money will be allocated within the limits decided by the economic planning commission on the distribution of funds between different types of education. The Directorate of Objectives within the Ministry advises on priorities between programmes which have been previously costed. Funds are then dispensed to the *académies*, which have some power to decide on distribution within the priorities established by the Ministry. Schools are given budgets to cover the materials needed for education.

This system of financing means that criteria are decided in terms of nationally established objectives rather than in response to requests at local or regional level. This may mean that, for instance, materials and buildings for science education can be underused when demand for science courses has not met the projections. It does mean also that a more equal distribution of resources between regions and areas is likely to occur.

These are considerable opportunities for central government to change priorities between different sectors and types of education. This may in part explain the great expansion of pre-school and lifelong educational provision in France compared with other industrialized countries. The centralization of finance does not necessarily obstruct the achievement of individualistic aims of education. It is possible in the French system for localized projects to be allocated generous finance. Whether this occurs is dependent upon the administrative and political processes described in the previous section.

Organization and Structure

The individualistic aims of education enunciated in 1975 require a structure of schooling which allows for a high level of access to schooling, wide opportunities for individual advancement through the system to achieve the ideal of equality of opportunity and also an emphasis on horizontal integration to permit a diversity of choices for children to develop in different ways. The French structure of education has been reformed since 1959 in ways which have brought a high degree of success in the realization of the first two aims. Attempts to attain the last aim have been far less successful.

Like the education systems of most countries at some point in their history, there was a distinction in France between mass elementary schooling and elite secondary education. The movement towards integrating these two sectors developed in the middle of the twentieth century. What is of interest is the particular form this reorganization has taken and the effects it has had on raising enrolment rates, equalizing opportunities and providing for diverse interests. On the one hand, compared with most other industrialized countries, there are high rates of participation in French education by children and young people between the ages of 3 and 19. On the other hand, a high degree of selection of pupils persists.

Compulsory education begins at the age of 6. Almost all children from 4 to 6 and 80 per cent of those from 3 to 4 years old attend *écoles maternelles* or classes attached to the primary schools. The expansion of these *écoles maternelles* occurred mainly in the 1960s and 1970s so that the proportion of children receiving nursery education is greater in France than in any other OECD country apart from Belgium. *Écoles maternelles* are provided by religious organizations as well as by the *communes* and are financed in the same way as primary schools. They are coeducational and free. However, classes are often much larger than in primary schools.

Primary education has been free, universal and compulsory since the 1880s. Up to 1959 elementary education was terminal for the majority of pupils. Classes up to that date were provided for children up to the end of compulsory schooling at 14. It was possible for pupils to attend an *école primaire supérieure* or *cours complémentaires* between the ages of 14 and 16 but these institutions were part of the elementary school system.

Since lower secondary school for all children began to be provided after 1959, first-level (primary) education has ended at the age of 11. Primary schools or, in some cases, the classes within them were single-sex but since 1964 have become increasingly coeducational. They enrol children on a neighbourhood basis. About 16 per cent of children were in private primary schools in 1979.

Before 1959 primary schools prepared children for the examination of the *certificat d'études primaires* at 14 and a minority for the selective examination for entry to the academic second-level school at 11. Since the development of common lower-second-level schooling in the 1960s, formal external examinations no longer influence first-level schools. But the allocation of children to grades within the primary school is related to their performance in school work. About 15 per cent of children repeated the first grade and 11 per cent the fifth and final grade in the mid-1970s. Attempts have been made to reduce grade repeating, including the expansion of pre-school education. The principle survives, however, that the promotion of children through the grades is related to academic achievement as well as to age.

Up to 1959, academic second-level schools, *lycées*, catered for pupils between 11 and 18 and above and were quite separate from the elementary system. *Lycées* had been established by Napoleon as nationally (as opposed to locally) supported institutions. They had been fee-paying and drew pupils from their own preparatory classes though in the twentieth century they gradually recruited more pupils from state first-level schools at the age of 11. Even then they selected only a minority of these pupils.

Attempts were made to introduce second-level classes for other pupils after 1936, but secondary institutions for the majority of children began to be introduced only after the 1959 Berthoin decrees. The first institutions were the *collèges d'enseignement général*, which provided classes for the 11–16 age group but were separate from the *lycées*, which continued as before. After 1964 genuinely common lower second-level schools – *collèges d'enseignement secondaire* (now called *collèges uniques*) – were introduced for all children in the 11–15 age group. The *lycées* became upper secondary schools enrolling a proportion of pupils who had completed lower secondary education. By 1969, when the minimum leaving age was effectively raised from 14 to 16, the majority of schools had begun to be reorganized on these lines.

The ideal of the *école unique* has been realized by the creation of a separate stage of lower-second-level schooling. All children from the same neighbourhood are in the same *collège unique* until the age of 15. The major issue has become the differentiation of various groups of pupils within lower-second-level schools.

There were three tracks (*filières*). Two tracks followed a similar type of general education course for four years with a distinction only between the number of extra subjects which might be taken by the pupils in the more advanced stream. A third track – the transitional and pre-vocational classes – consisted of about 25 per cent of pupils, who followed a more limited curriculum. These pupils almost always left school at some point in this course, since grade repeating meant that most reached the age of 16 before completing the course.

The internal structure of the lower secondary school was based on the principle of orientation. Children were assigned to one of the three tracks on the basis of counselling and guidance. The primary schoolteachers compiled dossiers on children which recorded academic performance, interests, attitudes and medical history after they had consulted parents and pupils. The dossiers were considered by guidance committees of primary and secondary schoolteachers, guidance counsellors, parent representatives and sometimes inspectors. In the first two years of lower secondary school – the observation cycle – there was continuous assessment by teachers, in consultation with parents and counsellors at some stages, to allow for transfer of some children between tracks before they entered the second two years of the orientation cycle.

Since the 1975 Haby Reform, the track system has been abolished in principle and the idea of mixed ability teaching has been proposed by the Ministry of Education for the observation cycle. In practice, many of the elements of the track system survive in a more flexible form. Mixed ability teaching has been left to the initiative of individual schools and has not been implemented very widely. There is an emphasis on remedial classes for slow learners which in practice leads to setting of children by subject rather than rigid differentiation in every subject. In the orientation cycle, optional courses are introduced which force a choice between second language or pre-vocational courses. The old distinction between the former top and bottom tracks is likely to persist through the choice of options.

There is clearly selection in the French school system, despite recent reforms, which affects the later opportunities of pupils. On the other hand, selection is overt, is performed thoroughly and carefully and involves consultation of pupils and parents. This contrasts with some national systems where selection is disapproved of by many educationists but is carried out covertly, informally and often in an arbitrary and unjust way.

The distinction between the pre-vocational courses and the other classes has meant that 25 per cent of children were shunted out of the system at the earliest possible time with restricted opportunity to climb back to mainstream schooling. The obverse of this is that 75 per cent of children were given a fairly similar educational experience up to age of 15. The transfer rate to upper second-level institutions is now about 75 per cent. Educational opportunities are kept open for a high percentage of pupils throughout the lower secondary state.

There were three types of upper-second-level education. 'Short' technical education of one or two years was provided in *collèges d'enseignement technique*. 'Long' technical took place in *lycées techniques*, while 'long' general education was provided in *lycées* – in both cases in three-year courses. More recently the technical institutions have become *lycées d'enseignement professionel* while the traditional *lycées* have been renamed *lycées généraux et technologiques*.

The *collèges d'enseignement technique* developed to supplement the apprenticeship centres which were established after 1919 to give part-time training to young workers. The professional *lycées* still perform this function. The 1971 Law on apprenticeship requires employers to release their young workers for part-time training in such establishments. The professional *lycées* also provide full-time vocationally orientated courses mainly for those who have left school at 16. A one-year course prepares mainly for unskilled work and attracts the least successful leavers from lower secondary schools. A three-year full-time course, which is also taken by part-time apprentices, leads to the *certificat d'aptitude professionelle* and qualifies students as skilled workers. Courses are divided into those that prepare for industrial, commercial, administrative and agricultural occupations. Though the *certificat d'aptitude professionelle* can be a qualification for further study, the courses in the colleges and apprenticeship centres are seen as terminal and leading to employment.

The traditional *lycées*, since their establishment at the beginning of the nineteenth century, have prepared pupils for the *baccalauréat* examinations – the entry qualification for higher education. Some *lycées* also have one- or two-year post-*baccalauréat* classes preparing for entry examinations to the elite higher education institutions, the *grandes écoles*. The *lycées* have continued to maintain these same objectives since they were truncated with the introduction of common lower second-level schooling.

The major change in the *lycées* since 1960 has been that branches of the *baccalauréat* have been introduced which have a technological orientation alongside the traditional academic courses. Such options are taken in both the general and the professional *lycées*. In the latter there are also some more specialized technical courses leading to the *brevet de technicien* or the *baccalauréat de technicien* in specialisms relating to particular occupations. These courses often involve experience in industry or commerce and are often terminal courses. But they have parity with the *baccalauréat* in that they are accepted entry qualifications to higher education. Such parity was promoted by the 1971 Law of Orientation of Technological Education, which was designed to raise the status of technological education.

The majority of French lower second-level school leavers enter some form of further education. About 35 per cent enter *lycées* and about 40 per cent enrol in the professional *lycées*. Though there are high retention rates in post-compulsory education, the failure rate in the final examinations is high. About 50 per cent fail the *certificat d'aptitude professionelle* and about 35 per cent fail the *baccalauréat*.

Since the mid-1960s the participation rate in French schooling has risen. Over 80 per cent of children begin schooling at least two years before it becomes compulsory at the age of 6 and 75 per cent have at least one year of further education beyond the minimum leaving age of 16. Thirty-five per cent embark upon courses at 16 which may lead to higher education.

Yet the processes of selection are very well defined and rigorous. Selection at the end of lower second-level schooling and at the end of upper second-level schooling assigns pupils quite firmly to particular paths of education. Opportunities for entry to higher education are affected quite considerably by selection decisions made at earlier ages.

The processes of selection have become much more careful and there are more opportunities for transfer from one path to another, though these are still limited. Recent policy decisions have concentrated on means of achieving more fluid transfers within the lower second-level school without removing the actual distinctions between courses, especially between the transitional classes and others.

Progress in the French school system is linked very much to academic attainment. Grade repeating means that classes do not contain children who are homogeneous in age. The concept of the chronological community of children is still absent. The school is essentially a selection agency for higher education and post-school occupations rather than an institution which attempts to encourage a sense of community among diverse individuals. Opportunities have been widened and selection has become less arbitrary and final but the role of the school in differentiating pupils according to preceived individual post-school futures predominates over the role of integrating the members of a future community.

The debates about school structure have emphasized on the one hand the need to relate schooling to the future occupational structure of the French economy. This perspective has predominated in the plans produced by the government. There has also been a demand that the school structure should continue to be reformed so as to maximize individual opportunities to gain entry to higher-status occupations. Such pressure has come from political groups, major teacher unions and parents. There are occasional protests – often from students – that schooling dehumanizes because it is directed towards the division of labour required by the economy but there are only fairly weak pressures to transform schools into communities of children with the aim of stressing the collective integration or the development of non-economic aptitudes.

Curriculum

One view of cultural lag is that values and attitudes change more slowly than institutions. The school curriculum, particularly, is a repository of such traditional values. In France, attempts have been made to reform the school curriculum in ways that are consistent with changing general aims. New subjects have been introduced and methods of examination have changed. But the dominant and traditional view of what constitutes worthwhile knowledge has changed far less.

The French school curriculum can be said to be guided by a conception of valuable knowledge which was developed by the encyclopaedists such as Diderot but which also had roots in medieval scholasticism. Eighteenth-century encyclopaedism was based upon the two principles of rationality and utility. Knowledge was valuable when it was logical and coherent, a conception derived from the influence of Descartes on French thought. Mathematics, languages, natural sciences and philosophy were worthy of study because of their rationality. Each could be argued to be useful in the improvement of human society and to have a utilitarian purpose.

These conceptions emphasize the intellectual aspect of learning and the universality of the knowledge to be acquired. Social, aesthetic, physical and emotional development and the possibility of differing interests between children were given little emphasis. All children were to learn as much as possible of a universally valid, rationally connected body of knowledge. The acquisition of this knowledge by as many children as possible was for the benefit of society as a whole.

The main issue was the sequence in which this knowledge should be transmitted through the school system. The curriculum of the primary school has traditionally been limited in scope. Half the timetable was devoted to French and arithmetic. There was also history, geography, observation (simple science) and drawing. Moral education had an important place but religious education was excluded from state schools by law.

There was an emphasis on learning fundamental rules and structures in French and arithmetic and essentially moral precepts in *morale* (ethics) and history. The stress was on intellectual understanding and on intellectual attainment. The teaching method emphasized the reading of a text, or perhaps the observation of a picture, drawing or object, and then questions. Children were tested frequently on the knowledge they had acquired.

There were concessions to the position of the primary school as a rural institution which taught the children of peasants who would follow their parents' occupation. The pressure of teaching was not intense except for those who attempted the *lycée* entry examination and in the year leading to the leaving certificate. History, geography and science teaching were to be related to familiar objects and conditions in the locality. But the teaching was also designed to give a common experience to all the future citizens of one nation.

Pressures to emphasize non-intellectual activities and more child-centred approaches have developed in recent years. In the *écoles maternelles* there is little attempt to teach formal skills until the year before entry to primary schools. In the 1970s, government circulars urged that children should develop oral skills and that subjects such as history, geography, observation and *morale* could be approached through interdisciplinary projects and 'curiosity awakening' methods. Physical education has a more important place. But the subjects of the curriculum have changed little and there is still an emphasis on the achievements of individual children according to standard criteria which is reflected in the continuance of grade repeating on the basis of performance.

The secondary school curriculum maintains many continuities with the Napoleonic *lycée*. There is a common core (*tronc commun*) which is followed by the majority of pupils from entry into the lower second-level school until nearly the end of the *lycée* course. This common core includes French (until the penultimate year of the *lycée*); history and geography; mathematics; a foreign language; and science. At no point in the first six years of general secondary education may students specialize to the extent of dropping major subjects in the humanities or science. The encyclopaedic tradition of a comprehensive curriculum for all pupils including most of the components of valuable knowledge has been preserved.

Before about 1977–8 in the lower-second-level school all pupils of the two top tracks studied the same subjects for the first two years with half the timetable being occupied with French, mathematics and a foreign language. Artistic education (art and music and technical/handicraft education) received three or four hours' teaching a week in total. Physical education, however, was timetabled for five hours a week throughout second-level education. The transitional classes for the least able 25 per cent were considered unable to cope with such a programme and were taught a less demanding curriculum by one class teacher.

In the third and fourth years distinctions were made between the two upper streams. The top track took one or two additional linguistic subjects – Latin, Greek, a second foreign language, or extra tuition in the first foreign language. The second stream concentrated on extra work in French, mathematics and the first foreign language. The pre-vocational (lowest) stream had a timetable consisting entirely of French, mathematics, science, technology and practical work.

There has been a significant change since the 1964 reforms of second level education, in that Latin and Greek lost the compulsory and central place they had in the selective *lycée*. Additional languages were the prerogative of the upper stream while in the lower stream the emphasis was on ensuring mastery of the basic subjects through extra tuition. The curriculum of the pre-vocational stream did not have an encyclopaedist character, which is a recognition that such a programme is not capable of being absorbed by all pupils.

The reforms introduced since the 1975 Haby Reform have modified this programme slightly. The transitional classes have been replaced by extra remedial work for those experiencing learning difficulties while technology has become an alternative option to classical or second foreign languages in the third and fourth years instead of being a self-contained course for those less able. The effect of this reform has been to emphasize a common curriculum in which all pupils spend similar amounts of time on the core subjects – French, mathematics, modern languages, history-geography, sciences, artistic and technical education and physical education. The rationale of these changes is the need to achieve equality by providing a similar curriculum for all pupils.

The modification of the curriculum to meet the varying interests of different children has received less attention. The 1975 Law allows schools to make their own curriculum choices for 10 per cent of the timetable periods in the light of the needs and interests of children. This option has not been taken up very widely. The encyclopaedist tradition has survived the democratization of lower second-level education at the cost of reducing the number and character of compulsory studies for most pupils.

In individual subjects, there are nationally uniform syllabuses for all children at the same state in each school. Syllabuses in French emphasize grammatical rules and the study of literary texts, though a little more encouragement has been given recently to linguistic creativity among children. Mathematics stresses the basic rules though there is also an orientation towards using these rules to solve practical problems. In history-geography attention is paid to non-European civilizations and the study of these subjects in France has never been as narrowly ethnocentric as in England or the USA.

There have been debates in recent years about changing the content of some syllabuses. The Rouchette Commission on the teaching of French in the 1960s for instance suggested an approach starting from the colloquial language of the pupils. The proposal, however, was an attempt to cater for pupils who were thought to be disadvantaged by their socio-economic background rather than support for a relativist philosophy of the curriculum. It was fiercely resisted.

Specialization occurs in upper second-level education, both between different types of institutions and within institutions. In the general *lycées*, a distinction was traditionally made between the philosophy-letters and mathematics-science courses. Economics-social sciences and mathematics-technology courses were introduced in 1960. The *baccalauréat de technicien* courses taken in the professional *lycée* include specialisms in various branches of engineering, medico-social sciences, administrative and commercial studies, music and information science.

All courses – including those for the *baccalauréat de technicien* – include the *tronc commun* similar to that of the lower second-level school, though in the final year French is replaced by philosophy. Different amounts of time are given, for instance, to mathematics in the philosophy-letters and in mathematics-science courses the content varies somewhat and different standards of attainment are expected in the final examination. Yet the requirement that all students follow a broad curriculum for their entire course is indicated by the necessity that candidates must pass in all subjects before the *baccalauréat* is awarded. (Even short vocational courses in technical colleges include general education subjects such as French, mathematics, science and languages.)

Since 1975 pupils may specialize in three major subjects and one minor subject in the final year of schooling. The development of the range of knowledge has led to some concession to specialization in the final year of the *lycée*.

The letters option had the highest prestige in the nineteenth and early twentieth centuries, reflecting the persistence of a humanist view of knowledge in spite of newer approaches based on encyclopaedism. Pressures to reduce the predominance of classics were resisted by *lycées*, especially the well organized *Société des Agrégés*, who received a sympathetic hearing from many politicians. The mathematics-science and social science courses did not enjoy the same prestige or the same popularity among the most ambitious students.

In the last twenty years the position of classics has declined considerably. Even within the philosophy-letters option it is possible to avoid Latin or Greek in favour of a second and third modern language. The links between economic planning and educational policy had allowed powerful economic groups to insist upon the introduction of technological options and a greater emphasis on pure science courses within general education.

These industrial and economic influences have operated also through student choices, presumably in the light of their perceptions of available career possibilities. By the mid-1970s there were more candidates for the mathematics and science specialisms of the *baccalauréat* than for the philosophy-letters and social sciences options. The numbers of students taking the technology options for the *baccalauréat* and the *baccalauréat de technicien* have grown considerably, to reach over a quarter of all candidates. The combination of economic interests in government and pupil choices seem to have defeated traditional attitudes and the power of upper second-level school teachers and their allies.

The French school curriculum has continued to be underwritten by a conception of the primacy of a standardized knowledge which is external to the experience of the students. The common core survives. Pupils are to acquire knowledge which is considered valuable because of its intellectual coherence and its value for society as a whole. But the boundaries of what is considered valuable knowledge have been extended specially to incorporate the technological knowledge required by industrial society. Similarly there has been some response to a regional cultural renascence and increased immigration by extending the list of modern languages to include Breton, Basque, Catalan, Occitan, Portuguese and Arabic.

These extensions are not incompatible with the rationality and utility which underline the encyclopaedic conception. Technological studies are seen to be based upon the intellectual coherence of mathematics and natural sciences while minority languages are just as capable of rigorous intellectual study as those which have traditionally predominated.

The demands for a curriculum which will reflect the individual interests or collective social interests of students have not been met as easily, especially when such studies do not have a clearly identifiable intellectual cohesion. Pleas by the ministry for an interdisciplinary and thematic approach have tended to be ignored by teachers. Physical education has been given a major place on the timetable but rarely appears to be taken very seriously by teachers or pupils. Aesthetic and practical subjects have been given only a minor role. The intellectualism and externalism of the encyclopaedic view seem to be well entrenched among teachers and outside groups.

Intellectualism, though challenged, is still supreme. The comprehensiveness of the encyclopaedic approach is under greater threat. The more the boundaries of worthwhile knowledge are expanded to include new subjects, the more difficult it becomes to offer total knowledge to all pupils. Specialization, which was the preserve of higher education, has begun to creep down into the *lycée*.

Teacher Education

French teachers are often thought to lack the autonomy enjoyed by their counterparts in some other countries. They are seen to be little more than executors of curriculum aims, content and methods which are dictated from above. In addition they are thought to be committed to the transmission of intellectual skills with little interest in other pedagogic problems. If these statements are valid then the nature of the teaching force makes it difficult to change the highly centralist and encyclopaedist traditions of French education in the direction envisaged by some of the new general aims of the 1970s.

French state school teachers are civil servants employed by central government. Salaries and conditions of service are uniform by grade throughout the country. Most grades of teachers may be transferred to any school in the country, though primary school teachers rarely move out of the department in which they were trained. These are important powers in ensuring the obedience of teachers to central government direction but also a valuable aid to government in ensuring equal distribution of teaching resources.

The counterpart of national uniform conditions of work is a highly stratified profession. There is a distinction between teachers who possess state teaching qualifications and security of tenure (though not in a particular school) and the unqualified auxiliaries who have no tenure or pension rights and often only half the salary of the qualified teachers. Before the late 1960s unqualified teachers were concentrated in primary schools, especially with the rapidly rising school population after 1945. The expansion of universal second-level education has shifted the auxiliaries to this level. State teaching qualifications are acquired with difficulty and this prevents the reduction of the number of unqualified teachers.

Traditionally there were two types of state qualified teachers. The *instituteurs* taught in primary schools and the *professeurs agrégés* staffed the *lycées*. The *agrégés* were then supplemented by *professeurs certifiés*, who also taught in the *lycées* though they were not as highly paid and could not teach the post-*baccalauréat* classes. With the introduction of non-selective lower secondary education, *instituteurs* were recruited, after further training, to teach the less academic pupils in lower second-level schools.

Strict divisions are maintained between these categories of teachers.

Agrégés receive double the salaries of the *instituteurs* and teach only half as many hours a week. Seventy-five per cent of the teachers in the *lycées* are *professeurs certifiés* who also teach the upper classes in the *collèges uniques*. The *professeurs d'enseignement général de collège* teach less academic children in the lower second-level schools. *Instituteurs*, without further lengthy training, are employed to teach the remedial classes.

The entry of teachers to a particular grade depends on the level of qualification obtained. Traditionally, *instituteurs* were recruited from lower secondary or upper primary schools at the age of 15 to the *écoles normales*, which were and are situated in each department. A general education up to *baccalauréat* level was provided along with teacher training. In 1972 the *baccalauréat* became a condition of entry to the *écoles normales*. Even then a strict competitive examination of an intellectual and academic nature limited entry. Success was related to potential teacher needs. Students were paid salaries while students in most other forms of higher education received no financial assistance. The lower status of the *instituteur* was emphasized by opportunities for the most able students to transfer from the *école normale* to higher levels of education.

The *école normale* course now lasts three years and leads to the *certificat d'études pédagogiques*. The first two years are spent partly on general education and lead to the first level diploma in higher education (*diplôme d'études universitaires générales – DEUG*), which is normally taken in universities. The academic level of first level (primary) and some lower second-level school teacher training has been raised so that lower level university qualifications are taken. But they are still trained separately from other grades of teacher in institutions outside the university system.

The *professeurs certifiés* are university graduates. They are recruited through the first part of the examination for the *certificat d'aptitude au professoriat de l'enseignement public du second degré (CAPES)*, usually a year after taking their degree. The first part of the *CAPES* examination is purely academic and is highly competitive. Less than 10 per cent of candidates succeed. Students then enter a regional teacher-training centre for a year of courses on education and practical training before taking the second part of the *CAPES*. A similar type of provision exists for technical college teachers.

The *agrégés* have passed the prestigious state *agrégation* examination, which is usually taken after university study beyond first degree level. There are one- or two-year courses preparing for the *agrégation* in the *écoles normales supérieures*. This examination is highly competitive and the pass rate is less than 5 per cent, based on the number of posts available. It is almost entirely academic apart from a requirement to give a formal lecture. *Agrégés* will have had no formal teacher training apart from their university studies. The majority of *agrégés* in fact tend to end up in higher education teaching, perhaps after a few years in a *lycée* while they complete a doctorate.

Differentiation between types of teachers is based on performance in academic examinations. This system is consistent with a Napoleonic concept of a career open to talents. Demonstration of intellectual quality leads to advancement. Even inspectors are appointed partly by these procedures. But the able and ambitious can rise in status by taking academic examinations at any time even after they have begun work. *Instituteurs* can and have become university teachers by such methods. But little reward is given to teachers with a deep understanding of educational theory or considerable practical teaching ability.

The differentiation of teachers according to performance in academic examinations does reinforce the primacy of intellectualism in French school teaching. It reinforces also the conservatism of higher-grade teachers, especially the *agrégés*, who resist structural and curricular reform which may undermine their position. Graduate teachers also resist recommendations from the Ministry on the introduction of mixed ability teaching when the grading of teachers has been linked to the ability levels of the pupils they teach.

The vertical organization of the teaching profession discourages school-based internal reforms. Different grades of teachers in second-level education are divided against each other and are represented by different teacher unions. Furthermore, there are few senior teachers who are encouraged and rewarded for taking responsibility for internal school management and leadership. Apart from the head and deputy head teachers, all teachers have privileges related only to their national grading, which is in accordance with the level of teaching of which they are judged to be capable. There is little incentive for teachers to become involved in pastoral or extra-curricular activities or to initiate curriculum reforms.

The structure of the teaching profession and teacher training is a great obstacle to some of the school reforms proposed in the 1970s. Despite central control, teachers can often in practice exercise much autonomy. An established teacher with little ambition for further transfer is in a fairly strong position *vis-à-vis* the inspectorate. There are limits to which the inspector can influence let alone dictate what the teacher does in the classroom. Well organised teacher unions can and do defend classroom teachers at national level. But the stratified nature of the profession, its training and professional associations, means that most reforms of educational structure and the curriculum will be seen as a threat by one or more groups of teachers. Such opposition may take years to overcome and means in practice that many government directives go unheeded in many schools.

Higher Education

Three issues have dominated debates about higher education in France, as in other countries, over the last twenty years. First there are questions of equal chances of access to higher education. Secondly there are demands that higher education should be related more strictly to the vocational demands of the changing economy. Thirdly there is the question of the relationship between the universities and the state especially centring on issues of participation and autonomy.

Universities in the 1960s became centres for criticism of the political and economic structures of modern society. These criticisms in France led to events in May 1968 which amounted almost to an attempted political revolution. These political disturbances, however, led to proposals to restructure French higher education in major respects. It has become more aligned to economic conditions but the other two issues, of access and of the relationship with society at large, have not been clearly resolved.

Before the 1960s there were two types of institutions for higher education in France: the *grandes écoles* and the universities. Since 1966 considerable changes have occurred in the organization and structure of the universities and new types of higher education have been introduced. The *grandes écoles* have changed little.

The *grandes écoles* are high level professional training schools preparing for specific occupations. Most were founded in the early nineteenth century. There are about 150 of these institutions of which around 30, mainly in the Paris area, have very high prestige. The *grandes écoles* are separate from the rest of the higher education system in that they fall under the influence of different ministries, they have separate entry procedures based on competitive examinations (the *concours*) and their students are state employees who are paid a salary.

Students are admitted to the *grandes écoles* after a highly competitive examination. Candidates prepare for these examinations in post-*baccalauréat* classes in the *lycées* over a period of one, two or three years. The courses in the *grandes écoles* usually last three years and they are similar to those of universities except that the *grandes écoles* often award their own diplomas, the entry is very selective and dependent on the number of places available and the student–staff ratio is very favourable.

The *grandes écoles* are elitist in every way. The academic and intellectual requirements for entry are much higher than for the university. The graduates of the *grandes écoles* quickly rise to the highest positions in the civil service and in private industry. The students come overwhelmingly from professional parents and are predominantly male.

The position of the *grandes écoles* has been threatened little by educational reforms. The existence of these elitist institutions may have reduced resistance to reforms of other types of higher education if only because the elite of French society was educated outside the mainstream university system.

The University of Paris was one of the major institutions of higher learning of medieval Europe. Other universities also developed. These were reorganized in 1896 and reduced to fifteen – one for each academy. However, Paris continued to have the greatest attraction and the largest number of students.

The traditional organization of universities was into faculties – letters, science, law, medicine and pharmacy. Faculties grew to an enormous size, especially in Paris. Student–staff ratios were high in the 1950s and 1960s – over 50:1 in some faculties. Contact between students and full professors – with a statutory teaching load of only three hours a week – became distant. The faculty-based system was associated particularly with the imparting of knowledge required for specific professions, compared with the *grandes écoles*, which were adapted to the wider intellectual education of a chosen elite despite their original vocational purpose. Universities found it difficult to adapt to the expansion of numbers after the Second World War.

Possession of the *baccalauréat* secured entry as a matter of right to any faculty of any university at least until 1965. In spite of the fact that failure rates in the *baccalauréat* were high, this encouraged the expansion as more and more students entered for the examinations, and strain on teaching resources of the most popular faculties, especially in Paris, increased. Courses lasting for three or four years led to the *licence* but over half the students failed to graduate. Failure rates in first or second year examinations were high. Fees were nominal but there were few grants or scholarships, which put additional pressures on many students.

The system of higher education was reformed drastically after 1968. The Minister of Education, Edgar Faure, in a Law of 1968, broke up the faculty system and reorganized several of the universities into smaller units, especially in Paris; dissolved the faculties of law and science and replaced them by departments; and grouped departments (which were often concerned with one specialism within a broader subject) into interdisciplinary *unités d'enseignement et de recherche*.

Students and junior staff were given elected representatives on university governing bodies, which helped to reduce the great power which had been wielded by deans of faculties and the professors. Universities were allowed more autonomy in the use of funds.

The pattern of courses was altered in 1973. The *diplôme d'études universitaires générales (DEUG)* is interdisciplinary and is taken after two years. This is followed by the *licence* after a further year or the *maîtrise* after two years. Within the third cycle of research studies for doctoral degrees, there is an examination at the end of the first year which students must pass to continue and there are two levels of doctorate. The *DEUG* is awarded by the universities, often by course work as well as by examination, though other degrees remain state examinations.

The other reform preceded the 1968 revolt. University institutes of technology were established in 1966 to encourage more students to aim at careers other than the traditional professions. Their prestige remained low and they have only attracted 10 per cent of all students in higher education though the number has grown in the 1970s.

The 1968 reform together with those of the early 1970s were in response to the 1968 students' revolt. Some of the student demands were met by giving more autonomy to universities, broadening studies and introducing student participation in university government. Other changes were clearly aimed at preventing a recurrence of the threat to political order which occurred in 1968. University teaching units were made much smaller and were geographically dispersed even within Paris itself. The reform of course structures was an attempt to encourage many students to find jobs after two years' study or after one year of postgraduate work rather than staying on and repeating studies.

These reforms also had economic features – which encouraged student protest. The university institutes of technology and the introduction of the two-year university diploma can be linked with attempts to persuade more students to aim at intermediate level technical jobs in industry rather than to aim at membership of one of the traditional professions. The utilitarian, economic perspective in French education has reappeared but in circumstances where continuation of old approaches were seen as a threat to political stability.

Certain reforms that might have been expected in 1968 were not carried out. University entry is still the right of the majority of *baccalauréat* holders, though a mark of 60 per cent rather than the bare pass of 50 per cent is required. Those who pass the *baccalauréat* may still enter university as a right but certain *baccalauréat* specializations are required for entry to certain faculties. But there is still overcrowding in faculties such as medicine, which is reduced by a high failure rate in the first two years.

Yet to have restricted university entry drastically would have been politically unwise in that it would have alienated many parents and their children. Furthermore, it would have been seen as a greater threat to the principle of equality of opportunity than measures which led to the truncation of courses after students had entered university. This was all the more important as students entering university up to 1968 were overwhelmingly the children of professional and white-collar workers. As in the school system, a careful balance has to be maintained between linking education to the needs of the economy and preserving or enhancing possibilities for all potential students to advance as far as possible within the educational system.

One further change has been the introduction of the concept of lifelong or recurrent education. The idea is that opportunities for education should be kept open even after the age when formal education is normally completed. It was argued further that all important knowledge could not be absorbed during the years of formal schooling. The ideal of equality of opportunity was thus linked to an encyclopaedic view of knowledge.

The first expression of government support came in the 1968 Law on higher education, which allowed certain universities to admit mature students who had not passed the *baccalauréat*. Several universities mounted courses reflecting the liberal ideal of lifelong education with an emphasis on education for leisure and the extension of the general or liberal education of adults.

The 1971 Law on lifelong education, however, emphasized the utilitarian aspect of the concept. All firms with more than 10 employees were to devote a proportion of their salary bill, initially about 1 per cent, later to rise to 2 per cent, to allow some of their workers to study full-time while receiving normal wages. Yet these studies were to be entirely vocational. Lifelong education was put in the context of the need for retraining workers in a rapidly changing technological economy.

University education has long been democratic and individualist in admissions. Students with a *baccalauréat* could enrol in any university. This principle has been retained with some modifications. In addition there are more opportunities for second-chance higher education through relaxed entry requirements for mature students. So far, however, there has not been a significant change in the social origins of university students.

Despite the post-1968 reforms, which allowed more student participation in university government, there has been less attention to individual aims after admission. New qualification structures and new course arrangements stress the relationship between higher education and economic planning. Government economic aims seem to have a stronger impact on the higher level of education than on the earlier stages of the school system.

Conclusion

Of the three individual rights aims – the right to schooling, equality of opportunity and individual development – which were stated in the 1975 Haby Reform, the French education system has been relatively successful in adapting to the first two. Provision has expanded so that access to education is open compared with other industrial societies. Central direction of resources, a traditional belief in the value of education for a united, progressive society and government intervention in industrial training have meant that pre-school education is highly developed and post-compulsory education both for school leavers and for adults is widely available. The traditions of a stong, interventionist central government have been entirely consistent with the widespread provision of education.

Similarly, the education system has been relatively successful in accommodating the ideal of equality of opportunity. Central allocation of resources has reduced the geographical inequalities found in some other education systems. Central direction of reform has meant that the structure of second-level education has become more egalitarian in a fairly short space of time. Even within schools, inequalities based on different curriculum offerings are less severe in France than in some other countries. The French encyclopaedist view of knowledge makes it easier than elsewhere to attempt to offer very similar curricula to the majority of pupils. Again, there is no basic conflict between traditions inherited from the eighteenth-century revolution and modern egalitarianism.

The third aim of providing for individual and group freedom is less easily accommodated. Central administration, a standardized curriculum and a stratified teaching profession are major constraints on the widespread promotion of the ideal of individual diversity within the French system. Very major changes in practices and prevalent attitudes would be needed to realize this ideal on a wide scale.

The three ideals may not, of course, be achieved in practice when other conditions are taken into account. Extra-educational pressures exist; governments and taxpayers may not be willing to allocate resources on a sufficiently large scale to education as a whole. Some parents are likely to find individual means of promoting the interests of their own children in the selective process at the expense of others. The labour requirements of industry are likely to exert an influence on selection and on the content of education.

Though this last influence finds some expression in stated aims of education, these extra-educational pressures should be considered separately from the formal education system. The failure or success of general aims of education may be explored profitably in the nature of the education system itself before the wider and less tangible social and economic influences are investigated.

Further Reading

J. Ardagh, *The New France: A Society in Transition 1945–1973* (Harmonds-worth: Penguin, 1973).

H. C. Barnard, *The French Tradition in Education* (Cambridge: Cambridge University Press, 1970).

N. Beattie, 'Parent participation in French education 1968–75' *British Journal of Educational Studies*, vol. 26, no. 1 (1978), pp. 40–53.

P. Bourdieu and J. C. Passeron, *The Inheritors* (Chicago: University of Chicago Press, 1979).

J. Capelle, *Tomorrow's Education: The French Experience* (Oxford: Pergamon, 1965).

F. S. Coombs, 'The politics of educational change in France', *Comparative Education Review*, vol. 22, no. 3 (1978), pp. 480–503.

E. Durkheim, *The Evolution of Educational Thought* (London: Routledge & Kegan Paul, 1977).

W. R. Fraser, *Reforms and Restraints in Modern French Education* (London: Routledge & Kegan Paul, 1971).

W. R. Fraser, 'The general reform of primary/secondary education (la réforme Haby)', *Western European Education*, vol. 7, no. 3 (1975), pp. 77–83.

W. D. Halls, *Education, Culture and Politics in Modern France* (Oxford: Pergamon, 1976).

J. Pujol, 'The lower secondary school in France: a note on the Haby reforms', *Compare*, vol. 10, no. 2 (1980), pp. 187–91.

J. Pujol, 'University reform in France', *Minerva*, vol. 7, no. 4 (1969), pp. 706–27.

Organizational and Statistical Appendix

France

Agencies of Administration

NATIONAL

Statutory   Ministry of Education.

Advisory   Le Conseil Supérieur de l'Éducation Nationale. Various standing committees on specific areas, for example, Le Conseil de l'Enseignement Général et Technique. Various commissions of inquiry on particular issues.

REGIONAL

Statutory   Académie Rectorates.

Advisory   Various representative advisory councils.

LOCAL

Statutory   Municipal councils of the communes.

Advisory   (School level) school administrative councils (conseils d'administration).

The Structure and Organization of the Educational System (1978–9)

Age	Level and stage	Types of institution	Number of institutions	Enrolments
25+	Postgraduate (1, 2 or 7 years)	Universities and institutions		
24	Higher (2, 3 or 4 years)	1 Universities	77	853,532 (1980)
		2 Grandes écoles	—	—
		3 Instituts universitaires de technologie	60	52,353 (1979)
20		4 Écoles normales primaires	—	—
19+	Upper secondary			
	General (3 grades + 1 or 2 grades)	1 Lycées généraux et technologiques	2,345 (of which 1,234 private)	1,079,008 (243,625 in private institutions)
16	Professional (1, 2 or 3 grades)	2 Lycées d'enseignement professionel		781,035 (163,003 in private institutions)

continued

Age	Level and stage	Types of institution	Number of institutions	Enrolments
15	Lower secondary (4 grades)	Collèges uniques	—	3,260,380 (578,642 in private institutions)
12 11	Primary (6 grades)	Écoles primaires (l'enseignement elementaire)	53,192 (of which 6,935 are private)	4,656,953 (658,736 in private schools)
6 5	Pre-primary	Écoles maternelles	15,297 (of which 322 are private)	1,856,605 (30,772 in private institutions)
2				

The Progress of Pupils through the School System

Age and admission and transfer procedures

Pre-school   Children are admitted at 2, 3, 4, and 5 years of age to free, state or private institutions. It is not compulsory.

First level   Children are admitted and required by law to attend state or private institutions from the age of 6. Five-year-olds may be admitted where pre-school institutions are not provided. Internal assessment and grade repeating.

Second level

Stage 1   Automatic transfer from primary schools to state or private institutions. Normal minimum age of transfer is 12 years but grade repeating in primary schools means that some children enter at an older age. Attendance is compulsory by law until the age of 16.

Stage 2   Entry is voluntary from the age of 16. Students are oriented towards different kinds of upper secondary education on the basis of internal school assessment (in marginal cases involving outside representatives) at lower secondary level.

Third level

Stage 1   Admission to institutions apart from the *Grandes Écoles* is usually at the age of 19+ and is on the basis of possession of the *baccalauréat* (national upper secondary examination) with appropriate branches of study (and sometimes grades). Admission to the *Grandes Écoles* is by competitive examination usually taken one or two years after the *baccalauréat*.

Stage 2   Stage 1 leads to a diploma after 2 years. Stage 2 leads to a *licence* (one year) of *maîtrise* (2 years) or to various diplomas (usually 3 years) in the *Grandes Écoles* or to 3rd cycle doctorates (4 years) in medicine, law or pharmacy.

Fourth level   Doctorate of the 3rd cycle (2 years) is required for admission to *Doctorat d'État* (5 years+).

Curricula

Pre-school   Integrated and child-centred learning (partly based on theories of Montessori and Decroly).

Last grade – preparation for work in reading, writing and arithmetic and sometimes in a foreign language.

First level

Stage 1   15 hours – French and mathematics.

6 hours – Curiosity-awakening subjects: history, geography, moral education, observation (science), handwork, modelling, music.

Stage 2   6 hours – Physical education and sport.

Second level

Stage 1   *Core* French (5 hours), mathematics (3 hours), foreign language (English, German, Spanish, Portuguese, Arabic, Italian, Russian or a French regional language) (3 hours), history/geography (3 hours), science (3 hours), art and music (2 hours), manual and technical education (2 hours), physical education and sport (3 hours).
Optional Either extra (remedial or extension) French, mathematics, modern language or new subjects (second foreign language, Latin, Greek).

Stage 2   *Core* French, history/geography, mathematics, science, modern language, physical education and (final year only) philosophy (level in each subject according to students' specialisms).
Specialisms One of: literary studies, economics and social studies, mathematics and physical sciences, mathematics and biological sciences, mathematics and technology, applied sciences (several branches), music, business and commercial studies, information science. Also, short technical courses (1 or 2 years) and long technical courses (3 years).

Third level

Stage 1   *Diplôme d'études universitaires generales* (2 years) – multidisciplinary with individual student combinations of a variety of courses (except for medicine, dentistry, pharmacy and the *Grandes Écoles*, which begin specialisms in the 1st cycle).

Stage 2   *Licence* (1 year) or *maîtrise* (2 years) in particular branches – letters, science, human sciences, administration, economic science, law, industrial studies, commerce.
6-year one-cycle courses in medicine, 5-year one-cycle courses in dentistry and pharmacy. Courses in *Grandes Écoles* are of one cycle of 4 or 5 years.

Fourth level 2-year courses leading to doctorate of the 3rd cycle (coursework and dissertation).
5 year + courses leading to *doctorat d'état*.
1- or 2-year professional diplomas (including teaching).

Teacher Education and Training

Type of institution	Qualification awarded	Level of school in which teacher can teach
Écoles normales primaires	*Diplôme d'études universitaires générales (DEUG)* + *Certificat d'études pédagogiques (CEP)*	Pre-primary and primary schools Remedial classes in lower secondary schools (after short in-service training)
Centres de formation	*Certificat d'aptitude pédagogique à l'enseignement de collèges (CAPEG)*	Lower secondary
Instituts preparatoires à l'enseignement secondaire (IPES) Universities	*Licence d'enseignement*	Lower secondary Upper secondary
Centres pédagogiques régionaux	*Certificat d'aptitude pédagogique à l'enseignement secondaire (CAPES)* Part I Part II	
École Normale Supérieure and other *Grandes Écoles*	*Agrégation*	Lower secondary Upper secondary Higher education (junior grades)
University	*Doctorat de 3me cycle*	Higher education (junior grades)
	Doctorat d'État	Higher education (senior grades)

UNESCO Statistical Information: France

UNESCO date of entry: 29 June 1946
Surface area (km²): 547,026
Population 1980 (millions): 53·71
Persons/km² 1980: 98
Rural population (%) 1980: 22·1
Births per 1,000 pop. 1980: 14·8
Deaths per 1,000 pop. 1980: 10·1
Infant deaths per 1,000 live births 1978: 11
Life expect. at birth 1979: 74 years
Pop. growth rate (% p.a.) 1975–80: 0·3

Est. illiteracy rate 15+ (%) 1980
  M: 0·5 F: 0·5 MF: 0·5
National currency: Franc
National currency per US $ 1980: 4·5160
GNP per capita in US $ 1979: 9,950
GNP per capita real growth rate
  (% per annum) 1960–79: 4.0
% agriculture in GDP 1979: 5
% industry in GDP 1979: 34
  of which manufacturing: 25

Data Series	1975	1977	1978	1979
Education				
Education Preceding First Level				
1 pupils enrolled	2,591,142	2,575,972	2,502,843	2,412,711
2 of which female (%)	—	49	49	49
3 teaching staff[a]	57,658	64,676	75,890	76,574
4 of which female (%)[b]	100	99	99	—
Education at First Level				
5 duration (years)	5	5	5	5
6 official age range	6–10	6–10	6–10	6–10
7 gross enrolment ratio (%)	109	111	112	112
8 pupils enrolled	4,601,550	4,618,436	4,647,552	4,650,954
9 of which female (%)	—	49	48	49
10 teaching staff[a]	204,311	201,759	230,634	232,405
11 of which female (%)[b]	68	68	65	65

12 pupils repeaters (%)	9	9	9	9
13 pupil/teacher ratio[a]	20	20	20	20
Education at Second Level				
14 duration gen. educ. (years)				
15 official age range gen. educ.	11–17	11–17	11–17	11–17
16 gross enrolment ratio (%)	84	83	83	84
17 pupils enrolled	4,890,152	4,948,694	4,976,489	5,007,508
18 of which female (%)	—	51	51	52
19 teaching staff	316,341	352,982	358,916	354,758
20 of which female (%)	—	—	—	—
21 pupils repeaters gen. ed. (%)	—	9	9	10
Education at Third Level				
22 students per 100,000 inhabit.[d]	1,970	2,050	1,921	—
23 students enrolled	1,038,576	1,086,938	1,020,503	—
24 of which female (%)	48	50	48	—
25 students scient./tech. fields (%)	39	39	39	—
26 foreign students	93,750	104,317	108,288	—
27 teaching staff	—	—	—	—
Public Expenditure on Education[e]				
28 total in nat. currency (000)	76,816,145	103,647,000	114,264,740	—
29 of which current expend. (000)	46,844,110	62,738,600	71,481,125	—
30 total as % of GNP	5·3	5·5	5·3	—
31 current expendit. as % current government expenditure	22·2	20·9	—	—
Science and Technology				
32 stock of university graduates per million inhabitants	28,894	—	—	—

continued

Data Series	1975	1977	1978	1979
33 stock of persons with complete second educ. per million inh.	—	—	—	—
34 scientists and engineers in R&D per million inh.	1,245	1,281	1,327	—
35 technicians in R&D per million inh.[f]	2,931	2,904	2,892	—
36 expend. on R&D as % of GNP	1·8	1·8	1·8	—
Culture and Communication				
37 book titles published[g]	—	31,673	21,225	25,019
38 circulation daily newspapers per 1,000 inh.	214	205	—	—
39 consumption (kg) newsprint per 1,000 inh.	7,627	10,927	11,465	11,555
40 consumption (kg) printing and writing paper per 1,000 inh.	26,771	12,658	36,149	37,676
41 cinema seats per 1,000 inh.	33·3	30·2	28·6	27·6
42 radio receivers per 1,000 inh.	326	325	328	337
43 TV receivers per 1,000 inh.	269	281	282	292
44 volumes in public libraries per 1,000 inh.	—	917	—	—

Notes:
[a] For 1975 and 1977, public education only.
[b] Public education only.
[c] For 1975, full-time only.
[d] The total number of students is overestimated due to concomitant enrolment in more than one institution.
[e] Expenditure of the Ministry of Education and the Ministry of Universities only.
[f] Including auxiliary personnel.
[g] For 1978, books only.
[h] Licences.

Source: Statistical Digest 1981 (Paris: UNESCO, 1981).

3

Education in the USA
Freedom to be Unequal

DAVID TURNER

In the USA education debates have frequently been acrimonious, and have never been finally resolved. In the process of deciding debates, at least temporarily, recourse has often been made to the supreme courts, either at the state level or the federal level. The principal role of the supreme courts is to decide whether particular activities are permissible under the terms of the relevant constitution. The practical consequence of this has been that many educational debates have been argued in terms of the constitution, and whether particular policies are or are not constitutional. The various constitutions, and particularly the federal constitution, have been of central importance in educational debates.

Inspired by the example of the French revolutionaries of the late eighteenth century, the founders of the new American Republic sought to incorporate the principles of equality, liberty and fraternity into its basic legislation. But it should be noted that the inherent tension between the principles of equality and liberty means that the liberty of each state to determine its own destiny can only be protected by circumscribing the power of the federal government, while the liberty of the individual can only be preserved by limiting both state and federal control. Equality can only be ensured by a central authority with the administrative resources to check that benefits are equally distributed and rights protected, and the financial resources to correct any perceived inequality. The pursuit of equality would therefore indicate that strong central authorities are required, while the protection of liberty suggests that the power of central authorities should be strictly limited.

The conflict between these two ideals of equality and liberty was felt early, and is exemplified by the different stances taken by A. Hamilton and T. Jefferson. Hamilton argued that the central federal government should have considerable power, while Jefferson fought to retain for each state the right to conduct its own affairs, and to protect individual freedom. Thus the Constitution (in the preamble) allocates responsibility for the common defence and welfare of the country to the federal government, while (in clause 9) it gives the states responsibility for services not specifically mentioned in the Constitution. The amendments to the Constitution are generally accepted to have been inspired by Jefferson, and are principally concerned with the protection of individuals' rights.

Of particular importance in the case of debates on education is the fact that education is not specifically mentioned in the Constitution, and that responsibility for education therefore rests with the states. Federal intervention in education can only be constitutional if it can be justified in terms of the 'common defense and welfare of the country' or in terms of securing individual rights, and particularly equality of individuals before the law.[1] In addition the constitutional prohibition on any link between the federal government and any church, intended to protect individuals from the kind of religious persecution Americans had sought to escape when leaving Europe, has had profound consequences for the provision of education, particularly private education.[2]

It should be noted that the exact wording or interpretation of the Constitution has not strictly been the source of educational problems. Educational problems have been identified by groups which have felt aggrieved because of their position with respect to existing provision, and they have attempted to arouse public support in terms of that grievance. But the most effective way of removing policies which have been offensive has been to secure a Federal Supreme Court ruling that those policies were unconstitutional, with the consequence that many educational debates have been couched in terms which refer to the precise wording or interpretation of the Constitution. This is exemplified by the case of the civil rights campaigners in the 1950s who intended to remove the perceived injustices in the treatment of the blacks in the USA. But the case was argued in the US Supreme Court on the basis of the exact interpretation of the Fourteenth Amendment of the Constitution which prevents states from passing legislation which differentiates between citizens on the basis of race or colour. However, since the Fourteenth Amendment does not apply to the administration of Washington DC, the civil rights case had to be argued in different terms there. In that case a ruling was secured under the terms of the Fifth Amendment, which applies to the federal government, and which had a very similar effect. Thus while the exact wording of the Constitution may not produce educational problems, or materially affect their outcome, it is of central importance in understanding how the debates are conducted and resolved.[3]

It is within the framework of the Constitution that the major issues of educational policy in the USA can be analysed.

Aims

The provision of education for all as a human right has dominated discussion in the USA since 1945. Indeed, American delegates were influential in ensuring that education was included in the United Nations Declaration of Universal Rights. But what exactly should constitute the education which is due to each individual as a right has been the subject of debate, a debate which originated long before 1945. For Jefferson the elementary schools were to provide for a minimum understanding of general issues, so that the citizens of a democratic state would be in a position to judge the policies put forward by their representatives. But, influenced by French revolutionary thinkers such as Condorcet, he thought that a major function of the schools was to select out the talented elite, and ensure that they received a suitable preparation for high office in the state.[4] Certainly, all children should have equal access to all levels of education, regardless of their origin, subject only to their ability to benefit from education beyond the primary level. But the prime concern of Jefferson was that all children should be at liberty to develop their talents to the fullest extent; education was to prepare children for their unequal responsibilities in the democratic state. It is clear that slaves were not included in this broad vision of an educated society.

Historically, Jefferson's view may be contrasted with that of Horace Mann, who emphasized the importance of a common school for the children of rich and poor alike. By equalizing the provision of education for all social classes he hoped that the moral tone of society could be raised. As secretary of its board of education he campaigned for the increased equalization of provision in education in Massachusetts.

Following the Kalamazoo court case in Michigan in 1874, which decided that it was permissible for public money to be spent on secondary education, the education system as a whole, and particularly the high school provision, underwent a rapid expansion.[5] It was in this context that John Dewey made his proposals on the aims of education. On the one hand he suggested that the curriculum should be geared to the needs of the individual child, thus stressing the freedom of the individual to develop at his or her own rate. But this aspect of his proposals was balanced by a concern for the social purposes of education, and the proposal that in a democratic society all should be educated to play their part.

During the 1930s and 1940s the Progressive Education Association had reflected this division between child-centred and society-centred aims by being fairly consistently split on the issue. H. Rugg, in 1947, observed that all seven aims of the association were concerned with child-centred aims, and the policy of the association was to avoid links with social reform movements. This remained the policy until the association was disbanded in 1955. But there were many critics of this policy: Dewey himself was critical of the excessive emphasis placed on the arts and self-expression by the association and George S. Counts delivered a speech to the association in 1932 entitled 'Dare progressive education be progressive?', in which he suggested that the main purpose of education should be the reformation of society. His address was enthusiastically received.[6] But the association did not move far from its child-centred traditions, which were strongly advocated by W. H. Kilpatrick. The most prominent curriculum theorists within the association stressing the importance of following the learner's needs were R. W. Tyler and H. Taba, whose works still exert considerable influence. S. Hook was outspoken in his criticisms of those he felt had betrayed the ideas of Dewey by narrowing them to a view of child-centred education.[7]

Besides these disputes within the Progressive Education Association, there were also those who criticized both groups from a more traditional standpoint. Neither child-centred educationists nor society-centred educationists emphasized the role of content or traditional disciplines in education. Before the Second World War, R. M. Hutchins maintained that once such traditional notions of discipline were abandoned the whole educational project was threatened by loss of standards. After 1945 the Report of the Harvard Committee, under the chairmanship of J. B. Conant, argued that education should be based on the inherent differences between subjects. A. Bestor argued from a similar position, and received support from those who feared a shortage of trained scientists at the height of the Cold War.[8]

Admiral H. G. Rickover was anxious to secure the reintroduction of formal instruction, in the pure sciences particularly, in the high schools. To this end he stated that Dewey, through his support of the child-centred curriculum, had given the child the freedom to avoid particular specialist branches of knowledge. But Rickover argued that this freedom denied a second and greater freedom, the freedom of able pupils to be stimulated intellectually by a formal introduction to areas of knowledge such as the pure sciences and foreign languages. It should be noted that while Rickover unjustly identified Dewey with the child-centred curriculum advocates, he did not move the discussion of educational aims away from its central focus, the balance between freedom and equality in the design of the curriculum.

Finance

Within the constitutional framework, direct federal financing of education as such was precluded. However, the federal government does have responsibility for the common defence and welfare of the nation, and federal financing of education could be deemed to be constitutional to the extent that the education supported in this way contributed to the national defence and welfare. On these grounds there is a long history of federal involvement in the finance of education.

The first Morrill Act of 1862 made provision for the allocation of land to the individual states by the federal government. The money from the sale of these lands was to be held in trust under specified conditions, and to be used to finance institutions of higher education, the 'land grant colleges'. Under subsequent legislation, further federal assistance was extended to the states on similar lines. The primary purpose of these institutions was to promote instruction in industrial and agricultural arts, and provide technical education appropriate to the needs of the area in which they were located. But in terms of the Constitution it is significant that the Morrill Act specifies the type of instruction which was to be encouraged, and includes the assertion that military sciences should not be excluded. The clear implication that federal involvement in higher education is justified in terms of the contribution education makes to the national defence is enshrined in the Act.[9]

Under the provisions of the first Morrill Act and subsequent legislation, every state founded at least one institution of higher education, and a number of them founded two or more. Some of these institutions were entirely new, while others represented a regrouping of sections of older institutions in such a way as to stimulate higher technical education. In both ways the study of technical subjects was encouraged. But the Morrill Acts did not restrict the activities of the land grant colleges to technical studies and many also offered courses in the humanities and social sciences. Many of them later became state universities, forming a very prestigious sector of public higher education.

Until 1958 federal funding of education on the grounds of national defence was limited to higher education and some specific vocational programmes. However, at the height of the Cold War, and following the launch of the first sputnik by the Soviet Union, the National Defense and Education Act was passed by Congress. Under Title III of the Act, federal monies were made available to the states for the provision of secondary education. This federal involvement was limited to the provision of mathematics, science and modern language courses, but the provision of large sums of money promoted curriculum development programmes which indirectly affected other curriculum areas.

Title III made money available to the states on a matched basis, a principle which had been incorporated into most previous Acts providing federal money for education. In terms of general principle, this meant that if a state spent a dollar on a project which qualified for aid, then a federal dollar would be added to it. This matched-dollar formula was circumscribed, however, by overall limitations on a state's benefit, calculated in terms of population, size and so on, to prevent the wealthiest states from taking undue advantage of the federal provision.

The issue of the balance between liberty and equality of the states is thus clearly illustrated by the provisions of the Act. The federal government provided money, but without directing how it must be spent, and without removing sovereignty from the states. However, the net effect was to make certain types of programmes available to the states at a reduced cost, thus influencing policy decisions. At the same time, wealthy states were prevented from gaining excessive benefits at the expense of states which were unwilling or unable to put in their own money by a limit on the maximum amount of money a state could receive.

The civil rights legislation of 1964 went rather further in terms of the range of curriculum areas in which federal financing was involved. Under the Act, money was made available for educational programmes which contributed to securing civil rights for all citizens, particularly blacks, on an equal basis. Money was provided for such remedial programmes as Headstart. In addition, the Act denied federal monies to any institution, for whatever purpose, if racial segregation or discrimination were practised in that institution.

This last point is of considerable importance, as it implies a monitoring by a federal agency of institutions which receive federal money. This kind of detailed monitoring could be seen as going beyond the range of activities permitted by the Constitution. Similar issues had been raised in the context of financing private, particularly church-run, schools. In the 1930s the Supreme Court decided that it was constitutional for public money to be spent on books used in educating children in church schools. But this public money could be spent only on educational materials and resources which were not linked with sectarian education. At first the case against the use of public money was based on the argument that even such support would class as state support for a church and was therefore proscribed by the Constitution. However, the Court made it clear that children had the equal right to benefit from public expenditure on secular education, whether or not they went to church schools. However, subsequently it was argued that, since the money could only be spent on particular areas of education, the government agencies would become involved in the administration of church schools, a link which was itself unconstitutional.[10] Here again, the central issue is whether supplying public money curtails individual freedom by increasing the power of the churches, increases individual freedom by making it economically viable to have the education of one's choice, decreases equality by permitting a separate denominational school or increases equality by providing uniform resources in schools of all types.

These questions of balance between equality and liberty are not only present at the federal level, but are also potent in the politics of state finance. The question of equality of provision between states has already been mentioned in the context of the National Defense and Education Act. But there is also the question of unequal provision within states. It is permissible for rich school districts to make better provision for education than poor school districts? This was the subject of the *Serrano v. Priest* case before the Supreme Court of California in 1971. The specific issue was whether it was constitutional (under the California state constitution) for the district of Beverley Hills to spend $1,223 per child per annum on education while Baldwin Park spent only $577. It should be noted that these differences, although large, are by no means extreme for California, much less for the USA as a whole. The California Supreme Court ruled that it was not constitutional, thus coming down in favour of equality of provision in education, rather than the liberty of each school district to make the provision deemed appropriate by the school board. Similar verdicts followed in a number of other states.[11]

Administration

Education is a responsibility of the state, but with the exception of a few specific areas such as teacher certification these responsibilities have been delegated to local boards. The fundamental unit of school administration in the USA has thus been the local school board, although state and federal money have been made available to the boards. In the interest of liberty, education has been the concern of the local community, and the education has been provided which that community felt was appropriate to its needs. In the context of finance, it has already been noted that this liberty of the local community is no longer considered sacrosanct, and increasing equality has been achieved, not least through the reduction of the number of local school districts. As the average size of school districts has increased, so the school boards have become less responsive to the demands of particular ethnic minorities. Before the First World War, communities of immigrant Germans were able to ensure that German was used as the language of instruction in schools within their local communities. Although the First World War had a particular impact on this group of immigrants, and they dropped their insistence on the use of German as the language of instruction, they were still able to secure instruction in German as a foreign language in their schools. From 1919 to 1968, subsequent immigrants, from Italy, Poland or Puerto Rico, were unable to implement similar policies.[12] The Bilingual Education Act of 1968, subsequently amended and extended by the 1974 Act of the same name, changed this situation considerably by providing federal money for programmes in bilingual education, mainly for children whose mother tongue was Spanish.

The decrease in the number of school districts has continued steadily since 1932, when there were 127,649. By 1980 there were only 15,766, with a corresponding increase in the average size of school district.[13]

One group which has traditionally had separately administered schools is the blacks. The Supreme Court case of *Plessy v. Ferguson* in 1896 resulted in a ruling that segregated facilities for blacks and whites were constitutional so long as the provision was equal. Although the original case referred to separate accommodation in trains, it was taken to apply equally to education, and between 1896 and 1954 many similar rulings were handed down, some of which applied specifically to education. In fact the black schools, with black staff, were comparatively poorly equipped, teachers were poorly trained and paid, and pupil–staff ratios were poor. In 1954 the Supreme Court ruled, in the case of *Brown v. Topeka*, that segregated provision was essentially unequal, and therefore unconstitutional. This decision, and the later civil rights legislation, resulted in *de jure* desegregation and a number of measures to reduce *de facto* segregation such as bussing.

The idea behind bussing was that children from predominantly black or white housing areas should be carried by bus to schools in other areas, in order to improve the balance between black and white in any school. However, formulating a policy to implement desegregation was the responsibility of local boards, and they faced a number of possibilities. Children could be bussed in both directions, or only in one, and bussing could be either optional or compulsory. Political considerations made local board members disinclined to upset groupings of white voters by introducing schemes which involved the compulsory bussing of white children to predominantly black schools. They therefore usually implemented schemes under which black parents could opt for their children to be bussed to predominantly white schools. The fact that this took the black children away from their home area, and that the schools they were bussed to retained their predominantly white ethos, was enough of a disincentive to black parents, and such schemes had minimal impact on the actual patterns of racial mix in schools.[14]

Such policies could be justified in terms of the fact that they preserved the liberty of parents to choose, although they did little to increase equality of provision. Other variations on this policy included the provision of well equipped and staffed schools in black areas, 'magnet' schools, which would attract white parents to opt for schooling outside their own neighbourhood.

In the late 1960s and early 1970s, disillusionment with the outcomes of desegregation as a policy led many in the black community to look for alternatives. Rather than aim for equality through integration, many sought liberty to achieve their own style of education in black neighbourhood schools. In New York, for example, they pressed for black school districts, in which blacks would control the education provided to their own children. However, this too became the subject of a Supreme Court case. The Court ruled that school districts could not be drawn up with the specific intent of producing school boards which represented local ethnic groupings.[15] The basis of the Supreme Court ruling is again a consideration of equality. Since the school board is elected by the school district, equality of political power between individuals is secured by having all school districts of equal size, since each elector in a small district has proportionately more political power. The court therefore ruled that drawing the boundaries of school districts could not take into account the ethnic background of the inhabitants of the area if that resulted in unequal school districts. The question was not simply one of the absolute differences between the sizes of electorates, because it would not be sufficient to demonstrate that worse discrepancies occurred elsewhere. In order for school districts drawn up on ethnic grounds to be constitutional, it would have to be demonstrated that the school districts were no more unequal than if ethnic considerations had not been taken into account. The difficulty of providing a proof which satisfied the conditions of the Supreme Court ruling served as an effective block to complete community control of schools in the 1970s. Several states did, however, pass legislation designed to facilitate the decentralization of school administration.[16]

Two groups which have been successful in securing increased equality in terms of educational provision have been women and the handicapped (both mentally and physically handicapped). Federal laws now prohibit the provision of federal funds for institutions which discriminate in their selection procedures against children on the basis of sex or handicap. In the case of the handicapped, this move towards integration into the common schools, or 'mainstreaming', is coupled with arrangements to set realistic goals for the education of the child, and for a review panel which includes the child's parents and should oversee the progress of the child. It is hoped that in this way the handicapped can receive an equal education while their special requirements are also safeguarded.

Organization and Structure

Twelve years of primary and secondary education are provided in the USA, and the majority of children attends all twelve years. At the end of the nineteenth century, when only a few children attended the full twelve years, the usual pattern of organization was an elementary school of eight years, followed by a high school of four years. Although this pattern persists in some areas, a more common arrangement now is a six-year elementary school followed by a three-year intermediate school (or junior high school) and a three-year high school (or senior high school).

The rapid expansion of high school enrolments, which took place at the beginning of the twentieth century, had promoted a number of changes in the way the schools were organized and offered courses. One important feature was the emergence of the accreditation boards. Broadly speaking, there are no public or state-organized examinations for students leaving the high school. The school is accredited, or approved, by the accreditation board, on the basis of staffing, of courses offered, of level of equipment, and of periodic inspection, and the school is then responsible for awarding a graduation certificate to the student. Assessment on the courses is then the responsibility of the school, and the final qualification is expressed in terms of 'credits', one full credit in a subject representing approximately five hours' study per week over the period of one year.

The major exception to the rule that there are no publicly administered, national examinations are the scholastic aptitude tests (SATs) which are being used increasingly, in conjunction with the high school graduation qualification, to select students for the more prestigious institutions of higher education.

The expansion of the high school led to concern over the provision of courses, which had originally been oriented towards the classics as the required qualification for college entry. When the colleges, following the lead of C. W. Eliot, president of Harvard from 1869 to 1909, dropped their insistence upon Latin and Greek, the ground was prepared for courses which offered individual students greater liberty.[17] They could choose their credit courses from a broad menu, although these were frequently grouped into suitable set programmes. This diversification was aided by the federal support given under the Smith-Lever Act of 1914 and Smith-Hughes Act of 1917, which provided money for specific types of vocational and technical education in the high schools.

In large school systems the result of this can be seen today in the presence of elective courses which are closely related to specific careers. The Norman Thomas High School in New York, which specializes in vocational courses for business and commerce, with courses on clerical work, word processing, computing and accounting for business and sales management, is an example. In Milwaukee each high school specializes in an area of vocational instruction – the media and visual arts, social services, applied technology, and so on. A majority of the courses offered are very closely tailored to vocational skills required in specific careers.

The corollary of this is that other high schools – in New York the Bronx High School for Science and Stuyvesant High School might be mentioned – specialize in college preparatory courses, while still other high schools have no particular specialism at all.

Such specialization between schools is restricted to large systems which have a large number of schools in relatively close proximity. In a smaller town, where one or two high schools serve the whole community, it is impossible. But in these cases course specialization within the schools is common, and many high schools offer vocational education of the Smith-Hughes type.

Coping with the inequalities permitted by such diversity and liberty has been a major problem in the USA, in terms of equality of opportunity and the satisfaction of the perceived needs of society. If high school graduation certificates are to be considered graded, with vocational schools or courses being regarded as second-rate, then children who enter vocational tracks at a relatively early age will thereby be excluded from higher education. On the other hand, if vocational courses are thought to have equal status with the traditionally academic courses, able students will be diverted into vocational courses where they can graduate with better grades. Such a development will not help those for whom the vocational courses were originally intended, those not intending to go on to higher education.

With regard to perceived social needs, much of the justification for federal aid for science, mathematics and language courses in 1958 was based on the small number of students electing for those subjects. Among those who did elect for them, very few studied more than two credit courses in any one language, or more than one credit course in each of biology, chemistry or physics. Since 1958, the number of students opting for these courses has, in fact, declined.[18]

In theory courses have been considered as nominally equal in status. In practice, selection has included an increased differentiation between courses as regards status, and increasing use has been made of SAT results by prestigious institutes of higher education. The result is that the system of high school education in the USA is highly stratified, and in 1983, in *A Nation at Risk*, the public and private schools of America were severely criticized for this.[19]

Various solutions have been advocated to reduce individual freedom in electives, most debate centring on compulsory requirements for graduation. Currently very few credits are compulsory in general. Typically, one or two credits per year in English language, physical education and US history, or civics, are obligatory. Particular universities, however, may have more specific requirements for entry into specialist courses. But authors such as J. B. Conant and the authors of *A Nation at Risk* have advocated an increase in this compulsory component, linked with increased variety in vocational electives, to raise standards and increase equality of educational opportunity.[20]

Higher Education

Since 1945 higher education has been greatly expanded, stimulated by federal aid in two ways. The GI Bill of 1946 made funds available for ex-servicemen to have grants for study in higher education institutions. Since then, this has been expanded into a federal system of guaranteed, low-interest loans for students. Individual states have also developed schemes of loans and grants. This combination of federal and state support has brought increased equality of opportunity in higher education.

In some states this equality is secured through state legislation which requires that any graduate of a high school within the state must be given a place at a university or college within the state if he or she requires it. On the other hand, it cannot be assumed that the student will gain entry to the university of his choice or that he will be retained in it beyond the first year. There is a well established hierarchy among the institutions. Even among degree-awarding universities there is a hierarchy, with the state universities at the top, and the private institutions being of lower status. The well established private universities, many of which date back to colonial times, are an exception to this general rule.

This differentiation between universities and colleges has been enhanced through the second type of federal funding. During the Second World War a large number of academics were involved, with army and navy scientists and engineers from the larger industrial corporations, in research work for the government, notably the development of nuclear weapons. From the beginning the implications of such work have given academics unused to working under conditions of secrecy and external direction serious cause for concern.

Since 1945, however, government and industrial funding of research projects has been a major source of revenue for the universities, and has stimulated competition between them for large contracts. Those universities with high status and a good academic record have been better placed to attract such funding. While this funding has principally been directed towards science and technology, the large foundations have also been significant in their funding of the social sciences.

The federal involvement in higher education, the increasingly total social provision by the universities, and the increasing complexity of the university administration have all helped to increase equality of opportunity for the students. But at the same time they have removed some of the opportunities for individual expression and recognition from students – liberties which were an integral part of the traditional model of university education. It is in part this identification on the part of students of the university with 'the establishment' which found expression in the student unrest in the late 1960s and early 1970s.[21]

In the community or junior colleges the USA has a post-secondary institution which is virtually unique to North America. (Japan has similar colleges.) These are two-year colleges offering a range of technical vocational and life adjustment courses. They have been rapidly expanded since 1945 to accommodate the increased aspirations of high school students. They do not award degrees, and are therefore well down the hierarchy of higher education institutions. Some degree of equality is maintained, however, as many of them offer two-year courses which lead to credits towards a four-year bachelor's degree after subsequent transfer to a degree-awarding institution.

Bachelor degree courses are typically four years long, with credits being given for courses successfully completed. Successful completion is assessed on course work, prepared essays and possibly final examination. The credit system of assessment is ubiquitous in the education system right up to the level of PhD, where a considerable part of the assessment is based on credits for taught courses.

Higher education has been one of the areas where it has been hardest to strike the balance between equality and liberty, and massive expansion has made the problem worse. Traditionally universities offered an extraordinary liberty and privilege to the prospective elite.

Expansion and increased funding, with all their promise of increased equality, have brought increased concern over the amount of liberty which society can afford to permit. In the 1950s the Senate Committee on Un-American Activities attempted to limit that liberty as far as possible. In the 1960s the general atmosphere was more liberal, but it was tragically clear that the differences of opinion over the balance between individual liberty and social need could still lead to bloodshed.

Teacher Education

The debates on teacher training in the USA have been closely linked with the debates on the aims of education. Depending on the ways in which liberty and equality were interpreted in the schools, different views of what constituted adequate preparation of teachers were held. Those who thought that the child should be free to develop at his own pace in a child-centred curriculum wanted the teacher to have the psychological and pedagogical skills to assess the child's development, and to tailor the curriculum to his individual needs. Those who thought the child should be stimulated by a rigorous introduction into formal academic study stressed the teacher's own academic ability and understanding of the subject of instruction. Those who thought that education should prepare the pupils equally for a place in a democratic society stressed the need for the teacher to have sociological skills and an understanding of social problems.

In specific terms, there was a division between those who thought that the principal component of teacher training should be professional training in the educational foundation subjects of sociology, history, psychology, and pedagogical methods, and those who thought that liberal education through a formal academic subject of the sciences or arts was more important.

There was general acceptance of the principle that all teachers should be graduates, and that they should be professionally qualified after study in postgraduate schools of education, a pattern that was previously well established for other professional groups. But, as Conant observed, there was little agreement as to what should constitute the professional education.[22] In particular, it was unclear whether philosophy of education, for example, should be offered as a course within the faculty of education or within the faculty of arts and sciences. Within the university the debate was conducted primarily between the professors of education on the one hand, emphasizing professional training within the faculty of education, and the professors of sciences and arts on the other, emphasizing preparation in a specific and single discipline. Conant himself advocated increased co-operation between the two groups, but stressed that he could see no justification for the exclusion of professors of sciences and arts from the preparation of teachers.[23]

The professors of education started from the better position, in that state teacher certification procedures generally included a requirement for professional education, but no specific requirement for general or liberal education. On the other hand, they had no claim to an esoteric area of knowledge that the professors of sciences and arts did not also have a claim to. In attempting to define such an area they identified specific pedagogical skills which teachers required. In this way it was hoped that a teacher education programme could be developed that was designed to give prospective teachers the minimum competence essential to be a teacher through competency-based teacher education (CBTE).

CBTE is open to the criticism that it does not develop the teacher through his own liberal education, but rather turns him into a pedagogical technician. However, it appears to have been fairly successful in defining a basis for professional education, and over half of the state-run programmes of teacher education are now competency-based.

On the other hand, professors of sciences and arts have not been unwilling to view the teacher as a pedagogical technician who transmits knowledge, but does not have any control over its generation and selection. For example, J. R. Zacharias, Professor of Physics at the Massachusetts Institute of Technology, was active in the development and promotion of teaching material for the Physical Science Study Committee course on physics, and the staff of the physics department of Florida State University were involved in running summer schools and in-service courses to show teachers how to use this material. The material was based on a series of films which were to form the main structure of the course, and which would limit the way in which the teacher could present the subject matter in class. Zacharias was quite clear in his own mind that technicians, such as film directors, should be used for their specific skills, but that responsibility for the content should rest with the scientists in the university departments.[24] In this context he clearly sees teachers as technicians whose skills are there to promote his subject matter rather than being involved in the selection of course material.

This separation between the professors in the sciences and arts and the high school teachers of the same subjects is less marked in Europe, where teachers at the upper secondary level have generally followed a more specialized degree course themselves, and been more fully socialized into the attitudes appropriate to subject specialists. It is interesting to note that the National Science Foundation took physics, chemistry and biology teachers from England to participate in the early summer schools which were intended to facilitate the implementation of the Physical Sciences Study Committee course and other revised science courses.

Curriculum

Debates on the curriculum have necessarily been linked with other aspects of the debates in education. Responsibility for the curriculum has rested with the state authorities, although this has generally been delegated to the local school boards. On the other hand, the broad influence of accreditation boards and the existence of a forum for curriculum debate in the National Education Association make it possible to speak of a national curriculum.

Pragmatic curriculum theory, as put forward by Dewey, stresses the method of solving problems, without specific restriction as to the kind of content on which it is to be exercised. It therefore does not provide for a curriculum which is based on subjects separated into discrete units or areas. What it does emphasize is that problems which pupils should learn about are problems taken from their own life, problems relevant to them, and problems of interest to them. Even these suggestions have been open to various interpretations, being used on the one hand to support the case for vocational education, and on the other the case for programmes which stressed the psychological and emotional adjustment of the child to the group he was in.[25]

School systems in large cities have enough schools and pupils in a geographically compact area to have specialist schools preparing students in specific academic or vocational areas. But nationally the trend has been towards comprehensive neighbourhood schools which provide a curriculum to cater for all children. In this there has been an increased emphasis on the equality of children, their right to equal access to courses, and the need for courses suitable to all children to be provided.

However, this development of courses suitable for all, which have generally included various general 'life adjustment' courses, has also come in for some severe criticism. Indeed, Conant is critical of school administrators who do not ensure that students follow a suitable mix of such courses and formal academic courses.[26] Others have gone further in condemning all such courses as 'Mickey Mouse courses'. Predominantly, this criticism of courses in the high school has been from professors of arts and sciences in the universities who have complained about the standard of preparation of the undergraduate students who come to them. In some cases, university departments have found it necessary to run introductory courses in subjects which the professors felt should have been covered in the high school, and which were inappropriate to the universities. Almost inevitably, these criticisms have been linked to criticisms of the teachers in the high schools, and of methods of teacher training.

The development of curriculum material based on the structure of the subject and designed by university specialists has already been mentioned. Those associated with these materials have gained some support from the psychological theories put forward by J. S. Bruner. Bruner has argued that the internal logic of the subject should form a basis for understanding the educational process, but that this internal logic can be simplified in ways which make it presentable to students of any age. At the Woods Hole Conference in 1959 Bruner associated himself directly with those involved in the development of courses aimed at reinstating the traditional academic disciplines in high schools.[27]

Conclusion

While the educational system of the USA has been developing, there has been a continual conflict between the ideal of liberty in development to meet state, local, or individual needs and the ideal of equality, either between individuals or between larger groupings. The rapid expansion of the system, particularly at the secondary level at the beginning of the twentieth century, and at the tertiary level since 1945, has brought other changes in the system. The conversion of the system of education from one which prepared a talented elite to a system of mass education has been associated with an increased emphasis on equality rather than liberty. Control by the states, and as their agents the local school boards, has been retained in the interests of promoting local participation in educational decision-making. But increased federal legislation and funding to reduce the inequalities between some groups in the society and the reduction in the number of local school boards suggest a gradual erosion of the framework within which local participation can be ensured.

The debates about education have been linked with other important social concerns, not least with freedom and inalienable rights and the expanding requirements for an industrialized society for technically qualified personnel. In view of these broader social issues the federal government has become increasingly involved in the finance of education, and in the provision of equal facilities for all.

The tendency towards an increased concern with equality has not

122 *Equality and Freedom in Education*

been without its critics, primarily those concerned with maintaining the standards of the elite, and the freedom of the individual to aspire to the elite through success in education. Here again, the federal government has been involved in the finance of programmes designed to promote an elite of talent.

These changes have brought about a change in the relationship between federal and state governments, which over the period from 1945 can be considered to have been mainly in the direction of increased federal involvement. But increased federal provision has had its critics and its opponents. The broader constitutional issues have been argued through the courts of the country. But there has also been a response to increased federal activity at the political level, with President Reagan committed to reducing the role of the federal government in the areas of health, education and welfare. In the political arena, the justification of such a reduction is that it would increase the liberty both of the states and of individuals.

Thus the precise balance to be struck between liberty and equality in education in the USA has long been a focus for attention, and the centre of legal, political and educational debates. It would be premature to conclude that the problem has finally been settled, and it is likely to remain the source of educational problems for a long time to come.

Notes: Chapter 3

1 US Constitution, Article 1, Section 8; C. Spurlock, *Education and the Supreme Court* (Urbana, Ill.: University of Illinois Press, 1955), p. 245.
2 First Amendment; Spurlock, op. cit., p. 247.
3 L. A. Graglia, *Disaster by Decree* (Ithaca, NY: Cornell University Press, 1976), p. 29.
4 H. J. Perkinson, *The Imperfect Panacea* (New York: Random House, 1968), pp. 8–10.
5 C. P. Hooker (ed.), *The Courts and Education* (Chicago: University of Chicago Press, 1978), p. 146. The case is *Stuart v. School District No. 1.*
6 D. Tanner and L. N. Tanner, *Curriculum Development: Theory into Practice* (New York: Macmillan, 1980), pp. 359–61. The speech became the basis for G. S. Counts, *Dare The School Build A New Social Order* (New York: The John Day Company, 1932).
7 S. Hook, *Education and the Taming of Power* (London: Open Court, 1974), and particularly the chapter entitled 'John Dewey and his Betrayers'.
8 Harvard Committee, *General Education in a Free Society* (Cambridge: Harvard University Press, 1946); D. Tanner and L. N. Tanner, op. cit., pp. 389–90.
9 R. Hofstadter and W. Smith, *American Higher Education: A Documentary History* (Chicago: University of Chicago Press, 1961), pp. 568–9.
10 N. C. Thomas, *Education in National Politics* (New York: David McKay, 1975), pp. 43–8.
11 P. E. Burrup and V. Brimley, *Financing Education in a Climate of Change* (Boston, Mass.: Allyn & Bacon, 1982), p. 211.

12 D. B. Tyack, *The One Best System* (Cambridge: Harvard University Press, 1974), pp. 254–5.
13 P. E. Burrup and V. Brimley, op. cit., pp. 101–2.
14 R. C. Rist, *The Invisible Children* (Cambridge: Harvard University Press, 1978), pp. 254–5.
15 L. J. Fein, *The Ecology of the Public Schools* (New York: Pegasus, 1971), p. 78.
16 M. Fantini, M. Gittell and R. Magat, *Community Control and the Urban School* (New York: Praeger, 1970), pp. 228–9.
17 E. A. Krug, *The Shaping of the American High School 1880–1920* (Madison, Wis.: University of Wisconsin Press, 1969), pp. 18–23.
18 Harvard Project Physics, *Project Report* (Cambridge: Harvard University Press, 1967), p. 28.
19 National Commission on Excellence in Education, *A Nation at Risk: The Imperative for Educational Reform* (Washington, 1983).
20 J. B. Conant, *The American High School Today* (New York: McGraw Hill, 1963).
21 J. Barzun, *The American University* (London: Oxford University Press, 1969), pp. 73–6.
22 J. B. Conant, *The Education of American Teachers* (New York: McGraw Hill, 1963).
23 ibid., p. 131.
24 J. R. Zacharias and S. White, 'The requirements for major curriculum reform', in R. W. Heath (ed.) *New Curricula* (New York: Harper & Row, 1964), pp. 68–81.
25 S. Hook, op. cit., pp. 125–7 draws a vocational conclusion from Dewey. Tanner and Tanner, op. cit., p. 615, quote Dewey's view of vocational education.
26 J. B. Conant, *The American High School Today* p. 23.
27 J. S. Bruner, *The Process of Education* (Cambridge: Harvard University Press, 1960).

Further Reading

E. Ashby, *Any Person, Any Study* (New York: McGraw Hill, 1971).
S. Bowles and Herbert Gintis, *Schooling in Capitalist America* (London: Routledge & Kegan Paul, 1976).
Raymond E. Callahan, *Education and the Cult of Efficiency: A Study of the Social Forces that have Shaped the Administration of the Public Schools* (Chicago: University of Chicago Press, 1962).
Carnegie Commission on Higher Education, *Toward a Learning Society: Alternative Channels to Life, Work and Service: A Report and Recommendations by the Commission* (New York and London: McGraw Hill, 1973).
J. S. Coleman, *Equality of Educational Opportunity* (Washington, DC: United States Office of Education, 1966).
L. A. Cremin, *The Transformation of the School* (New York: Knopf, 1961).
Merle Curti, *The Social Ideas of American Educators*, new edn (Totowa, NJ: Littlefield Adams, 1974).
D. Fellman, *The Supreme Court and Education* (New York: Columbia Teachers College Press, 1960).
Edward McGlynn Gaffney (ed.), *Private Schools and the Public Good: Policy Alternatives for the Eighties* (Notre Dame: University of Notre Dame Press, 1981).
M. Gittel and A. G. Hevesi (eds), *The Politics of Urban Education* (New York: Praeger, 1969).

C. Jencks, Marshall Smith, Henry Acland, Mary J. Bane, David Cohen, Herbert Gintis, Barbara Heyns and Stefan Nicholson, *Inequality: A Reassessment of the Effect of Family and Schooling in America* (Harmondsworth: Penguin, 1975).

C. J. Karier, Paul C. Violas and Joel Spring, *Roots of Crisis: American Education in the Twentieth Century* (Chicago: Rand McNaly College, 1973).

Diane Ravitch, *The Great School Wars: A History of the Public Schools as Battlefields of Social Change (New York City, 1805–1973)* (New York: Basic Books, 1974).

Diane Ravitch, *The Troubled Crusade. American Education, 1945–1980* (New York: Basic Books, 1983).

C. Silberman, *Crisis in the Classroom: The Remaking of American Education* (New York, Random House, 1970).

Joel Spring, *The Sorting Machine: National Educational Policy since 1945* (New York: McKay, 1976).

US Department of Education, *Progress of Education in the United States of America, 1978–1979 and 1979–1980)*, publication no. E–82–14020 (Washington, DC: US Government Printing Office, 1982).

F. M. Wirt and M. W. Kirst, *The Political Role of American Schools* (Boston, Mass.: Little, Brown, 1972).

Organizational and Statistical Appendix

USA

Agencies of Administration

NATIONAL

Statutory Legally education is a matter for the individual states, except for federal provision on grounds of 'defense and welfare' of the USA. However, note Department of Defense schools, overseas, and 1979 creation of a Department of Education from old Department of Health, Education and Welfare.

Advisory National Institute of Education, established by Congress in 1972 to research and advise on teaching and learning, educational policy and organization, dissemination and improvement of practice. In addition over 20 national advisory committees in existence in 1980, on topics such as bilingual education, adult education, Indian education, women's education, vocational education, black higher education, post-secondary education, etc.

REGIONAL

Statutory State legislature enacts laws on elementary and secondary education. Within these laws, details of regulations usually defined by a state board of education, and carried out by a state superintendent of education and staff in a state department of education. Statutory duties usually include distribution of state monies for education, interpreting school laws, and certifying teachers.

Advisory Services to local superintendents and school boards carried out by officers of state board and state department of education.

LOCAL

Statutory Considerable delegation of state authority and responsibility to local boards of education of from 5 to 7 members appointed by higher officials or elected by local citizens who, with the local superintendent of schools, and within state guidelines, determine curriculum, appoint teachers, provide and maintain school buildings and provide school transportation.

Advisory   Local supervisors in larger districts; for smaller districts, regional service districts or regional centres provided by state.

The Structure and Organization of the Educational System (1978)

Age	Level and stage	Types of institution	Number of institutions	Enrolments
Over 22	Level 4	Public and private universities offering two or more years for master's degrees and 5 years or more for doctorate.	486 institutions (325 private) of which 427 (229 private) have a doctoral programme	overall total public: 703,205 overall total private: 337,512 amounting to 1,080,717
	Level 3 Stage 2	Private and public colleges and universities offering bachelor courses of 4 years.	1,941 4-year institutions (1,391 private)	Total overall total, public 8,785,890
	Stage 1	Mainly 2-year junior colleges offering 2- or 3-year courses (vocational and academic)	1,193 2-year institutions (of which 224 private)	overall total, private, 2,474,112 amounting to 11,260,002
18+	Level 2 Stage 2	Municipal upper secondary schools and private schools (mainly religious), three years, grades 9–12.	25,300	15,556,000 (public: 14,156,000)
15	Level 2	Municipal lower schools, with private schools	Grades 7 and 8 are counted as 'elementary'	

continued

Age	Level and stage	Types of institution	Number of institutions	Enrolments
12	Stage 1	(mainly religious) offering a 3-year course.	or 'secondary' depending on the local structure, which may be 8–4 (elementary) but is usually 6–3–3 (lower secondary)	
6 5	Level 1	Municipal elementary schools. Admission at age 6, normally providing a 6-year course.	62,900	Kindergarten–Grade 8: 32,005,000 public: 28,455,000
3	Pre-school	Nursery and kindergarten, private and public, age of admission 3–5		Nursery 1,822,000 Kindergarten 2,762,000

The Progress of Pupils through the School System

Age and admission and transfer procedures

Pre-school   Voluntary. Application by parents. School admits. Most states provide kindergartens for 5-year-olds. Note particulary 10,000 Headstart centres partly financed by federal funds for children of poorer families.

First level   Admission at age 6. Emphasis on basic skills and knowledge, some in-class measurement of academic attainment and standardized tests. No formal examination for admission to second level. Some guidance and counselling now expanding at first level. Transition usually at 12 years.

Second level

Stage 1   In-class grades awarded. Introduction of sustained guidance and counselling services, reviewing pupil's physical, emotional academic and career development. Emerging choices begin to define category of courses to be followed by pupil in Stage 2, but no formal, set examination for transition and admission to Stage 2.

Stage 2   At about Grade 10, most pupils are choosing between a pattern of academic courses leading to university; a vocational programme leading to employment of post-secondary training; or general programme combining academic and vocational elements. Strong guidance counselling services. In several states, students have completed minimum school attendance time before Grade 12, but nationally three-quarters of students remain in school to complete high school graduation credit requirements.

Third level

Stage 1   Admission normally from 18, but early placement possible for advanced or brilliant students. Admission to 2-year junior college normally with high school graduation, but possible without. Admission to university or liberal arts college on basis of high school grades, and often on basis of scores in standardized tests of attainment, such as the Scholastic Aptitude Test (SAT), and the American College Testing Program.

Stage 2

Fourth level Entry to postgraduate courses, including professional schools, from about age of 22, with quality requirements based on first degree, often supplemented by standardized tests such as the Miller Analogy Test.

Curricula

Pre-school   Emphasis on adjustment to peers, language acquisition and enjoyment of stories, music or crafts.

First level

Stage 1   No national curriculum. Some standardization through textbook choice. Curriculum core of language arts (i.e. English), mathematics, science, social studies, and physical education. Normally some experience of craft or home economics courses, possibility of a foreign language, music and likely state or local requirement for American or state or local history, and perhaps particular required courses in anti-narcotics or sex education.

Second level

Stage 2   Curriculum core in language arts, maths and science and the social studies. Probability of required physical education and certain locally required courses (e.g. state history or health education). Elective range of courses in aesthetic areas, craft, additional academic courses likely to be extensive. Increasingly, state testing of minima in reading, writing and mathematics.

Stage 2   Curriculum division into academic track, vocational-technical track and 'general education', a mixture of academic and vocational studies likely to have been established for most pupils. But curriculum core of language, arts, maths and science, and the social studies typically retained for all pupils. In addition to state minimum competency testing, and textbooks, SAT and ACTP tests have standardizing effect.

Third level

Stage 1   Junior colleges; and liberal arts colleges. Vocational training courses; and general education.

Stage 2   General education typically continues into bachelor programmes, with specialization in a 'major' lasting two years. Curriculum under control of higher education institutions.

Fourth level   One-year courses for Master's degrees and three or four year courses for PhD and professional schools. Specification of curriculum by academics, but in professional areas minima required by state licensing authorities will be covered.

Teacher Education and Training

Type of Institution	Qualification awarded	Level of school in which teacher can teach
Pre-service 1,300 institutions in 1980 offered teacher education courses in, mainly, the public and private universities. Some state colleges, which have developed from state normal schools.	**1 *Academic qualifications*** A four-year bachelor's degree the minimum in all 50 states, with typically 2 years of general 'liberal arts' education in first two years, and education-linked courses in second two years. Typically more time spent by elementary school teachers on clinical and education courses than by prospective secondary school teachers.	Certificates classified by state, on basis of speciality within bachelor degree, in terms of a licence for: (a) teaching certain subjects, and/or (b) teaching at certain institutional levels, e.g. kindergarten/elementary/secondary. In addition, certificates classified by state as (i) permanent, i.e. with tenure, (ii) probationary or, (iii) temporary, though precise nomenclature varies from state to state.
In-service (a) Teachers' centres and (b) about half the states require formal academic study of education in local colleges or universities after initial appointment to teaching.	2 State licensing, once minimum academic bachelor degree obtained, permits entry to teaching, but 20 states require a postgraduate degree within 10 years of entry to teaching. In practice, about half the licensed teachers in the USA hold both bachelor and master's degrees.	

UNESCO Statistical Information: USA

UNESCO date of entry: 30 Sept. 1946
Surface area (km²): 9,363,123
Population 1980 (millions): 227·64
Persons/km² 1980: 24
Rural population (%) 1980: 23.0
Births per 1,000 pop. 1980: 16.2
Deaths per 1,000 pop. 1980: 8·9
Infant deaths per 1,000 live births 1977: 14
Life expect. at birth 1979: 74 years
Pop. growth rate (% p.a.) 1975–80: 0·9

Est. illiteracy rate 15+ (%) 1980
  M: 0·5 F: 0·5 MF: 0·5
National currency: dollar
GNP per capita in US $ 1979: 10,630
GNP per capita real growth rate
  (% per annum) 1960–79: 2·4
% agriculture in GDP 1979: 3
% industry in GDP 1979: 34
  of which manufacturing: 24

Data Series	1975	1977	1978	1979
Education				
Education Preceding First Level				
1 pupils enrolled	5,141,000	4,800,000	4,800,000	4,800,000
2 of which female (%)	—	—	—	—
3 teaching staff	—	—	—	—
4 of which female (%)	—	—	—	—
Education at First Level[a]				
5 duration (years)[b]	6	6	6	6
6 official age range[b]	6–11	6–11	6–11	6–11
7 gross enrolment ratio (%)	—	—	—	—
8 pupils enrolled	26,846,000	25,652,000	—	—
9 of which female (%)	—	—	—	—
10 teaching staff	1,354,000	1,330,000	—	—

	A	B	C	D
11 of which female (%)	—	—	—	—
12 pupils repeaters (%)	—	—	—	—
13 pupil/teacher ratio	20	19	—	—
Education at Second Level[a]				
14 duration gen. educ. (years)[b]	6	6	6	6
15 official age range gen. educ.[b]	12–17	12–17	12–17	12–17
16 gross enrolment ratio (%)	—	—	—	—
17 pupils enrolled	20,546,000	20,342,000	—	—
18 of which female (%)	—	—	—	—
19 teaching staff	1,109,000	1,130,000	—	—
20 of which female (%)	—	—	—	—
21 pupils repeaters gen. ed. (%)	—	—	—	—
Education at Third Level				
22 students per 100,000 inhabit.	5,238	5,192	—	5,245
23 students enrolled	11,184,859	11,285,787	—	11,569,899
24 of which female (%)	45	49	—	51
25 students scient./tech. fields (%)	25	—	—	—
26 foreign students	179,350	235,544	263,940	—
27 teaching staff	670,000	—	—	—
Public Expenditure on Education				
28 total in nat. currency (000,000)	100,700	120,700	140,400	152,200
29 of which current expend. (000,000)	96,800	109,900	131,000	142,600
30 total as % of GNP	6·6	6·3	6·6	6·4
31 current expendit. as % current government expenditure	29·8	30·0	—	—

continued

Data Series	1975	1977	1978	1979
Science and Technology[c]				
32 stock of university graduates per million inhabitants[d]	10,797	11,397	11,501	—
33 stock of persons with complete second educ. per million inh.[d]	4,379	4,453	—	—
34 scientists and engineers in R&D per million inh.	2,494	2,595	2,685	2,854
35 technicians in R&D per million inh.[e]	206	207	305	—
36 expend. on R&D as % of GNP[f]	2·2	2·2	2·2	2·3
Culture and Communication				
37 book titles published	85,287	—	85,126	—
38 circulation daily newspapers per 1,000 inh.[g]	287	287	284	282
39 consumption (kg) newsprint per 1,000 inh.	38,907	41,652	45,392	46,177
40 consumption (kg) printing and writing paper per 1,000 inh.	46,672	59,375	63,846	65,603
41 cinema seats per 1,000 inh.	—	—	—	—
42 radio receivers per 1,000 inh.	1,934	2,052	2,036	2,040
43 TV receivers per 1,000 inh.	586	624	633	635
44 volumes in public libraries per 1,000 inh.	—	1,782	—	—

Notes:
a Including special education.
b The educational structure allows for other alternatives.
c Not including data for law, humanities and education.
d Economically active persons in 1974, 1976 and 1978 respectively.
e Higher education sector only.
f Current expenditure only.
g English-language dailies in 1975 and 1977.
Source: Statistical Digest 1981 (Paris: UNESCO, 1981).

4

Education in the USSR
Equality and the 'New Soviet Man'

J. TOMIAK

Addressing the All-Russian Teachers' Congress in 1960, Nikita Khrushchev declared: 'We are now fulfilling two historical tasks: the creation of the material and technical basis for communism and the education of a new type of man.' He argued as many Soviet leaders did before him as well as after him that the two tasks were intimately and organically connected. Indeed, whether one looks back upon the growth and development of Soviet education over the last sixty-odd years, examines its present aims, principles of control and administration, its structure, contents and methods, or looks at its prospects for the future, one finds that the essential elements of coherence and unity are given to it by a consistent and continuous stress placed upon the concept of a New Soviet Man. When the Communist Party of the Soviet Union (CPSU) adopted its Third Programme for the building of communist society at the Twenty-Second Congress in October 1961, the moulding of the new man was, again, identified as the principal task in the spheres of ideology, education, instruction, science and culture in a long-time perspective. Its constituents were clearly defined as the shaping of a scientific world outlook, labour education, affirmation of communist morality, promotion of proletarian internationalism and Soviet patriotism, all-round and harmonious development of the individual, elimination of the survivals of capitalism in the minds and behaviour of the people and the exposure of bourgeois ideology. Formally, one can trace the origin of it all to the utterances of Lenin, both before and after the October Revolution. Logically and substantively, these aims and objectives of Soviet education ought to be seen as clearly identifiable guidelines formulated at a high level of generality and, as such, retaining lasting relevance to the process of formulation of educational policy.

Aims

Lenin's own conception of the role of education in building a communist society is manifestly clear: education was one of the component parts of the struggle that the communists were waging against the old order and its foreign enemies; it was a bourgeois lie that schools could stand above politics and simply serve society as a whole; once capitalism had been eliminated the Soviet schools had to become the chief instrument for building a socialist and then a communist society. Beyond the immediate objectives facing the communist authorities in the period following directly the Revolution and connected with the effective destruction of the old educational order, there were long-term considerations, linked to the attainment of crucial political, cultural, social and economic objectives. From the educational point of view, this was a question of not mastering, merely, a given body of knowledge, but, more significantly, the question of acquisition of the right kinds of socially and economically relevant skills, politically relevant attitudes and forms of behaviour, of developing an entirely different *Weltanschauung*, in other words of creating a New Soviet Man.

This was an extremely far-reaching and ambitious programme of action and it was quite clear to Lenin himself that enormous difficulties would have to be encountered if it was to be realized. His analysis of the principal elements involved in pursuing so ambitious a goal led him to the conclusion that the key elements were the teachers. This explains why so much attention was given to the education and training of Soviet teachers right from the very beginning of the Soviet state by the Commissariat of Education (*Kommissariat Narodnogo Prosveshcheniya*) under Anatoly Lunarcharsky and why so many efforts have been made ever since by the Soviet educational authorities and the Soviet government to reorient the teachers towards the new aim and to instil in them the new values. Yet the teachers themselves were the product of their own upbringing and had received the education permeated by the traditional values and an outlook upon life which had little to do with a radical scientific-utilitarian philosophy of life. The danger, therefore, was that while paying lip-service to the officially declared objectives, they would not be able to change to the extent that they would be in the position to internalize the new revolutionary values and change their patterns of behaviour. This is precisely what has been happening over the years and the gulf between the officially proclaimed norms and the actual beliefs which individuals tend to hold, has not closed. In Marxist terms, the false consciousness has tended to persist. Deeply rooted, it has continued to exist despite the constant stress on the Marxist values in the official documents, such as the main educational laws and regulations, in which regular references were made to the education of the younger generation in the spirit of communism, to the good provision of basic knowledge of science, and to a successful fusion of study with socially useful labour. This is as true of the Basic Principles of Uniform Schooling for Workers proclaimed in 1918, or the 1959 Statutes on the Eight-Year School and on the Secondary General Education Labour Polytechnical School with Vocational Training, as it is of the more recent Statutes of the Secondary General Education Labour Polytechnical Schools of 1970 or of the Fundamentals of Legislation of the USSR and Union Republics on Public Education of July 1973, which came into force on 1 January 1974. Article 47 of the Fundamentals had again to reiterate the former exhortations by stressing that the pupils and students were under the obligation systematically and deeply to master knowledge and practical skills, to attend classes, to fulfil within a prescribed time all the assignments specified by the curricula and study plans, to raise their ideological and cultural level, to take part in socially useful labour, to be well disciplined, show respect for the rules of socialist community, protect and strengthen socialist property and be intolerant towards any manifestations of antisocial behaviour.

Scrutinized in so far as its substance is concerned, Soviet education is a composite whole. General education (*obshchee vospitanie*), based upon the concept of all-round, harmonious development of all pupils, embraces five main aspects. Intellectual education (*umstvennoe vospitanie*) aims at the mastering of all the subjects of instruction, the acquisition of a conscious scientific and materialistic outlook upon life, mastering the dialectical method, developing orderly and systematic habits of thought and study. Moral education (*nravstvennoe vospitanie*) aims at the development of a conscious communist morality in every individual, at instilling in the pupils the feelings of Soviet patriotism and love for the homeland and its peoples and for the Communist Party of the Soviet Union and at cultivating the readiness to defend the socialist fatherland at all costs, conscious discipline, respect for work and physical effort. Polytechnical education (*politekhnicheskoe vospitanie*) aims at giving the younger generation a knowledge of the most important branches and general principles of the techniques, technology and organization of socialist production, equipping the young with habits of work by offering the experience of socially productive work, thereby eliminating the differences in esteem beween mental and physical effort, at cultivating the ability to assimilate changes brought about in working methods as a result of scientific and technological progress, and creating, in this way, a basis for a continuous increase in the productivity of labour. The view of

Nadezhda Krupskaya was that polytechnical education was not a separate teaching subject but that it should permeate every discipline and be reflected in the choice of content and teaching method in every subject of the curriculum, the natural sciences as well as the social sciences. Only if all these disciplines were linked with each other and with practical activity and especially with labour instruction could education acquire a truly polytechnical, as distinct from either a bookish or a monotechnical, character. Aesthetic education (*esteti-cheskoe vospitanie*), as another ingredient of harmonious general education, aims at developing appreciation of the different forms of art and particularly of social realism in art and at enhancing performing art skills among those who are particularly talented in this direction. Finally, physical education (*fizicheskoe vospitanie*) aims at the strengthening of the pupils' health and physical strength through a wide range of physical activities and exercises during PE lessons and participation in extracurricular events.

An important influence in formulating the aims of communist education in the 1920s and the 1930s was exercised by Anton Makarenko. While stating that the aim of education was the fullness of human personality, he stressed that in his view and in the light of his long experience of working with difficult and abandoned children and youths the correct Soviet way was to organize everywhere strong and properly integrated collectives as the means for moral education and the promotion of proletarian morality. Collective training, which subordinates the individual to the needs and the requirements of the collective, promotes strong and conscious discipline within the collective, provides for the circulation of the leadership from one member of the collective to another and allows for appropriate rewards as well as deserved punishment, was to characterize the system. All the socially useful work as well as academic study was to be based upon the collective effort of well integrated and well disciplined teams of pupils and students. Strict observance of the accepted rules of conduct and an agreed code of behaviour, manifestly strengthened by an effective use of symbols and ceremonials, were to become the chief features of youth organizations, which were to intensify further wholehearted commitments and dedication of the younger generation to the process of building a communist society. Yet the individual members were not to lose all their distinctiveness. They were rather to seek their fulfilment within and through the collective effort of the group as a whole, which he defined as a 'treasure of individual identities'. More recently, V. A. Sukhomlinsky, a Ukrainian pedagogue of growing popularity, continued along these lines by arguing that the spiritual worlds of the collective and of the individuals who constituted it were forged by a reciprocal interaction.

And yet education in the collective, by the collective and for the collective, in the sense that Anton Makarenko wanted to promote it, has not generally succeeded in producing a deeper change in the personality of Soviet citizens. As Nikita Krushchev pointed out in his speeches in the late 1950s, individualism and egoistic behaviour had not been eliminated, the devotion to collective goals could not be said to be universally held, there still was widespread contempt for manual work and physical effort among the Soviet people and the ability and willingness to work efficiently in different kinds of collectives had not become a universal pattern of behaviour. More important, even Krushchev's own attempts at reforming Soviet education and reorienting the young generation once more towards a collective basis of organization, based on his own, no doubt genuine concern, did not – despite all his zeal – bring about the fundamental change in the inner consciousness of the Soviet citizens that he had envisaged.

The need for education in the mother tongue has always been stressed by progressive Russian educators such as Ushinsky. Lenin accepted it as a fundamental principle of Soviet education, with the important proviso that while it was national in form it had to be socialist in content. The 1937 constitution formally declared the right to 'instruction in schools in the native language' for the citizens (Article 121); growing population mobility and the appearance of new industrial areas with mixed population resulted in the reformulation of this right in the 1977 constitution to 'the opportunity to attend a school where teaching is in the native language' (Article 45). Instrumentally, as over a hundred different nationalities inhabit the Soviet Union, the policy had to differentiate between various stages of cultural development characteristic of the particular groups. The 1927 Law on the subject distinguished between four groups of nationalities: the first, consisting of small and dispersed tribes with no written language of their own, were to be taught through the medium of Russian; the second, consisting of peoples living in larger compact groups, but without a national literary culture, were to be taught in the mother tongue at the primary level and in Russian at the secondary level; the third group, containing large nationalities with their own distinctive cultures, were to have schools teaching in the mother tongue at both the primary and secondary (though not higher) levels; the largest nations, with their own historical and cultural traditions, were to have educational institutions at all levels teaching in the mother tongue. Subsequent developments in this aspect of education provided increased opportunities for teaching in the mother tongue to some sixty distinctively different nations and nationalities, at least for the younger children.

The need for a more integrated union and consolidation of equal peoples in a single multinational state and their close effective co-operation in political, economic and cultural development, however, also has important consequences for educational policy. There is need to place special emphasis upon the culturally and socially integrative forces. The advantages and, indeed, the indispensability of everybody mastering the Russian language have constantly been stressed by the Party and the state organs of power. Three arguments have been put forward consistently, but with a renewed vigour more recently, to make sure that all Soviet people speak, read and write Russian well. It is argued that, first, Russian is the most important language in the USSR, as some 130 million people, more than half of the total population, speak it already as their mother tongue – no other language occupies a similar position; second, Russian language and literature are among the most important and impressive in the whole world; third, the process of building a communist society, and also that of a more rapid urbanization and industrialization, would be inconceivable without a good and universal knowledge of a common language, which in any case is already more or less known to the majority of the people. Hence a special emphasis is put upon the training of teachers of Russian in the nationalities' schools (*natsional'nye shkoly*), upon the growing need for bilingualism among the non-Russians, and upon the Russian language requirements in the entrance examinations to higher education establishments. Learning Russian, mastering it well, even becoming bilingual, doesn't necess-arily mean affecting adversely one's original ethnic allegiance or an automatic change in one's ethnic identity. It may, however, under specific conditions be the first move towards it. It is quite significant that several more millions of Soviet people name Russian as their mother tongue than give their nationality as Russian. In the 1970 census of population 129 million declared themselves Russian; 141·8 million named Russian as their mother tongue, while at the same time there were 41·9 million who said that Russian was the second language of which they had a good command. In the 1979 census 137 million people, out of the total population of 262 million, stated that Russian was their mother tongue. In addition, 16·3 million non-Russians named it as their mother tongue, while 61·3 million persons listed Russian as a second language which they spoke fluently. All in all, therefore, 215 million individuals should speak Russian fluently – 82 per cent of the entire Soviet population.

Administration

The recent, far-reaching and fundamental reforms touching upon every aspect of educational provision in the country would have been difficult to implement without a definite move for a greater rationalization of effort at the centre. Up to 1966 pre-school and general school education was administered by the separate ministries of education of the Union republics and autonomous republics. In that year the Ministry of Education of the USSR (*Ministerstvo Prosveshcheniya SSSR*) came into existence to meet the growing need for an overall synchronization of effort in tackling educational problems in a uniform way throughout the whole of the Union. The new ministry was explicitly charged with the responsibility for ensuring communist education of children and youth and providing for their spiritual, physical and aesthetic development; managing pre-school education, primary and secondary education of general character as well as out-of-school education; promoting and co-ordinating pedagogical research work in the country; elaborating and carrying out measures concerned with the further development and improvement of the system and presenting the corresponding proposals for the consideration of the government; specifying the targets for both short- and long-term plans in collaboration with the councils of ministers of the republics; determining the content of general education and of labour training for the pupils; improving the curricula for secondary schools of general education; preparing and publishing school textbooks; rendering assistance to the republics of the Union in improving the management of individual schools and pre-school and out-of-school educational establishments; and fostering the professional skills of teachers and developing foreign relations in the field of education.

In addition, a Council for the Problems of Secondary Schools of General Education (*Sovet za problemy srednikh obshcheobrazovatel'nykh shkol*) was created at the same time in order to give consideration to all important problems in education and in particular to formulate plans of development and school regulations and to determine school curricula. A Board of Authorities was constituted at the ministry to review regularly the development of education and pedagogical research, while the ministry's Scientific Council on Teaching Methods (*Uchebnometodicheskiy Sovet pri Ministerstve Prosveshcheniya SSSR*), consisting of outstanding scientists, pedagogical science researchers, distinguished teachers and representatives of educational associations, was set up to provide a forum for discussing innovation in the light of experience and the results of research work currently concluded.

Parallel with it went the measures to co-ordinate and integrate educational research. The Academy of Pedagogical Sciences

(*Akademiya Pedagogicheskikh Nauk*) up till then officially of the Russian Soviet Federated Socialist Republic, became, as the Academy of Sciences, a USSR institution and was made responsible for its work to the newly instituted Ministry of the USSR. The rationale for this change was obvious. For many years, and with increasing emphasis, Soviet scientists and sociologists have been drawing attention to the speeding up of the tempo of scientific and technological change. The concept of scientific-technological revolution, framed in the early 1950s, came to dominate all discussions at the highest levels in the 1960s and found its way into important CPSU programmes and resolutions. A report resulting from the Academy of Sciences conference in 1964 was largely dominated by an analysis of its consequences, while most of the papers presented by Soviet sociologists ten years later in the World Congress of Sociology devoted to the theme of 'science and the revolution', in Toronto, used the concept to analyze not only economic and social change but also changes in education deemed necessary to keep up with the growing speed of scientific and technological change. The sheer impact of the expected increase by a factor of between 15 and 25 in the volume of knowledge between 1960 and 2000 was bound to have immediate educational consequences. Clearly, the real issue was not how to squeeze more and more material into the already overloaded syllabuses, but how to devise new methods for independent learning and the acquisition of new knowledge, skills and aptitudes in one's own time.

The USSR Academy of Pedagogical Sciences is the main centre of pedagogical research work, upon which the educational reforms of different kinds are subsequently based. It now has fourteen research institutes, staffed by the country's best scholars and researchers: for general pedagogy, general and educational psychology, general problems of education, the contents and methods of instruction, child and adolescent physiology, school equipment and audio-visual learning aids, adult general education, pre-school education, the education of physically and mentally defective children, labour training and vocational guidance, artistic education, and the teaching of Russian in non-Russian schools. All institutes engage in both basic and applied research in the field of pedagogical sciences. The Academy institutes are divided into departments specializing in a particular aspect of educational development – for example, the Department of Moral Education and Character Training within the Institute of General Pedagogy. The institutes are controlled, guided and financed by the Academy. The research work is conducted in several pedagogical laboratories located in experimental and ordinary schools and, generally, oriented towards the solution of current problems at the different levels of education. At the head of the Academy is its president, a position occupied first by the Academician Vladimir Potemkin and, subsequently, by Professor I. A. Kairov in the years 1946–67, Professor V. M. Khvostov, a historian, till 1971, then Professor V. N. Stoletov and now Professor M. I. Kondakov. Among the fifty-odd full members and over seventy corresponding members are found the most distinguished scientists working in the fields of pedagogy, psychology, child physiology, sociology and economics of education as well as teaching methods of all the subjects in the school curriculum. The research staff employed in the Academy's institutes totals more than 1,600.

While the Ministry of Education of the USSR is the highest body in the field of administration of education, each of the fifteen Union republics has its own ministry of education, subordinate on the one hand to the council of ministers of the particular republic and on the other to the Ministry of Education of the USSR. The autonomous republics have their own ministries of education. The ministries of education at these levels are responsible for making plans for developing the necessary networks of pre-school institutions, schools and out-of-school educational establishments in their respective areas, draw up regulations concerning school education and school work and supply and maintain school equipment. They guide and control the regional and local district and municipal departments of education, responsible for the direct control of the work of individual pre-school institutions and schools. The latter bodies, which are also subordinate to the local soviet of working people's deputies, have jurisdiction over the directors of schools in their areas and maintain their own staff of inspectors of schools, each inspector being assigned to a number of schools. The inspector's duty is to visit each school at the very least twice during the course of each year and check on the proficiency of the director and the teaching staff, and to ascertain that all the laws, rules and regulations are properly observed and all the instructions implemented. The local district and municipal departments of education are also responsible for appointing teachers to schools and providing help to the teaching staff in solving any major problems as well as for providing pedagogical assistance through the district or municipal methodological section, organized locally by a council of experienced teachers, who guide the work of the methodologists. Also concerned with the education and upbringing of schoolchildren, both at school and at home, are the local Party branches, trade-union and Young Communist League organizations in the various productive units and state or collective farms, which maintain close ties with the schools, often offering financial and practical assistance.

The Ministry of Higher and Secondary Specialized Education of the

USSR (*Ministerstvo Vysshego i Srednego Spetsial'nogo Obrazovaniya SSSR*) exercises overall supervision of all the higher education institutions in the country (*vysshee uchebnye zavedeniya – VUZy*), which include universities, polytechnics and monotechnical institutes, as well as secondary specialized education establishments. The ministry is responsible for the cohesion and effectiveness of the educational process and in particular for the specification of the conditions for admission of students to all establishments, the preparation and approval of curricula, as well as the lists of specializations taught, methodological directives concerning the organization of instruction, the establishment of procedural methods for the recruitment of staff, supervision of the organization of instruction leading on to scientific research and higher degrees, the publication of a large proportion of textbooks used in higher education and the preparation of building plans for universities and other higher education establishments. Administratively and financially some institutions may be also subordinated to respective republican ministries of higher and secondary education (or republican state committees in some republics) or to other Union ministries. Medical institutes are thus controlled by the Ministry of Health of the USSR, while higher education establishments in agriculture, transport and communications come under the corresponding ministries and those in art under the Ministry of Culture. The All Union Council for Higher Education (*Vsesoyuznyi Sovet po Vysshomu Obrazovaniyu*) is a permanent body set up to deal with the fundamental problems of education at this level in wider and long-term perspectives. Its main tasks are to study and assess the prospects of development of higher education for a period of 3–5 years in some detail and 10–15 years ahead in a more general way, to work out recommendations concerning organization of the study process, to define the ways of promoting effective research in the basic sciences and in the crucial applied problems, to determine ways of improving the scientific qualifications of the teaching and research staff and to make recommendations on improving the administration of the country's system of higher education. At the local level, in all the larger cities there are rectors' councils, consisting of rectors of all the *VUZy* in a city, and they co-ordinate higher education in their respective areas.

The secondary specialized education establishments are generally subject to the ministries of higher and secondary specialized education of the Union republics (or republican state committees) or to other ministries in much the same way as the institutions of higher learning, depending upon the specialization. They are, however, opened, reorganized or closed only by agreement with the Ministry of Higher and Secondary Specialized Education of the USSR and the USSR Ministry of Finance.

The State Committee of the USSR Council of Ministers for Vocational-Technical Education (*Gosudarstvennyi Komitet Soveta Ministrov SSSR po professionalno-tekhnicheskomu abrazovaniya*) controls and guides the work of all vocational-technical schools (*professionaleno-tekhnicheskie uchilishcha – PTU*) in the whole country. The committee works out standard curricula for each trade or specialization and determines the number of students to be trained in each field in close contact with the state planning authorities. It is the responsibility of each council of ministers in the Union republics to present detailed estimates of the additional requirements in its skilled labour force to the USSR Council of Ministers and the USSR State Planning Commission (*Gosplan*) every year. The estimates must cover all productive units, institutions and organizations located in the given republic, irrespective of the actual administrative body which controls them. The estimates are added up to indicate an overall figure for the additional requirements in each category of specialization for the whole of the country. This, in turn, becomes the basis for the elaboration of the detailed figures for the number of skilled workers to be trained in a particular specialization in a given vocational-technical school.

Rigorous planning of the development of the national economy has been one of the principal features of the Soviet system since the late 1920s. From the moment the decision was taken to concentrate on the building of communism in one country before the banner of the world revolution could be raised, under Joseph Stalin, planned growth of the material and technical foundations of communism through the development of science and technology, mechanization and auto-mation, coupled with a steady rise in the productivity of labour, has been considered by the Party leadership and the government to be the principal task of Soviet society in the economic field, side by side with the effort to educate all Soviet people in the spirit of Soviet patriotism and proletarian internationalism and to develop in them a high level of political consciousness, a communist attitude to public property and to work, the readiness to defend the gains of socialism and an irreconcilable attitude towards bourgeois ideology. Manpower plan-ning, necessitating the preparation of adequate numbers of skilled workers, technicians, technologists and scientists for the different branches of the economy and the different kinds of specializations, had to be very closely integrated with the five-year plans for economic and social development. Five decades of experience in this direction have enabled the planning authorities fully to develop and improve centralized economic management by the state, to elaborate effective

146 Equality and Freedom in Education

forms and methods in planning techniques and to train the personnel indispensable in ensuring proper functioning of the accepted procedures on such a scale.

In connection with this, frequent references are made to the economic aspects of education, starting with S. G. Strumilin's pioneering study on the subject. In his work published in 1924, he arrived at the conclusion that two or three years of formal education raised the qualifications and therefore helped to increase the productivity of the workers by some 20–30 per cent. His book was reprinted in 1957 and stimulated interest in education as an investment among other Soviet researchers working in this field, notably V. E. Komarov and V. A. Zhamin. Scientific coordinating conferences on the economics of education began to take place in the 1960s and the Problem Laboratory for Socio-Economic Research in the Field of Education was created at the Moscow State Pedagogical Institute, named after Lenin. Research work there led to the conclusion that in the early 1960s as much as 27 per cent of the growth in national income could be attributed to investment in education and – what was particularly important – that an additional year of schooling was worth two or three times as much as one spent in training on the job. The longer the period of education, the less wasted effort in production, less unwarranted mobility, the greater the productivity and the greater the opportunity to earn higher wages by a worker. According to the USSR Central Statistical Board's data, the number of men with higher and a complete or incomplete secondary education employed in the economy increased between 1939 and 1970 nearly fivefold and the number of women in the same category in the same period more than sixfold. In 1977 three-quarters of both men and women gainfully employed had a higher or a complete or incomplete secondary education behind them, and in 1979 the proportion in the case of both sexes exceeded 80 per cent. Progress was by no means uniform throughout the country and the Central Asiatic republics were lagging behind other regions; there were also significant though greatly reduced differences in this respect between the urban areas and the countryside, but due to the fact that the last decade was particularly characterized by the growth of large cities and a rapid increase in the proportion of urban population, and – at the same time – a real exodus from the rural areas to towns on the transformation of rural settlements into urban-type centres, some improvement was possible. Nevertheless, the urban-rural dichotomy still persists, with its social, economic and educational repercussions, differences in lifestyle, opportunities and expectations.

Finance

The sources of funds for educational expenditure in the USSR are state budgets, overwhelmingly those at the republican and local – and to a much smaller extent – at the Union level; some money comes from the contributions of parents to their children's maintenance in crèches, kindergartens, boarding schools or young pioneer camps in the summer, as well as from the trade unions and state economic enterprises. Funds obtained from the local soviets' budgets constitute more than a half of the total. Local soviets have large sums of money at their disposal, made up first and foremost of profits from the different units of production and economic organizations and, to a minor extent, of personal income tax paid by the better off, state duties and local taxes and dues. Planning procedures require that the budgetary appropriations in the case of schools of general education are calculated by the city, district or regional departments of education and by the ministries of education of the Union and autonomous republics, on the basis of estimates of expenditure forwarded annually by all educational establishments; in the case of vocational-technical schools they are calculated by the State Committee of the Council of Ministers of the USSR for Vocational-Technical Training; and in the case of secondary specialized and higher education establishments they are calculated by the USSR and Union republic ministries and departments to which they are formally subordinated. They are subsequently submitted to the ministries of finance of the appropriate republics in the case of schools of general education and to the Ministry of Finance of the USSR in the case of vocational-technical schools, secondary specialized and higher education establishments. The average cost per pupil or per student being worked out centrally and the funds being provided by the single stage budget, a basic equality of educational provision for the whole of the country can be evaluated.

The principle of determining remuneration centrally – both wage rates and salaries, as well as the differentials in terms of periodical increases for experience, supplementary payments for special responsibilities or additional remuneration accruing to those working in more remote or less easily accessible areas, or those with higher academic qualifications – permits the government and the planning authorities to use remuneration as an important lever to influence an individual's choice of occupation and place of employment. This applies to all employed in the national economy, including teachers and other groups. Scales are nationally determined for a period of time and subject to collective bargaining with the authorities. In general, it is the case that the salary scales of teachers are fixed, depending upon experience, below the average monthly money wages for manual workers and the remuneration for non-manual workers. Four increments are given at the completion of five, ten, fifteen and twenty-five years of work in schools. Teachers with higher education behind them receive salaries which are considerably higher than those paid to teachers with secondary specialized education. Pay is between 10 and 20 per cent higher for those who are employed in the Urals, in Kazakhstan and in Central Asiatic republics, and up to 70 per cent higher for those working in the Soviet far north. Senior instructors in higher education establishments receive much higher remuneration than the teachers in schools and extra payments (50 roubles per month) are allocated to those with a Candidate of Science degree. Teachers who have been awarded the title of Merited Teacher or Heroes of Socialist Labour receive additional payments.

Organization and Structure

Reference is always being made to the fact that, in the USSR, education is a truly public domain which is the concern of the whole nation. The state, the family, the schools and social organizations of various kinds work consistently together to provide the upbringing and education of the young generation. In accordance with the views of Anton Makarenko concerning the unity of all pedagogical and educational efforts, close collaboration between school and family, teachers and parents, is continuously presented as an indispensable condition for proper communist upbringing and education. The Basic Principles of Legislation in the USSR and the Union Republics on Marriage and the Family of October 1968 declared that, while the state and society were rendering all-round help to the family in the bringing up of children in the form of a network of nursery schools, kindergartens, children's homes and boarding schools, the communist education of the rising generation and the development of its physical and spiritual potential was a major duty of the family. The legislative measures taken in this respect were aimed at promoting the family education of children in organic unity with their social education in a spirit of devotion to the motherland, a communist attitude towards work and the preparation of children for active participation in the construction of a communist society. In a similar vein, the Bases of the Legislation of the USSR and the Union Republics on Public Education of 1973 stipulated that the task of pre-educational establishments was to help families by offering children a harmonious education, protecting and strengthening their health, preparing them for entry into school and creating for wives and mothers such conditions as would enable them to play an active part in social and productive life. Section 11 of the same law identified the rights and duties of parents and guardians regarding children's upbringing: parents, on the one hand, were required to send their children to school as soon as they attained the required age and to create conditions suitable for the children to receive general education and vocational training, and, on the other hand, were entitled to take part in discussions concerning children's education and upbringing, to organize out-of-school activities in the schools attended by their children and to elect – or be elected to – parents' school committees.

Organizationally, well back in 1919 the Eighth Congress of the Russian Communist Party, whose deliberations were powerfully influenced by both Lenin and Krupskaya, laid down the long-term fundamental aims and principles of the fully developed Soviet system of education. This was to consist of a network of pre-school institutions such as nurseries, kindergartens and children's homes; free, universal and compulsory schools of general education for all children of both sexes between 8 and 17 years of age, and universities and other institutions of higher learning which were to be open to all who could profit from study at this level. While the original idea was to establish everywhere under Soviet power the unified labour school as the one and only form of educational experience common to all children, practical considerations enforced a much more realistic, though at the same time much slower, pace of development. Universal primary education was attained only in the 1930s; eight-year incomplete secondary schools came in in 1958; ten years of education available to all became a reality only at the end of the 1970s.

However, sustained progress enabled the Soviet authorities to introduce two very important reforms within the field of universal and compulsory education during the 1970s: the shortening of the primary school cycle from four to three years and the increase in diversification in general and professional education for the older adolescents over the age of fifteen.

Pre-school establishments in the Soviet Union include permanent and seasonal nursery schools, combined nursery-school-kindergartens, kindergartens, playgrounds and orphanages. They provide care and education for children under 7 years of age. Nurseries (*yasli*) accept children between 6 months and 3 years of age. The children are divided into small groups according to their age. They are looked after by specially trained nurses and teachers. Kindergartens (*detskie sady*) are divided into three age groups, with no more than twenty-five children in each group: juniors (from 3 to 4 years of age), intermediate (4–5) and seniors (5–6). Of special importance has been the recent formation of the group for children between 6 and 7, aimed at preparing them for school attendance from the age of 7. This came into prominence because of the adoption of new curricula and programme schedules and the shortening of the cycle of primary education from four to three years.

The pre-school education sector is considered to be an essential part of the entire system of public education, as its first stage, laying down the foundations for the all-round and harmonious development of all children. At the same time it is designed to meet the needs of the family, by enabling women to do socially productive work and supplement the family income, as well as to offer young mothers opportunities for improving their education or gaining further professional qualifications. The specific tasks, content and methods of education at this level are regulated by the kindergarten syllabus, elaborated by prominent educationists and child development experts working in the Pre-school Education Institute of the USSR Academy of Pedagogical Sciences, jointly with the representatives of the USSR Academy of Medical Science. The syllabus lays down a theoretical basis for the content of pre-school education, having particular regard to the transition between kindergarten and school. Special attention is devoted to the educational process. Naturally, special attention is paid to children's health and promoting physical fitness, but developing their mental abilities, early speech training with a special emphasis on improving the child's auditory skills, powers of observation and playing and working in a collective are strongly emphasized. Moral education at this level is directed towards the children's acquiring the positive qualities of being polite, showing respect to adults, being truthful and responsive, and developing love towards the motherland. Individualistic orientation is discouraged and egoism and selfishness are not tolerated.

Children attend kindergartens from nine to twelve hours a day, depending upon the parents' time and circumstances. Some establishments have facilities for children to stay overnight, at their parents' request. Three or four meals are provided per day, depending upon how long the child stays in the kindergarten. The basic principle of combining work with play is strictly observed. Children aged between three and four normally have ten short lessons, of from fifteen to twenty minutes, per week; children aged from 5 to 6 receive as many as fourteen lessons per week, devoted to the introduction of the basic skills of literacy and numeracy, art, music, practical work and physical education. Accepting responsibility for the satisfactory fulfilment of tasks is taught by appointing each child in turn as monitor to take care of plants or pets, to serve and clean up, or to do simple gardening. Despite the harshness of the winters, spending at least some time in the fresh air is a must, unless absolutely impossible.

Parents pay for the education of their children at this level according to their ability to pay. The cost of maintaining a child in a kindergarten has increased to some 480 roubles per year from 410 roubles in the early 1970s, of which about 380 roubles is allocated by the government.

Kindergarten teachers are trained either in special secondary pedagogical schools, numbering over 200, or in the departments of pre-school education operating in thirty-four pedagogical institutes.

By far the most important and fundamental reform of the Soviet system of education after 1945 was the one attempted in 1958 following the criticism of the shortcomings of the system by Nikita Khrushchev. His main point was that instruction in schools and other educational establishments was divorced from life, and that this could not be tolerated at the stage of intensive efforts to build a communist society. The main task of school must be the preparation of the younger generation for life and for useful work and the inculcation in youth of a deep respect for the principles of socialist society. In an elaborate memorandum, which appeared in *Pravda* in September 1958 and was followed a month later by the publication of the Theses on Strengthening the Ties of the School with Life and Further Development of the System of Public Education, Krushchev insisted that every boy and every girl must come to realize that in studying at school they must prepare themselves for work, for creating values that are useful to man and society. Everyone, regardless of the position occupied by his parents, must have only one road in front of him – that of study and, after the acquisition of the appropriate knowledge, that of work. The schools were unfortunately concentrating too much on preparing the older pupils for entering a university or an institute. This was leading to one-sidedness and resulted in serious shortcomings in educational work. The schools tended to limit themselves to verbal methods of instruction and did not pay the necessary attention to accustoming the young people to take an active part in socially useful work. As a result, many boys and girls considered that the only road suitable for them was to continue their education in a higher education establishment, or, if the worst came to the worst, in a special secondary education establishment. They only very unwillingly went to work in factories, steel mills, or collective or state farms, while some even considered it degrading to do any manual work. As a solution of the problem Khrushchev proposed that all young people should join in socially useful work on a regular basis and that education in the fundamentals of science should be linked with productive work in industry or in agriculture. Instruction from the very first years must, however, prepare the children psychologically for taking willingly an active part in socially useful activities.

Within six weeks of the publication of the Theses, the Law on Strengthening the Ties of the School with Life and Further Development of the System of Public Education in the USSR was passed. It sought to introduce a reform along the lines suggested by Khrushchev. In the first place universal and compulsory education was extended from seven to eight years. Second, it decided that complete secondary education for young people aged 15 or 16 would be carried out on the basis of combining study with productive work. This type of education was to be given in three kinds of schools: schools for young workers and rural youth, which were to offer part-time education in out-of-work hours; secondary general education labour polytechnic schools with productive training, which were to give three years of full-time education, following eight years of compulsory general education; and secondary specialized education establishments, which were to provide both general and specialized secondary education on a full-time as well as a part-time basis. Production training and socially useful work was to be carried out at instructional and production workshops in industrial enterprises, on collective or state farms, or in workshops in schools.

Bridging the gap between physical and mental work with the help of study combined with production training proved, however, difficult in practice. Industrial enterprises found that they could not easily provide adequate facilities and meaningful enough schemes. Teachers, parents and pupils began to develop doubts about the value of working experience of an inadequate kind. The result was that in 1964 there came a return to a two-year course in the upper grades of the general secondary education school, with a corresponding drastic reduction in the time spent on industrial training and productive work. Polytechnical education, practical training and courses in theory and practice of production were, however, not abandoned. Proper attention was rather directed towards finding better means to a more effective solution of the problem with the help of new initiatives, which were first to be rigorously tested experimentally.

The 1969 Law on Shortening the Primary Phase of Education reduced the first cycle of education from four to three years. The decision to do so was based upon prolonged research into young children's learning by Soviet educational psychologists working under the leadership of N. A. Menchinskaya, D. B. Elkonin, L. V. Zankov, A. Lyublinskaya and S. M. Yazykov. School practice and experimental research indicated that the new children's experiences and their cognitive abilities were much greater than the traditional syllabuses in primary education had allowed for in the past. There was also evidence that in the 1960s children had been developing quicker, both physically and intellectually. The reduction of the course of primary education by one whole year – from four years to three – was nevertheless a bold step. It meant that the whole course of secondary education could then be extended by one year and the specialized teaching of individual subjects could begin at the age of 10 and not 11, as before – an important innovation, even though an allowance has to be made for the fact that compulsory education in the USSR starts at the age of 7. The real point was that a full use was made by the reformers of the potentially most significant work of I. P. Pavlov and L. S. Vygotsky. Pavlov argued that in studying comprehension and assimilation one is led to the conclusion that the ability to assimilate associations (seen as part of the reflex theory and as analysis and synthesis) depends upon an active state of the brain and the ability to use and apply associations in practice. Vygotsky's work on concept formation and language development and the importance of the acquisition of speech led him to the conclusion that the stages of individual growth, linked rigidly to chronological age in Western theories, can in fact be significantly accelerated by education and equally well retarded by the lack of it. A road was, therefore, open for a much greater use of the powers of abstraction in the primary school curriculum and a much greater use of pupils' mental powers at this level of education. Further impetus was added to investigations leading in this direction by the studies of V. Luria and A. N. Leontiev on the formation of abilities, and of A. V. Zaporozhets and P. I. Zinchenko on attention in children and this, in the end led to structural reforms in the system.

The explosion of aspirations, identifiable in the USSR to the same extent as in many other countries, coupled with the axiom of potential equality of scholastic achievement among all children with normally functioning brains, itself a feature of paramount importance in Soviet educational psychology since its beginnings, has recently paved the way towards a much more positive solution of the problem of diversification in upper secondary education.

Recent structural changes at this level of education are based upon the guidelines laid down by the Twenty-Fourth Congress of the CPSU in March 1971 and the provision contained in the ninth five-year plan (1971–5) for making general education at secondary level available to all. The 1972 Law on the Completion of Transition to Universal Secondary Education and Further Development of the General Secondary School and the Law on Further Improvement of the System of Vocational Education of the same year laid down the lines to be followed in extending to everybody access to secondary education and the gradual change-over to training skilled workers with secondary-level education. A new type of vocational school came into existence as a result of this, a school in which side by side with vocational education the students receive secondary general education and on completing the course receive both a secondary school leaving certificate as well as a professional-vocational qualification in a particular occupation. At the same time as this new type of school is gradually being developed, the professional-vocational schools offering a one- or two-year course continue their existence; in these, students who have completed a ten-year school or an eight-year school obtain their vocational training.

Differences between rural and urban environments have always characterized the vast territories which constituted the Russian Empire and today form the USSR. Lenin considered that communism could not be attained in the country until such differences were eliminated. Even the six decades of Soviet power could not, however, remove the contrast between the town and the countryside. The 1973 Law on Measures for Further Improvement of the Working Conditions in the Rural General Education Schools accepted that there were rural schools where educational standards were lower than those of urban schools and spelled out the measures which are now being implemented to improve education in the village schools, attended nowadays by 22 million pupils, which is half the total number of schoolchildren in the country. Improvement in this field is envisaged as an important step towards the solution of problems concerning the socio-political, cultural and economic development of the rural environment and the levelling out of substantial differences between such areas and the urban environment. Specifically, in the years 1974–80, the state authorities were to construct in the rural areas new general education schools with a total capacity of 7,250,000 places and provide boarding facilities for 772,000 pupils. The collective farms were to build, at their own expense, schools for some 2,000,000 pupils, while receiving for that purpose from the State Bank of the USSR a long-term credit repayable over fifteen years. An area of over 6 million square metres was to be set aside for building houses for teachers in rural schools. Planned investment in the construction of new state farms has now to include specific provision for building large schools of general education, properly equipped with workshops, specialized subject rooms, libraries and modern learning aids. The Central Committee of the CPSU and the government have approved the initiative taken by the Young Communist League to direct into rural areas voluntary teams of young workers, students, and pupils in their final year of schools, during their summer holidays, in order to help with the construction of new schools there.

The existence of schools for specially gifted, high-ability children in the Soviet Union has for many years been attracting the attention of Western educators. The original and mistaken idea that the whole system was turning 'elitist' and that it was introducing rigorous selection procedures at a time when other systems in the West were moving away from it or abandoning it altogether has been dispelled. Careful and detailed accounts of the ongoing debates and controversies and of the actual nature and extent of the adopted measures have indicated more clearly the character of the recent changes. Admittedly, certain kinds of schools of a special kind for highly gifted children have been in existence in the Soviet Union for a very long time – schools for youngsters with exceptional artistic ability. As artistic talent undoubtedly requires proper cultivation and intensive care from a very tender age, such schools have consistently received full support from the Soviet authorities and their existence has always been considered quite compatible with that of the unified labour school in the 1920s and with that of the secondary general education labour polytechnical school in more recent times.

The schools for children with superior intellectual ability, particularly in the fields of mathematics and the natural sciences, or foreign languages, constituted, however, a different category and their advocates had to use entirely different kinds of arguments for their creation and promotion. Naturally, supporters of any scheme leading to the earliest possible recruitment of potential talent and to any well designed programme for the intensive cultivation of it in an academic environment conducive to rapid intellectual advancement claim that it is in the interests both of the child and of society.

Towards the end of 1960, Academician M. A. Lavrentiev, chairman of the Siberian branch of the USSR Academy of Sciences at Novosibirsk, proposed that in the interest of speeding up scientific and technological progress in the country boys and girls with a special talent for mathematics should be selected early and be given an opportunity to cultivate their talent in this and related fields in special schools, where they would be taught by and remain in very close academic contact with outstanding mathematicians and scientists, working in the forefront of scientific research in the USSR. The voice of the founder of *Akademgorodok*, the famous Siberian academic city, whose capital cost was equal to the annual budget of all British universities put together at that time, was bound to be listened to, particularly as he appeared to have the support of the President of the Academy of Science of the USSR itself, Professor M. V. Keldysh, as well as several of his colleagues in the Academy, notably Professors Sakharov, Kolmogorov and Semenov.

On the other hand, strong opposition to selection at or before the age of fifteen was naturally to be expected from the traditional believers in equal opportunity, who argued that setting apart some gifted children and making them feel exceptional was ideologically unacceptable. The battle between the 'differentiators' and the 'egalitarians' was protracted but the scientists at Moscow State University managed to organize the First All-Russian Mathematics Olympiad in 1961, while those in Novosibirsk prepared the First All-Siberian Mathematics and Physics Olympiad in 1962. A year later the Statute on the All-Russian Mathematics and Physics Olympiad was issued and officially approved. Ever since, the olympiads in these two subjects, to which, subsequently, those in chemistry, astronomy, geology, linguistics and arts subjects were added, have been taking place annually, selecting the most gifted young people.

Meanwhile, successful competitors began to enter special classes attached to some universities. These were organized as mathematics and physics boarding schools (*fiziko-matematicheskie shkoly*), consisting of grades eight, nine and ten as a rule. The curricula in such schools cover all subjects, but much more time is given, in addition, to an intensive study of mathematics and the sciences. Lessons are often given by the best scientists and university professors; special stress is put upon original approaches to the solution of problems. Small groups of pupils study under conditions approximating to work in a university, as the schools try to develop rigorous and creative scientific thinking and mathematical logic. Intellectual games are employed and, in their last year, the pupils begin to participate in scientific work in the laboratories. The pressure of work is great and criticism has been expressed that the talented young scientists sometimes lack time and encouragement to pursue with rigour the language and literature syllabuses. Some critics have tried to argue that the pupils recruited do not replicate the different social groups in the population, that the children of well educated parents are overrepresented and that rigorous demands make for a high drop-out rate. The fact remains that schools of this type continue to operate and receive very strong support from certain quarters. Outstanding talent must be identified and taken proper care of at an early age, it is argued, in the interest of society as a whole, as the greatest discoveries and the most consequential formulations of new theories are often the work of brilliant young individuals. As the evidence shows, many former pupils from the mathematics and physics boarding schools quickly join the ranks of the top Soviet scientists and research workers. The principle of serving the process of building a communist society and subordinating personal interest to that of the collective interest, instilled in the minds of the pupils in accordance with the teaching of Anton Makarenko, is considered to constitute a good enough guarantee that the products of such schools do not become the nucleus of a self-centred elite.

Curriculum

Curricula in the ten-year general education labour polytechnical schools include the full range of subjects: humanities, natural sciences, mathematics, labour training, representational art, music and sport. Expressed cumulatively over the ten grades, the weekly load totalled 330 periods in 1959, 310 in 1964 and after the new curriculum was introduced in 1966 it came to a total of 276 periods, plus 18 periods devoted to options. The fact that the curriculum in schools teaching in Russian consists of seventeen subjects, while in schools teaching in other languages it includes eighteen subjects, should not obscure its polytechnical character, as the teaching of all subjects is directed towards combining study with work and establishing very close links between theory and practice, and includes for the upper grades labour training in workshops or production centres. Over the past decade the content of education has been updated and new learning aids and improved methods of instruction have been introduced. Significant changes have been introduced in the syllabuses in the humanities, mathematics and the natural sciences. This was accomplished not by adding new material but by the modification of the structure of courses and by enhancing their theoretical level. This was rendered possible by the reduction of the primary cycle from four to three years, which made specialist subject teaching possible from an earlier age. In particular, the new syllabuses in mathematics for the fourth and fifth grades unified and closely combined the elements of arithmetic, algebra and geometry and those for the higher grades were redesigned to permit the application of mathematical knowledge in the study of physics and chemistry.

The syllabuses in physics put greater stress upon polytechnical orientation, laboratory experiments and practical work in physics. Syllabuses in biology put emphasis upon the understanding of agricultural production, cultivation of plants, livestock breeding and the elements of agronomical biology. Those in chemistry put emphasis upon the importance of industrial and technological processes. The history course was designed to provide an integral view of the historical process, while an effort was made to exclude excessive descriptiveness in the geography syllabus. A new course, the fundamentals of the Soviet state and legal system, was introduced in the eighth grade, in the 1975–6 school year. Labour instruction in the senior grades now takes the form of practical courses in metalwork, electrical engineering, radio-electronics, agricultural chemistry, or learning to drive a car. Labour training in the top two grades takes into account the local production pattern and many large industrial enterprises have workshops equipped with machinery. Since 1974 a considerable number of interschool training and production centres (*mezhshkolne uchebno-proizvodstvenne kombinaty*) have come into existence to acquaint the older pupils with industrial processes and with the jobs done by the workers in local factories of different kinds and to provide an opportunity for vocational guidance. They have been placed under the control of the educational authorities, while the directors of the nearby factories have been authorized to set up and equip them as training workshops, resource rooms and laboratories; to form formally organizational subdivisions of their enterprises, and to assign to them skilled workers, engineers and technicians to provide instruction and to organize productive work for the pupils.

In addition, optional courses have been devised for the upper grades: language and literature, history, social studies, mathematics, physics, biology, chemistry, labour training, or, in additional fields, psychology, ethics and aesthetics. In fact there are option courses of two different kinds: complementary courses, designed to supplement the body of knowledge included in the ordinary courses in the different branches of knowledge and directed towards a further study in depth of the selected aspects of the different subjects of the standard curriculum; and special courses, concerned with specific themes or topics which can be handled quite separately from the ordinary syllabuses.

Teacher Education

Soviet teachers clearly play the key role in Soviet education, but the tradition of treating teachers with great respect goes much further back into the past. Russian revolutionary writers of the nineteenth century such as N. G. Chernyshevsky and N. A. Dobrolyubov regarded the teachers' work as the best example of service to society. Konstanty Ushinsky wrote that each child develops mentally and spiritually under the direct influence of the teacher's personality and that nothing can replace the teacher's beneficial influence on his pupils. Lenin argued that teachers in a communist state should be placed at a level at which they had never been put before and that one had to do it by providing opportunities for the spiritual progress of teachers, high-quality training for the profession, and improving teachers' material well-being. Mikhail Kalinin stressed, years later, that the teacher's authority should be increased by the cultivation of a most profound respect for him among all age groups of the population and by surrounding him with 'an aura of general esteem'. Anton Makarenko demanded from the teacher decisive qualities of leadership and dedication to the communist cause and for the teacher universal support and respect.

The political leadership in the USSR stresses regularly that the successful solution of all the important tasks facing the system of education in the country depends above all upon the teacher, his ideological conviction, professional skill and general cultural standards. Teachers' educators stress that the Soviet teacher is first and foremost an ideological educator, responsible for developing among young people a scientific, political and civic outlook. The Statutes of the Secondary General Education School emphasize the leading role of the teacher in the school, where he 'performs the honourable and responsible state task of the instruction and communist upbringing of the young generation'.

There are some 2·9 million teachers working in the USSR, over 70 per cent of whom are women. Teachers are trained in secondary specialized pedagogical schools, of which there are over 400, in 200 pedagogical institutes, or in the universities. All the Union republics now train their own teachers. The autonomous republics have their own pedagogical institutes and the autonomous areas of the far north have their own pedagogical schools. The students of all these establishments are local inhabitants.

Secondary specialized pedagogical schools (*pedagogicheskie uchilischcha*) train primary school teachers, who receive general secondary education and pedagogical training. Long-term plans envisage ultimately the training of all teachers at higher education establishments, but it is accepted that the pedagogical schools will still for a long time train teachers for grades one, two and three and for pre-school establishments. The students may be admitted after the completion of an eight-year school for a course of four years, or after the completion of a ten-year school for a two-year course. The four-year course includes general education subjects as well as the study of anatomy, physiology, child hygiene, child and educational psychology, pedagogy, children's literature, and teaching methods in primary or pre-school education. Special stress is put on drawing, modelling, workshop training and learning to play a musical instrument. The study of theory is augmented by teaching practice in schools. The two-year course concentrates upon educational theory and teaching practice. Music, singing and physical education teachers for the primary grades and eight-year schools are trained at special pedagogical music schools and pedagogical schools of physical education. All students who complete their course of study and pass the final examination receive diplomas giving them the right to teach in the primary grades as well as the right to enter a higher education establishment for further training, after teaching for a period of three years.

The pedagogical institutes (*pedagogicheskie instituty*) are higher education establishments training teachers to teach in grades 4–10. In many pedagogical institutes the students prepare for teaching two subjects, in which case their course lasts five years; those preparing to teach one subject study for four years. The institutes accept students who have successfully completed a secondary general education school or a secondary specialized education school and have passed their entrance examination. The curricula include socio-political subjects, pedagogic subjects and the subject or subjects of specialization. The first group includes the history of the CPSU, political economy, philosophy and scientific communism. The pedagogic subjects embrace general pedagogy, history of education, general psychology, child and educational psychology, child physiology and school hygiene. The study of educational theory includes an examination of the aims and tasks of education; a scrutiny of the aims and content of intellectual, moral, aesthetic, polytechnical and physical education; discussing the characteristic features of the system of education in the USSR and in other countries; giving consideration to the teaching and learning process and the alternative methods of exposition as well as studying the forms and methods of educational work in extracurricular activities and youth organizations. Lectures have to be supplemented by extensive reading. Current issues are discussed in seminars, with students presenting papers and reports on educational problems of different kinds to the group, followed by general discussion of the issues raised. An important role is played by the teaching practice, which may include work in a pioneer camp and extend from twenty to thirty weeks. In order to graduate, the students, until recently, had to pass their state examinations in the specialist subject of their choice and in the methodology of teaching it, in pedagogy and in scientific communism.

According to recent regulations the students now have the option of writing a thesis instead of taking a state examination in pedagogy and in teaching methods. After obtaining the diploma, the students are allocated jobs in schools, the most successful ones managing often to obtain positions in areas of their own choice. In many pedagogical institutes there are also evening departments and correspondence departments. The course of study there is one year longer than in the day departments and admissions quotas regulate student numbers. Universities are also an important source of supply of new teachers, particularly in so far as the teaching of languages and social sciences is concerned. In comparison with the pedagogic institutes, students in the universities receive a more specialized training in a particular subject, such as English, mathematics or physics, and the study of pedagogy and teaching methods tends to receive less emphasis.

Considerable attention is devoted to the advanced training of practising teachers. New curricula and syllabuses have been introduced for teachers' refresher courses in the different subjects. The actual content depends upon the length of service and special interests of the participants. Teachers have always been strongly encouraged to improve their professional qualifications and to update their knowledge. An important new development is the periodic certification of teachers, introduced in 1974, which requires that every teacher is certified once in every five years. This is being done with the help of the local institutes for the improvement of teachers' qualifications (*instituty usovershenstvovaniya uchitelei*) and methodological centres (*metodicheskie kabinety*), where practising teachers acquaint themselves with the recent developments and progress made in their subjects as well as with new teaching techniques.

Higher Education

The 1958 Law on the Strengthening of the Ties of the School with Life stressed particularly strongly that Soviet higher education establishments had played a most important role in the development of science and technology in the country. Indeed, in the creation of hundreds of thousands of experts and specialists who had passed through the *VUZy* it saw one of the biggest achievements of the Party and the Soviet state. At that time just over 2 million students were enrolled in the institutions of higher learning in the USSR. They were studying in 727 establishments, which included then 39 universities. Twenty years later over 5 million students were enrolled in 856 *VUZy*, including 65 universities with over 600,000 students. The expansion proceeded at an even speed, in a planned way. No student unrest accompanied the growth, despite the fact that competition to get into higher education was intensifying. In 1950 eight out of ten secondary school graduates succeeded in getting in; in 1960, not even three out of ten; in the early seventies, two out of nine were admitted. Competition at this level certainly became very intense. The higher education establishments in the Soviet Union include several categories. They are the universities (*universitety*), offering courses in all the different subdivisions of knowledge, from mathematics to soil sciences and from Oriental studies to journalism; there are the polytechnics (*politekhnicheskie instituty*), large and well-known establishments, training technologists in a large number of specializations and consisting of many faculties; there are technical institutes (*tekhnicheskie instituty*), specializing in mining, metallurgy, oil production, machine building, land, water and air transport and communications, and food and light industries; there are agricultural institutes (*sel'skokhozyaistvennye instituty*), specializing in agronomy, agrochemistry, zootechnology, forestry and the mechanization of agricultural production; there are medical institutes (*meditsinskie instituty*), specializing in the different subdivisions of the medical sciences; pedagogical institutes (*pedagogicheskie instituty*); and schools of fine art (*khudozhestvennye instituty*), specializing in fine art, applied art, music, the theatre or cinematography. About half of the total number of students study engineering; some 10 per cent, agriculture; and nearly 40 per cent, the liberal arts. There are three different kinds of study: full-time day, evening, or correspondence courses. The latter form of study has for years been known as 'the Soviet way'. Today some thirty independent evening and correspondence institutes and 1,200 evening and correspondence departments in universities and other higher education establishments offer a choice of 300 professions. The students receive generous help in the form of days off from work with pay and up to four months off to prepare and defend their diploma work. The drop-out rate in this form of study is, however, considerably higher than in full-time courses, the whole course has to be covered in a much reduced number of lectures in comparison with daytime study, and special arrangements have to be made to cover the absence of the students from their place of work. Voices, therefore, have been raised suggesting a better selection of students, excluding certain kinds of studies from part-time courses and placing a greater reliance upon the full-time form of study. Equalizing educational opportunities for access to higher education in social and geographical terms is being given special attention. Opening up new universities and other *VUZy* in hitherto less developed areas and regions is giving an increased chance to people living there to study at this level. Workers' faculties (*rabochye fakul'tety*), operating in most of the *VUZy*, are seeking to increase the proportion of students from families of industrial workers and workers on the state and collective farms. Young workers entering these faculties on the recommendation from the Party, the Komsomol or the trade unions receive scholarships. After completing a nine-months preparatory course, they take the entrance examination and, if successful, begin a normal course of study. The curricula at all higher education establishments consist of three major subdivisions: the social sciences, including history of the CPSU, political economy, dialectical and historical materialism and scientific communism; a basic course of study in the branch of knowledge in which the student specializes; and a range of related subjects, determining the type of specialization.

The duration of study is strictly regulated and in full-time study it is not less than four years and not more than six and a half years, depending on the specialization. Each student must complete his or her course within the prescribed time and, although sick leave may be granted, it may not exceed one year for the whole course of study. Examinations and tests are held regularly at the end of each semester, but homework assignments and laboratory work in many subjects are also taken into account in assessing students' progress. The work load is heavy and may consist of over thirty hours of lectures, seminars and work in laboratory per week in the first three years; it declines in the fourth year and more substantially in the fifth year, which is devoted to the preparation of the diploma work by each student. The theme of this work must be approved and the writing of it is undertaken with the help of guidance given by the student's scientific adviser. When the thesis is ready, the student presents it to the university or the *VUZ* and must defend it in an oral examination before a board of examiners consisting of professors and representatives of the appropriate ministry. If the defence of the thesis is successful, the student is awarded the graduate qualifications, that is, the diploma. The subsequent allocation to jobs is in the hands of a state commission on the basis of requirements presented and vacancies notified to the respective ministries by individual units of production.

The achievement of universal secondary education is exerting increasing pressures upon the higher education system. Both parents and students themselves see the undisputed advantages attached to the possession of a diploma as an indispensable precondition for upward social mobility. The *VUZy* and particularly the universities have, however, expressed their determination not to allow a stream of *beznadiezhnykh troyechnikov* (hopeless average pupils) to swamp the establishments of higher learning. In the early 1970s proposals were made instead to reorganize higher education by splitting the five-year cycle into two stages: the first, of three years, providing a broad training of theoretical nature and in the basic skills for a particular specialization, and the second, for outstanding students, offering advanced theoretical knowledge, leading to the acquisition of research and design skills. Although by 1982 no measures had, as yet, been taken to implement such a change, certain new types of higher education establishments had come into existence. These are the so-called plant-technical institutes (*proizvodstvenno-tekhnicheskie instituty*), which constitute an integral part of large industrial plants. Students there base their studies upon a programme which integrates practical work in production and related theory. The plant-technical institutes are opened in the places where the particular industries are located, so that the students have the opportunity to examine all the problems in their actual productive setting and direct their attention towards their solution on the spot. At the same time much greater emphasis is being placed upon the importance of research and awarding higher degrees to highly talented researchers. The number of higher degrees awarded went up very dramatically in the last two decades. Among the postgraduate students (*aspiranty*) who after at least three years of further study and research were awarded the degree of Candidate of Science (*Kandidat nauk*), in the 1970s, were those specializing in technology, economics, physics, mathematics, biology and agriculture. The degree of Doctor of Science (*Doktor nauk*) requires many years of intensive research and the writing of a substantial thesis; as a result only about one doctor's degree is granted for every ten candidate degrees.

The maldistribution of the higher education establishments in the USSR in the 1950s from the geographical point of view was sharply attacked by Nikita Khrushchev soon after he became First Secretary of the CPSU, in the Twentieth Congress. The time was ripe, he argued, to re-examine the geographical distribution of the *VUZy*, most of which were concentrated in large towns, instead of being more evenly dispersed throughout the country and in the proximity of the centres of production, where the need for specialists was greatest. An especially intolerable state of affairs prevailed in regard to the higher educational establishments in the field of agriculture, many of which were also located in large towns. He instructed the ministries concerned to work out a plan for the creation of a wide network of institutions in higher education to cover the whole of the Union. As a result, the 1960s and 1970s saw the creation of many new establishments in Kazakhstan, in the Central Asiatic Republic and in Siberia.

The late 1970s brought with them the creation of the so-called science centres. At their base lies a determined attempt to promote a more intensive collaboration between the best universities located in key geographical centres, and the experts working there, and the scientific branches of the Academy of Science, established in the very hearts of areas abounding in natural resources of different kinds and offering an opportunity for intensive economic development. The best example still remains the rapidly expanding University of Novosibirsk and the integration of the work done there with that undertaken in the neighbouring scientific research institutes, operating under the auspices of the Siberian branch of the Academy of Sciences at Akademborodok. Recently, its work and organization have been replicated and applied in the other newly established science centres: in North Caucasus, the Urals and the Soviet Far East. Additional science centres are now being established well away from the traditional centres of industrial and other forms of economic activity, in the Asiatic territories, rich in oil and other resources. In the expectation of increased opportunities for a fuller exploitation of these resources, the centre of gravity of scientific and technological innovation and advancement is steadily shifting eastwards.

Further Reading

J. R. Azrael, *Soviet Nationality Policies and Practices* (New York: Praeger, 1978).

J. Brine, M. Perrie and A. Sutton, (eds), *Home, School and Leisure in the Soviet Union* (London: Allen & Unwin, 1981).

U. Bronfenbrenner, *Two Worlds of Childhood: US and USSR* (Harmondsworth: Penguin, 1971).

R. Conquest (ed.), *Soviet Nationality Policy in Practice* (London: The Bodley Head, 1967).

N. T. Dodge, *Women in the Soviet Economy* (Baltimore, Md: Johns Hopkins University Press, 1966).

J. Dunstan, *Paths to Excellence and the Soviet School* (Windsor: National Foundation for Educational Research, 1978).

S. Fitzpatrick, *The Commissariat of Enlightenment*, (London: CUP, 1970).

S. Fitzpatrick, *Education and Social Mobility in the Soviet Union, 1921–1934* (Bloomington, Ind.: Indiana University Press, 1979).

N. Grant, *Soviet Education* (Harmondsworth: Penguin, 1976).

N. Hans, *The Russian Tradition in Education* (London: Routledge & Kegan Paul, 1963).

B. Harasymiw (ed.), *Education and the Mass Media in the Soviet Union and Eastern Europe.* (New York and London: Praeger, 1976).

N. I. Isayev, *National Languages in the USSR: Problems and Solutions* (Moscow: Progress Publishers, 1977).

N. P. Kuzin and M. I. Kondakov, *Education in the USSR* (Moscow: Progress Publishers, 1972).

D. Lane, *The Socialist Industrial State*, (London: Allen & Unwin, 1980).

G. W. Lapidus, *Women in Soviet Society* (Berkeley, Calif.: University of California Press, 1978).

V. Lenin, *On Youth* (Moscow: Progress Publishers, 1970).

E. G. Lewis, *Multilingualism in the Soviet Union* (The Hague and Paris: Mouton, 1972).

L. Liegle, *The Family's Role in Soviet Education* (New York: Springer, 1975).

M. Matthews, *Class and Society in Soviet Russia* (Harmondsworth: Penguin, 1972).

M. Matthews, *Education in the Soviet Union: Policies and Institutions since Stalin* (London: Allen & Unwin, 1982).

M. Matthews, *Privilege in the Soviet Union*, (London: Allen & Unwin, 1978).

W. Medlin, W. M. Cave and F. Carpenter, *Education and Development in Central Asia: A Case Study on Social Change in Uzbekistan* (London: Brill, 1971).

K. Nozhko *et al.*, *Educational Planning in the USSR* (Paris: UNESCO, 1969).

F. O'Dell, *Socialisation Through Children's Literature: The Soviet Example* (Cambridge: Cambridge University Press, 1978).

J. Riordan, *Sport in Soviet Society* (Cambridge: Cambridge University Press, 1977).

J. Riordan, *Soviet Sport: Background to the Olympics* (Oxford: Blackwell, 1980).

S. M. Rosen, *Education and Modernisation in the USSR* (London: Addison-Wesley, 1971).

H. C. Rudman, *The School and the State in the USSR* (London: Macmillan, 1967).

S. G. Shapovalenko, *Polytechnical Education in the USSR* (Paris: UNESCO, 1963).

W. Shimoniak, *Communist Education: Its History, Philosophy and Politics* (Chicago: Rand McNally, 1970).

G. Simon, *Church, State and Opposition in the USSR* (London: Hurst, 1974).

B. Simon and J. Simon (eds), *Educational Psychology in the USSR* (London: Routledge & Kegan Paul, 1963).

G. Smirnov, *Soviet Man: The Making of a Socialist Type of Personality* (Moscow: Progress Publishers, 1973).

J. J. Tomiak, 'Fifty-five years of Soviet education', in G. T. Cook (ed.), *The History of Education in Europe* (London: History of Education Society/Methuen, 1974), pp. 37–51.

J. J. Tomiak (ed.), *Soviet Education in the 1980s* (London: Croom Helm, 1983).

J. J. Tomiak, *The Soviet Union*, World Education Series (Newton Abbot: David & Charles, 1972).

J. J. Tomiak, 'The university in the Soviet Union', in M. D. Stephens and G. H. Roderick, *Universities for a Changing World* (Newton Abbot: David & Charles, 1975), pp. 160–73.

E. K. Vasileva, *The Young People of Leningrad* (New York: International Arts and Science Press, 1976).

M. Yanovitch, *Social and Economic Inequality in the Soviet Union* (London: Martin Robertson, 1977).

M. Yanovitch and W. A. Fisher (eds), *Social Stratification and Mobility in the USSR* (Washington, DC: International Association of Scholarly Publishers, 1973).

J. Zajda, *Education in the USSR* (Oxford and New York: Pergamon, 1980).

Organizational and Statistical Appendix

USSR

Agencies of Administration

The Supreme Soviet of the USSR.
The Councils of Ministers of the USSR.

Statutory USSR Ministry of Education.
USSR Ministry of Higher and Secondary Specialized Education.
USSR Ministry of Health and other ministries (responsible for higher educational establishments within their competence).
State Committee for Vocational Training of the Council of Ministers of the USSR.

Advisory USSR Academy of Pedagogical Sciences.
Scientific Research Institutes of the USSR Academy of Pedagogical Sciences.
USSR Ministry of Education Inspectorate.
Council for the Problems of Secondary Schools of General Education.
Board of Authorities of the USSR Ministry of Education.
Scientific Council on the Methods of Teaching of the USSR Ministry of Education.

REGIONAL

Statutory Supreme Soviets of the Union and Autonomous Republics.
The Councils of Ministers of the Union and Autonomous Republics.
Ministry of Education of each Union Republic and Autonomous Republic.
Ministry of Higher and Specialized Secondary Education in Union Republics.
State Committees for Vocational Training in the Republics.
Departments of Education in regions, territories and national areas.

Advisory   Republic Ministries of Education Inspectorate.
Regional branches of the Union of Teachers and Workers in Education.

LOCAL

Statutory   Departments of Education of the executive committee of the local Soviets of Working People's Deputies in cities and districts.

Advisory   Local inspectorate.
Heads and teachers.
Local branches of the Union of Teachers and Workers in Education.

The Structure and Organization of the Educational System (1980–1)

Age	Level and stage	Types of institution	Number of institutions	Enrolments
	Level 4	Universities Polytechnics Monotechnical institutes Research institutes		(Included in level 3)
22	Level 3	Universities Polytechnics Monotechnical institutes	80 } 883	5,230,000 (including 2,970,000 studying full-time 2,260,000 studying part-time or by correspondence)
		Adult evening schools preparing students to complete secondary education	12,500	4,800,000
17	Level 2 Stage 2	Top sections of complete secondary education schools	56,200 complete secondary education schools (ages 7–17)	32,300,000 in complete secondary education schools (ages 7–17)
	Grades IX–X(XI)	Specialized secondary education establishments (15–19)	4,383	4,610,000 (including 2,890,000 full-time, 1,720,000 part-time or correspondence)

continued

	2 months	
Permanent kindergartens-nurseries (ages 2 months-7 years)	83,600	11,077,000
Permanent nurseries (2 months–3 years)	12,100	873,000

Age	Level and stage	Types of institution	Number of institutions	Enrolments
15	Level 2	Vocational-technical secondary schools (15–17/18)	4,300	2,160,000
		Vocational-technical schools (15–17)	2,772	1,450,000
	Stage 1	Upper sections of incomplete secondary education schools		
		Upper sections of complete secondary education schools		
	Grades IV–VIII	(both providing general education for five years)	41,200 incomplete secondary education (8-year) schools	6,100,000 in incomplete secondary education (8-year) schools
10	Level 1	Primary schools	32,500	600,000
		Lower sections of incomplete secondary education schools.		
	Grades I–III	Lower sections of complete secondary education schools (all providing general education for three years)		
7	Pre-school	Permanent kindergarten (for children aged 3–7 years)	32,100	2,389,000

The Progress of Pupils through the School System

Age and admission and transfer procedures

Pre-school   Application by parents for admission to nurseries (children aged from 2 months to 3 years), run by health departments; kindergartens (chidren aged 3–7 years), run by the local departments of education, state or collective farms, or enterprises; nurseries-kindergartens combined (children aged from 2 months to 7 years). Seasonal nurseries or kindergartens, operating in harvest time. Parents pay according to income.

First level   Elementary grades of the primary, eight- or ten-year school (I, II and III); admission at the age of 7 to the district school on 1 September: the district (city) departments of education inform parents which school the child is to attend; on enrolment the parents must present the child's birth and health certificate, transfer by satisfactory level of attainment to the next grade (in practice automatic at this level): some schools are two-shift schools; the parents have the right to choose the language of instruction for the child.

Second level
Stage 1   Grades IV–VIII in the eight- or ten-year school; admission upon successful completion of grade III (in practice automatic at age 10+); transfer from grade to grade by satisfactory level of attainment; pupils' progress is assessed each quarter; pupils with three unsatisfactory marks for the year repeat the grade; general progress and the examinations taken in grade VIII largely determine the kind of school attended after the age of 15.

Stage 2   Admission to grade IX of a secondary general education ten-year school, secondary specialized school, secondary vocational school or a vocational school at the age of 15+, according to the individual candidate's attainment, wishes and teachers' advice. Most courses operating on both full-time and part-time basis.

Third level
Stage 1   Admission to universities and other higher education establishments open to those who have satisfactorily completed full secondary education, obtained a certificate of maturity and passed a competitive entrance examination. Transfer by satisfactory standard of attainment from one year to the next, measured by written assignments, tests and examinations.

Fourth level   Admission to postgraduate courses by selection, after gaining a diploma.

Curricula

Pre-school   *Kindergarten*   play, health habits, educational games to develop correct speech patterns, develop character traits, accustom the child to work and play in a collective, language, music and singing, drawing and modelling, physical exercises.

Senior group (children aged 6+) preparation for school: reading and simple arithmetic, in addition to the above.

First level

Stage 1   *Grades I–III* (All uniform curricula, based upon polytechnical principles.) Mother tongue, Russian (for children taught in non-Russian tongues), arithmetic, nature study, art, music and singing, physical education, labour training. 24 periods per week, each period lasting 45 minutes.

Second level

Stage 1   *Grades IV–VIII* (All uniform curricula, based upon polytechnical principles.) Mother tongue and literature, Russian language and literature (for pupils taught in non-Russian tongues), mathematics, history, Soviet state and law (grade VIII), geography (grades V–VIII), biology (grades V–VIII), physics (grades VI–VIII), technical drawing (grades VII and VIII), chemistry (grades VII and VIII), foreign language, art (grades IV–VI), music and singing (grades IV–VII), physical education, labour training, options (2 periods in grade VII; 3 periods in grade VIII per week). 27–30 periods per week (excluding options) of 45 minutes each.

Stage 2   *Grades IX and X* (All uniform curricula, based upon polytechnical principles.) Mother tongue literature, Russian literature (for pupils taught in non-Russian tongues), mathematics, history, social studies (grade X), geography (grade IX), biology, physics, astronomy (grade X), chemistry, foreign language, physical education, labour training, elementary military training, options (4 periods per week). 32 periods per week (excluding options) of 45 minutes each.

Third level

Stage 1   *Universities, polytechnics, monotechnical and other institutes*
1   Socio-political subjects: history of CPSU, political economy, dialectical and historical materialism, scientific communism.
2   The study of general sciences constituting the basis for the study of specialized subjects (e.g. mathematics–physics–chemistry): or history–language–literature.
3   Specialized subjects (e.g. literature of the people of the USSR; history of the Russian language; zoology or inorganic chemistry), including work in laboratories.
     4 to $6^{1}2$ years of study, depending upon specialization (full-time), leading to a *Diplom*.

Fourth level   *Universities, polytechnics, research institutes* Postgraduate courses of advanced scientific training leading to a higher degree, lasting not less than 2 years, involving advanced study of a particular specialization and a dissertation.

Teacher Education and Training

Type of Institution	Qualification awarded	Level of school in which teacher can teach
Secondary pedagogical schools	*Diplom* of secondary pedagogical school, entitling to teach in pre-school education establishments.	Pre-school education establishments
Pedagogical institutes (departments of pre-school education)	*Diplom* of pedagogical institute, entitling to teach in pre-school education establishments.	
Secondary pedagogical schools	*Diplom* of secondary pedagogical school, entitling to teach grades I–III.	Grades I–III in primary schools and in incomplete or complete general secondary education schools
Pedagogical institutes	*Diplom* of pedagogical institute entitling to teach grades I–III.	
Pedagogical institutes	*Diplom* of pedagogical institute, entitling to teach in secondary schools in the field of specialization.	Grades IV–VIII in complete or incomplete general secondary education schools.
Universities	University *diplom*, entitling to teach in secondary schools in the field of specialization.	
Pedagogical institutes	*Diplom* of pedagogical institute, entitling to teach in secondary school in the field of specialization.	Grades IX and X(XI) in complete general secondary education schools.
Universities	University *diplom*, entitling to teach in secondary schools in the field of specialization.	

UNESCO Statistical Information: USSR

UNESCO date of entry: 21 April 1954
Surface area (km²): 22,402,220
Population 1980 (millions): 265·54
Persons/km² 1980: 12
Rural population (%) 1980: 35·2
Births per 1,000 pop. 1975–80: 18·3
Deaths per 1,000 pop. 1975–80: 9·0
Infant deaths per 1,000 live births 1974: 28
Life expect. at birth 1979: 73 years
Pop. growth rate (% p.a.) 1975–80: 0·9

Est. illiteracy rate 15+ (%) 1980
    M: 0·5 F: 0·5 MF: 0·5
National currency: rouble
National currency per US $ 1979: 0·7463[a]
GNP per capita in US $ 1979: 4,110
GNP per capita real growth rate
    (% per annum) 1960–79: 4.1
% agriculture in GDP 1979: 16
% industry in GDP 1979: 62
    of which manufacturing: —

Data Series	1975	1977	1978	1979
Education				
Education Preceding First Level				
1 pupils enrolled[b]	8,403,162	10,718,000	11,301,000	11,953,000
2 of which female (%)	—	—	—	—
3 teaching staff	730,723	—	—	—
4 of which female (%)	100	—	—	—
Education at First Level				
5 duration (years)	8	8	8	8
6 official age range	7–14	7–14	7–14	7–14
7 gross enrolment ratio (%)	97	98	99	101
8 pupils enrolled	35,960,941	34,053,000	33,640,000	33,576,000
9 of which female (%)	—	—	—	—

continued

Data Series	1975	1977	1978	1979
10 teaching staff[c]	2,399,299	2,354,000	2,335,000	2,325,000
11 of which female (%)[c]	71	71	71	71
12 pupils repeaters (%)	1	0	0	—
13 pupil/teacher ratio[c]	18	17	17	17
Education at Second Level				
14 duration gen. educ. (years)[d]	2	2	2	2
15 official age range gen. educ.	15–16	15–16	15–16	15–16
16 gross enrolment ratio (%)	105	106	104	104
17 pupils enrolled	10,738,197	10,782,200	10,484,900	10,216,500
18 of which female (%)	—	—	—	—
19 teaching staff	—	—	—	—
20 of which female (%)	—	—	—	—
21 pupils repeaters gen. ed. (%)	1	1	0	—
Education at Third Level[e]				
22 students per 100,000 inhabit.	1,908	1,952	1,961	1,970
23 students enrolled	4,853,958	5,037,200	5,109,800	5,185,900
24 of which female (%)	50	—	—	—
25 students scient./tech. fields (%)	—	—	—	—
26 foreign students	43,287	55,237	62,942	—
27 teaching staff	317,152	—	—	—
Public Expenditure on Education				
28 total in nat. currency (000)	27,747,100	29,906,300	31,304,700	32,155,400
29 of which current expend. (000)	23,415,900	24,956,300	26,219,900	27,009,800
30 total as % of GNP[f]	7·6	7·4	7·4	7·3
31 current expendit. as % current government expenditure	—	—	—	—

Science and Technology				
32 stock of university graduates per million inhabitants[g]	37,253	40,694	—	—
33 stock of persons with complete second educ. per million inh.[g]	52,357	56,544	—	—
34 scientists and engineers in R&D per million inh.[h]	—	—	—	—
35 technicians in R&D per million inh.	—	—	—	—
36 expend. on R&D as % of GNP[i]	4·8	4·5	4·6	4·6
Culture and Communication				
37 book titles published	78,697	85,395	84,727	80,560
38 circulation daily newspapers per 1,000 inh.	397	396	—	—
39 consumption (kg) newsprint per 1,000 inh.	5,262	4,255	4,390	4,346
40 consumption (kg) printing and writing paper per 1,000 inh.	4,947	5,073	5,123	5,117
41 cinema seats per 1,000 inh.	481	—	—	473
42 radio receivers per 1,000 inh.	217	290	287	303
43 TV receivers per 1,000 inh.	—	—	—	—
44 volumes in public libraries per 1,000 inh.[i]	5,982	—	—	—

Notes:

a Commercial rate.
b For 1977, 1978 and 1979, including children under 3 years.
c Including general education at the second level.
d The educational structure allows for another alternative.
e Including evening and correspondence courses.
f As percentage of the Net Material Product.
g Specialists only, employed in the national economy.
h Scientific workers.
i 'Expenditure on science' mainly from the national budget. Expressed as a percentage of the Net Material Product.
j Data for 1975 refer to 1974.

Source: Statistical Digest 1981 (Paris: UNESCO, 1981).

5

Education in the People's Republic of China
Tradition and Change

PAULINE CHAN

In any discussion of Chinese education in the 1980s, the conventional hypothesis that Mao Tse-Tung and those who supported and those who disagreed with him played a leading role in educational policy shifts during the previous thirty years helps to put the issues in perspective. As far as goals and educational aims are concerned, a rigid, static goal structure cannot be found as such in the Chinese situation. Nevertheless, it is possible to identify a range of general goals and aims which have remained fairly constant and because of their high level of abstraction allow for possible policy choices. However, the implementation of the goals specified by the Chinese leadership has not been easy. Theories of policy implementation suggest that the more complex goals are, the greater the number of actors involved (with potentially very different interests and values), the less chance there is that a policy will be actually implemented. Moreover, specific conditions, unforeseen events and unexpected outcomes have to be taken into account in understanding the development of a particular social system with education as one of its subsystems. Therefore, for the purpose of analysis, it is assumed that ideas and goals of the leadership are of decisive importance in the evolution of Chinese education.

Aims

The present system of Chinese education has its foundations in Chinese communist ideology which is based on Marxism-Leninism and Mao Tse-Tung's thoughts. It provides first of all an ideological framework within which educational aims and ultimate goals are defined. The basic concepts of dialectical materialism, the unity of theory and practice, and the idea that all men are educable provide a rational construct upon which the Chinese leaders based the development of an educational system that would contribute to national construction.

Intrinsic to the nature of socialist education is the important assertion that education should be combined with productive labour to develop the entire personality. In addition, there is recognition of the role played by education as a social organization within the infrastructure and, therefore, subordinate to national economic development. Moreover, its class character affirms the notion that education in a socialist context is ultimately political.

Guiding principles for education were first laid down in the Common Programme of 1949 before the adoption of the Constitution in 1954. But it was mainly on the general principles of Mao (in *On New Democracy*, 1940) that the aims of the revolution, to build a new society and a new state for the Chinese nation, were set forth. According to the Common Programme (Chapter V, Articles 41–9), the government was to try to build a new democratic culture and to set up an educational system which was national, scientific and popular. The major tasks were specified as 'raising the cultural level of the people, training personnel for national construction work, liquidating feudal compradore, fascist ideology and popularizing the ideal of serving the people'. Education, therefore, was regarded not only as a right for all, irrespective of sex or nationality, but also an effective tool to mobilize the people in the class struggle to continue the revolution. 'To intellectualize the proletariat, and proletarianize the intellectuals' had always been the intention of Mao so that all his educational reforms were to reflect 'democracy for the people and dictatorship over the reactionaries' (*On the People's Democratic Dictatorship*, 1949).

In 1957 and 1958, Mao Tse-Tung stated clearly the goals towards the achievement of which the education revolution should strive. He claimed that education must serve proletarian politics and be combined with productive labour. It must be possible for everyone who gets an education to develop morally, intellectually and physically and become a worker with both a socialist consciousness and culture.

Priorities for educational development were spelled out. In order these were: to equalize educational opportunities; to strengthen education for the working people and for the cadres of workers and peasants in schools of all levels; to establish technical vocational education while providing revolutionary political education for the intellectuals. It was anticipated that the consolidation of a national independent educational system would best meet the needs of planned political and economic development by producing a sufficient number of literate skilled workers who were devoted to the cause of building socialism (*Kuo Mojo*, 1950).

Since the founding of the People's Republic of China in 1949, despite some educational successes, many problems still exist. It will be difficult, if not unlikely, for the educational system of the 1980s to meet the needs of national development as defined by the leadership. The constant changes in Chinese educational policy over thirty years not only reflected the inconsistency among the leadership but also gave rise to instability in the development of education.

During the period of reorganization between 1949 and 1952, change and innovation were informed by egalitarian ideals intended to reduce the three major differences in Chinese society, namely between town and countryside, between worker and peasant, and between mental and manual labour. These ideals provided a rationale as well as the motivation for emphasis on quantitative changes. Efforts were made to modify the Yenan[1] model into one for the nation as a whole and to set up more *minpan*[2] schools as well as worker-peasant schools to supplement the system of formal education. As a result, educational opportunities, especially at the base of the educational pyramid, were greatly increased, thereby reducing to some extent inequalities which existed in the provision of education for people in urban and rural areas. But the adoption of the Soviet development strategy in 1953 as the First Five-Year Plan shifted the emphasis to quality and academic achievement and concentrated on the development of education at the tertiary level in the urban areas. The anti-rightist campaign of 1958 reinstated the previous policy and refuted the Soviet approach by putting politics in command. The Great Leap Forward movement that followed called for the mass implementation of the work-study system and introduced an open-door policy and the 'three-in-one'[3] organization of the schools. During this period, the agricultural middle schools were first started. However, economic crises and natural disaster forced the leadership to adopt a more selective approach by slowing down expansion and reducing enrolment to primary schools but expanding spare-time education instead. A kind of 'key school'[4] system was designed to concentrate development. The so-called 'two-track' system of education began to evolve. During the period 1963–5, as the ideological contradictions over production and revolution, over class solidarity and the class struggle, and over study and productive labour became more apparent, and as the increased educational differentiation into the 'two educational systems and two labour systems' grew, power struggles within the Party intensified. This is more commonly known as the 'two-line' struggle.

The Cultural Revolution, which began in 1966, brought about a decade of radical changes as well as disruption. Its slogan was to 'destroy the old and establish the new' and in the revolutionary process of 'struggle-criticism-transformation' to transform the super-structure of Chinese society. Drastic measures were taken to extend educational opportunities in rural areas by vigorously implementing the policy of 'walking on two legs' when factories and communes were encouraged to run schools best suited to local conditions and needs. The open-door policy of mass recruitment was applied so that workers and peasants with practical experience were elected to study not only in schools but also in institutions of higher education. With the setting up of revolutionary committees based on a 'three-in-one' combination of the worker-peasant-soldier to operate the schools, Party workers and propaganda teams entered the schools to supervise teaching. This policy went further. Attempts were made to unify teaching, scientific research and production in schools of all levels by Party workers and propaganda teams setting up and running their own workshops, factories and farms. Furthermore, the 'down to the countryside' movement aimed mainly at remoulding teachers and youth to accept a proletarian outlook. They were required to participate in collective labour for a fixed period of time during each term. In addition, the period of schooling was shortened to five years for the primary school, to four or five years for the middle school and to two or three years for higher education at the university level. The number of subjects was reduced, top priority being given to the study of revolutionary theories. All entrance exminations were abolished and the open-book examination system was introduced. It was a planned attempt to integrate theory with practice by incorporating into the curriculum Mao's idea of the revolution in education, that is, by involving all, teachers and students, workers and peasants alike, in the three revolutionary movements of class struggle, struggle for production and scientific experiment.

By 1975, criticism of these revolutionary changes was rife. The Great Debate on the Revolution in Education focused on the issue that unless academic standards were raised it would be impossible for the country to become a modern industrial state by the end of the century. Immediately after the death of Mao in 1976 and following the liquidation of the 'Gang of Four', under the new leadership of Hua Guofeng, new policies were announced in the autumn of 1977 to incorporate Deng Xiaoping's four modernization[5] goals. According to the Constitution of 1978, education was given an immediate task for the new period of training a large contingent of working-class intellectuals and of raising the scientific and cultural level of the entire nation by greatly improving the quality of education at all levels so as to produce qualified personnel who were both 'red and expert'. Under the umbrella of the 'four fundamental principles' – socialism, proletariat dictatorship, Party leadership, and Marxism-Leninism and Mao's thought – the concept of 'walking on two legs' was to be interpreted more flexibly by utilizing every possible resource to realize policy objectives.

Based on the primary desire to improve the quality of education and to raise the level of teaching, standards and academic excellence were made the object of all learning. Emphasis was shifted to the standardization and professionalization of learning and teaching. A highly competitive examination system which was monitored by the Centre (The State Council, the Planning Commission, and the Ministry of Education) was reintroduced. With official acknowledgement of the differences in ability and individual effort, streaming and the key-point school system were to be implemented at the various levels. Power was restored to the education bureaux at the provincial and local levels. Above all, attempts were made to raise the social, political and professional status of the teachers, whose expertness was once again to be valued. It is obvious that these measures all aimed at keeping education development in pace with the requirements of national economic development. Following this, the training at high-speed of the large number of skilled and professional workers needed for economic advancement meant a great effort had to be made by the state to mobilize and co-ordinate efforts made by the central authorities and local administration, by industrial and agricultural units and by intellectuals with the purpose of providing education in a variety of forms, including both full-time and part-work, part-study schools.

As far as the correct handling of the relationship between political consciousness and professional competence is concerned, the debate of 'redness versus expertness' continues to dominate public discussion. Although in the early 1980s the leadership still adheres to Mao's basic principles of 1958 in making a correct political orientation primary, with the study of science and culture as a necessary outcome of a correct political consciousness, the search for a middle ground where both 'red' and 'expert' are integrated is not going to be easy. The question of how to implement effectively a policy of combining education with productive labour has yet to be answered. To say how productive labour and scientific research can be integrated into the school curriculum without disrupting the normal process of learning and study requires from the top not only a clear indication of its development strategy but also an honest assessment of the present system with regard to its long-term and immediate goals in relation to social and economic reality. Continued fluctuations in educational policy only create confusion and instability. Contradictions within education cannot be resolved unless the conflicts between the rival leadership groups receive attention, especially since the groups represent very different theoretical concepts and interpretations of Marxist ideology and describe the actual Chinese context in different ways.

What follows will focus on educational practice as exemplified in the administration, organization, and content of education in order to reveal the possible areas in which further adjustments could be made if education were to contribute substantially to the progress of modernization.

Administration

Education is to serve the people, but the Chinese Communist Party defines the interests of the people within the overall concept of socialist construction. As laid down in the Constitution of 1978, the Party's leadership acts in accordance with the principles of mass participation, democratic centralism and collective leadership, and also permits the Party to dominate the entire education system.

Mao first developed the 'mass line' style of leadership to enable the Party to gain legitimacy by eliciting the support of the masses.[6] A process of regularized communication and interaction between the cadres and the masses in sessions of 'criticism and self-criticism' in both Party committee meetings and people's congresses was claimed to be a self-correcting device preventing the development of party elitism. The Party was and is thus best held to represent the interests of the masses, thereby establishing the pre-eminence of Party leadership. In Chinese terms, democratic centralism is referred to as 'democracy under centralized guidance' with the individual being subordinated to the organization, the minority to the majority, the lower level to the higher level and the entire Party to the decision of the Central Committee. Democracy is delegated to Party congresses when members of the Party committees at all levels are elected by secret ballot from a list of candidates approved by the higher levels of the Party. To ensure democratic consultation, each level of Party leaders has to report to the entire membership of that level on all issues such as the plans, programmes and experience of that particular Party unit. Above all, internal Party criticism is recognized as a right of all Party members. Respect for collective experience makes collective leadership a preference so that members of a specific unit, as Party members, meet, discuss and reach consensus decisions to be transmitted to non-Party members of the same unit.

After the death of Mao, education was centralized again into a bureaucratic hierarchy made up of four levels: the Centre, the provincial level, the county level, and the local organizations within cities and communes. Each level of the system controls what is below and is controlled by what is above.

The highest level of administration is the national Ministry of Education located in Peking. Through the Planning Commission, the Minister of Education reports directly to the State Council. Once the goals have been set, they are transmitted to the Ministry which, in consultation with the Planning Commission, prepares a series of directives to be handed down to provincial bureaux of administration. The Ministry of Education is functionally subdivided into seven offices over which the Minister presides. The office of foreign affairs deals with visiting delegations and exchange visits by Chinese nationals to foreign countries. The planning office is in charge of long-term planning and acts closely with the Planning Commission. The higher education office is responsible mainly for university education. It offers supervision and leadership in all matters ranging from the approval of the curriculum to the development of textbooks and the appointment of the teaching and research personnel. The development of the first and second levels of education is centred in the elementary and secondary education office, which prepares texts, reviews curriculum plans and makes personnel assignments. While the mid-level technical specialisms office deals with all aspects of technical schooling, the worker and peasant office is responsible for developing adult education and for organizing spare-time education. In order to keep the Ministry of Education abreast of the needs and requirements of other ministries, a liaison office acts as a co-ordinating agent by communicating between the other ministries and the Ministry of Education especially in sponsoring educational institutions of their own. The State Council, the Planning Commission and the Ministry of Education are commonly referred to as the 'Centre' by the bureaucrats outside Peking.

At the provincial level, six different departments of the provincial education bureau perform functions similar to the various offices in the Centre. The higher education department administers all institutions of higher learning in the province. While supervising the curriculum and the national college entrance examination, its main role is to provide leadership in planning and for innovations. Other than for supervision and evaluation of the curriculum, the elementary and secondary education department has responsibility for integrating the activities of the extracurricular organizations, namely the Communist Youth League, the Red Guards, and the Little Red Soldiers, into a system which supports the school formal learning programmes. The workers and peasants department at this level focuses on basic literacy classes and middle-level courses in agricultural techniques. The curriculum department conducts regular meetings with teachers in various areas to discuss standards and goals before reporting to Peking. The other two departments are personnel, which is responsible for the assignment of staff to schools and for the enrolment of students, and finance, which supervises the preparation of the budget and allocation of funds. In practice, the provincial organizations have little influence on effecting change, except by implementing policies formulated at the higher levels.

The county education office at the municipal level provides services similar to that of the provincial education bureau only on a smaller scale. Except for the three municipal bureaux of Peking, Shanghai and Tianjin which are directly responsible to the Ministry of Education, other municipalities report to the education bureau of the province in which they are located. Neighbourhood committees administer and operate elementary and middle schools in each school district. In the communes, there is an education office with personnel for specific responsibilities. The brigade or the production team elects a person to run local primary schools.

This hierarchical administrative structure of the education system is reinforced by standardized processes in which decision-making is guided by rules and set criteria. Though there is informal division of responsibility between the central and the provincial education bureaux and the local school administrations in the determination of how best to translate national goals into practice to suit local needs and circumstances, there is a tendency for Party members who are also members of interlocking directorates to formulate policy and then to administer it through a bureaucratic machinery which is not necessarily composed entirely of Party members.

Moreoever, parental involvement is essentially supportive and is initiated most of the time by the professionals in schools. Formal interaction between the schools and the parents is limited to the general meetings (twice a year) at the school and initial home visits by the teachers to obtain background information. On the other hand, the local community under the leadership of Party committees is responsible for helping student organizations set up children's palaces and neighbourhood centres for extracurricular activities, and for supporting the political and moral education of young people. It is significant that both family and community participation in the process of formal education is mobilized only when it is necessary to pursue specified goals, which may be subject to continuous adjustment whenever there is a shift in policy preferences.

Centralization is an important principle in Communist ideology to ensure that the Party controls the development of education. This hierarchical structure, at best, provides an efficient system of resource allocation which maximizes contributions to meet the needs of national development, since it facilitates central planning and decision-making. But when the central government lacks the funds to support a desired educational activity it becomes necessary to enlist local support. Besides, centralized control of professional functions is extremely difficult. The success of the educational process relies on the quality of teachers as well as the correct motivation of the learner. Effective implementation of present educational policy calls for a systematic process of decentralizing education sufficiently to encourage local initiative as well as to gain the co-operation of local teachers in support of the general line of national development.

Finance

Education is financed mainly by the state; in terms of public spending on education, according to the 1979 state budget, 10·8 per cent of the total expenditure was spent on culture, education, health and science, probably leaving no more than 5 per cent for education. Even in terms of the GNP percentage, the Chinese admit that only a rather small part was spent on education (around 2·09 per cent in 1978 as compared with Japan's 5·4 per cent and the United States' 7·4 per cent in 1971). The argument for an increase in state investment in education to promote economic development is not groundless.

In budget deliberations, again the State Council and the Planning Commission make all the large-scale manpower training decisions based on national surveys to determine what type of personnel the country needs. These goals are then transmitted to the Ministry of Education, which in turn produces a proposed budget, derived initially from subprovincial-level recommendations, for approval by the State Council. Accountability is interpreted as requiring local schools to justify each item included in any proposed budget, which has to be reviewed by the finance department of the provincial education bureau before it is sent to the Ministry for final approval. If cuts are made in a province's educational budget by the Centre, the education bureau can decide whether to distribute the reduction equally among all its schools or to meet certain schools' budgets fully while cutting back on others. It is important to note that locally raised funds constitute a considerable part of total spending. Individual communes are encouraged to add a portion of their own funds to the school budget. Therefore, it is possible that, for some units, educational expenditure will exceed national norms. In this way, the more developed industrialized areas can afford to provide better education, while the poorer rural areas tend to be ignored, suffer from shortage of educational resources and therefore lag behind in their educational development. This poses a very serious problem reflected in a widening of the gap between urban and rural development, not to mention the contradiction it poses in terms of egalitarian principles.

The state pays teachers' salaries and about one-third of school building costs. Based on a 'needs analysis' method of calculating the amount each student is required to pay for his or her education, only about 30 per cent of those studying in the elementary and middle schools receive scholarships from the schools they attend. It is quite common for families to pay for the education of their children. The average cost of education per child per term is estimated to range from 7·50 to 12·00 *yuan*[7] in the urban areas from 6·00 to 10·00 *yuan* in the rural areas. The schools usually assist students according to the average income per family member per month – roughly 12·00 *yuan* for urban and 10·00 *yuan* for the rural families. About 75 per cent of the students attending the secondary specialized schools receive financial aid, while government grants are made available to students in institutions of higher education. Full-time schools, especially the 'key schools', are financed by the state, while part-work, part-study schools have to rely on local finance as well as funds augmented by the income obtained from students' work projects.

Under the economic circumstances of the 1980s, unless there is a significant increase in productivity per worker, a high commitment to education in relation to available resources will be unrealistic. To incorporate educational plans into a national economic manpower strategy, training programmes represent a more positive step toward the equalization of educational opportunities, especially in the rural areas where the struggle for survival still prevails.

Organization and Structure

Education at different levels is organized in accordance with Party directives based on the policy of 'walking on two legs'. Pre-school education is provided in both the public and community-run kindergartens. The former are maintained by government agencies, army units (the People's Liberation Army), and by industrial and mining enterprises. The latter are set up by neighbourhoods in the cities and by communes (or their production brigades) and teams in the countryside. They take children from 3 to 7 years old. Depending on local conditions and needs, they are either day-care or boarding schools for infants, or both, or kindergartens attached to primary schools. In addition, during the busy farming seasons temporary infant classes are organized in the countryside.

First-level education is compulsory and universal. It admits children aged 7, but in some cities children of 6 or $6\frac{1}{2}$ years old are enrolled. It lasts for five years. Under the campaign to provide universal primary education, schools and classes are run in various ways according to local conditions, and special attention is paid to the admission of over-age and girl students, especially in the frontier regions.

Second-level education is provided in a variety of schools. The general secondary schools offer a total of five years of schooling which is divided into two stages: three years in the junior middle school and two years in the senior middle school. It is intended that, if possible, the senior school should be increased to three years. Its main objective is to prepare students for higher education, while the secondary professional schools are responsible for preparing professional personnel. Through training, the students acquire a secondary education and vocational instruction. The period of schooling is from three to four years for schools taking junior school graduates. In general, the secondary professional schools enrol only local students because jobs are assigned to graduates according to their specialization and the locality in which they live. Some schools admit students from neighbouring provinces on condition that they will return to their province to work after graduation.

Schools are further divided into two tracks: the full-time day schools which are financed and run by the state, and the part-work, part-study schools which are locally funded. This policy of the two kinds of educational system is said to be an immediate answer, adopted by the Party, to the gap between rural and urban educational provision as well as to the ultimate elimination of the differences between manual and mental labour. Each kind of school has a role to play: full-time day schools concentrate on raising educational standards, while the part-work, part-study schools popularize education. It is claimed that the development of Chinese education is geared to building a complete professional and technical education system in anticipation of certain changes in the labour recruitment system.

Around the country, at all levels, 'key schools' are designated as model institutions to raise standards and to ensure a high quality of education. About twenty of these schools are run directly by the Ministry as national key-points, others are under the administration of the local education bureaux but authorized by the Centre. All 'key schools' have more competent teaching staff and better teaching facilities. While admitting existing differences between 'key schools' and regular schools, the Chinese leaders argue against a 'one set' national unified development with an even distribution of resources.

On the contrary, they claim that the development of key-point areas makes full use of the advantages gained from their standards and concentrates resources as quickly as possible to produce a large group of specialists to carry out the work of the 'four modernizations'. This policy has widened the gap between the 'key schools' and the other schools, but according to a high authority it will in the long run narrow the gap, when the 'key-point areas' are sufficiently developed to support the less developed schools.

Enrolment reforms were announced officially in October 1977, in regulations which spelt out admission policies at various levels. Admission to kindergartens remains limited only by the availability of facilities. Entry to primary schools is based on the 'neighbourhood school principle'. But once a school's potential student population exceeds the school's capacity, examinations are used to screen candidates. Political attitudes and physical health are the second and third criteria for admission. National standardization of the secondary entrance examination was under consideration, to rank students according to academic ability and special interests so that they could be assigned to different types of schools. The 'key schools' select students mainly on the basis of academic excellence revealed in the results of the entrance examination and the grades obtained in the previous school. The candidate's political and moral behaviour as shown in the report by former teachers, staff, and students of the school last attended and his or her satisfactory physical condition are also considered. Since each criterion is used sequentially, failure at one stage implies elimination from further consideration. A conventional examination schedule for all academic subjects is being restored in schools: a mid-term test and a final examination are given in every semester and report cards are issued twice a year. Promotion depends on passing the final examination at the end of each school year in a number of subjects. Failure to get through the make-up examinations (those for candidates in the promotion examinations who are given a second chance) means repeating the year's work. According to the general plan, all examination and tests are supposed to be used as a pedagogical device for defining the levels at which the students operate best, but in practice they become effective means of selecting the better students for higher education. The implication of this process of selection has social implications as well as political significance which the Party leaders have yet to define.

In school, children are grouped according to their ability. But the way in which they are streamed is determined by the individual school. Some prefer the two-stream system of dividing the students into 'fast' and 'average' classes, or 'regular' and 'make-up' classes; others use the three-stream method by adding a 'slow' class to the other two streams. The rationale behind this is said to be that it was a way of discovering not only those students who need extra help, but also methods of teaching which can be adjusted to the educational level of the pupils. It was, however, to cope with the problems arising from a serious deterioration of educational quality and the emergence of varied standards among students that the Minister of Education, Jiang Nanxiang, in 1979, warned against the possible drawbacks of streaming, such as an overemphasis on that portion of students graduating to higher levels, while neglecting the slow class. Reports have revealed that there were cases when students gave up and just 'drifted along'.

Curriculum

The political mission of education requires it to develop productive labourers with a socialist consciousness. Therefore, politics remains a central component of the curriculum. Politics is seen in terms of 'building socialism', which implies that education should be designed not only to impart a knowledge of skills that will enable the individual to make an effective and useful contribution to the economic development of the country but also to inculcate a certain world view that governs the motivation of the individual and provides a context in which to apply acquired skills. Thus, participation in productive labour is viewed as an invaluable pedagogical tool both in enriching classroom experience and in inculcating attitudes that promote individual social-political development. Work experience counts, when it is carefully planned, towards career opportunities and an enlightened choice of careers.

Curricula are laid down by the Ministry and textbooks are prepared by the provincial or local education departments. The kindergartens are set the task of equipping children mentally and physically for the primary school. Instruction in the three Rs is combined with organized activities for the purpose of generating a collective spirit among the children as well as respect for authority. The kindergartens serve as an effective socializing agent at this stage of early childhood. Children learn by emulation; they perform interesting tasks about the school and learn to help others.

A typical curriculum at the provincial primary school level includes Chinese language, mathematics, music, fine arts and physical education. Natural science and politics are added from the fourth grade onwards. In urban schools, foreign language instruction begins at the third grade. English is the most popular foreign language studied. According to the official guidelines, the school year lasts nine and a half months, including half a month of physical labour in the fourth and fifth grades in the form of participation in either factory or farm work.

In the general secondary schools, fourteen subjects are offered throughout the five years. They include the Chinese language, mathematics, foreign languages, politics, physics, chemistry, biology, history, geography, basic knowledge of agriculture, physiology and hygiene, physical education, music and fine arts. In the senior middle school, students are divided according to their major studies either in the advanced sciences or in the liberal art subjects. The school year lasts for nine months. Junior middle school students are required to spend six weeks on manual labour per year, while the senior middle school students have to undertake eight weeks of productive labour per year or one month per semester. Labour assignments in these schools form part of the curriculum and have the purpose of raising the consciousness of pupils. In the case of the part-work, part-study schools, the purpose is to fulfil labour requirements since the wages earned by students revert to the school for maintenance.

The secondary professional schools train middle-level specialists for modern production. There are 347 specialities in eight professions: 242 in engineering, 25 in agriculture, 11 in forestry, 12 in medicine, 34 in finance and economics, 1 in physical education, 20 in arts and 2 in teacher training. The basic curriculum consists of four categories of required courses: political science, general literature, basic courses for specialists and specialized courses. Practical work in appropriate settings is set up either by the school on a non-profit basis or by community units and is required. The proportion of practical work varies according to the speciality. The school year lasts for ten months and the courses range from two to four years.

Unified curricula for all full-day primary and middle schools are being planned at the Centre. These specify not only the teaching plan and materials but also the period of instruction and length of schooling. The move towards standardization is intended to raise the quality of education and to ensure academic standards, but it leaves little room for flexibility and variation which would allow the school curriculum to reflect local needs and circumstances. In view of the Party's commitment to the policy of 'walking on two legs', centralized control over the curriculum produces uniformity and rigidity; instead of reinforcing local initiative, it creates compliance to set rules on the one hand and competition on the other.

The relationship between education and productive labour is clearly defined in terms of the student's moral-political development, on which curriculum theory is based. However, the pressure to ensure that bright students develop substantially and to emphasize academic excellence creates concern among the authorities who want to combine the two components in a more utilitarian manner. Regulations relating to the time devoted to labour and to formal study of academic subjects are hotly debated. There is disagreement on the optimum mix of work experience and intellectual study in the total educational process of individual students.

Teacher Education

The development and improvement of teacher training is regarded as fundamental to the achievement of raised standards and the expansion of education. Teachers at different levels of the education system, it is held, should all receive a basic training. Both the infant normal and secondary normal schools (types of secondary professional schools) admit graduates from the junior middle school. The former trains teachers for the kindergarten and the latter for the primary school. The course of training lasts for a period of three years. Usually, normal schools have experimental primary schools and kindergartens attached to them for teachers in training to do their teaching practice. In 1978, there were 161 teachers' colleges and normal universities, which offer a four-year programme to train teachers for the middle school. A shorter course of three years is given in the teachers' institutes. They all take graduates from the senior middle school. All teachers in training receive the people's grants-in-aid. In addition to educational theory and practice, the training is designed to cultivate in student teachers high political, moral, cultural and scientific standards. At the third level, teachers are selected from college graduates and from among postgraduate students. They are expected not only to teach but also to undertake research.

Attempts by the authorities to reconcile mental and physical labour to further the construction of the socialist state involve various measures by the government to upgrade the status of the teachers. Education bureaux appoint all teachers. Each teacher is posted to a particular job in accordance with the individual's special abilities and the demand of schools in the area. Transfer between schools of the same level, and particularly from one level to another, requires the approval of the provincial education bureau through its personnel department. Teaching staff are not free to change jobs; they must wait for the local units to make a request, which has to be approved by the provincial authorities.

As an integral part of the upgrading programme to strengthen teaching personnel, teachers who had been transferred to other work units are sent back to their original schools to meet the demand for qualified teaching staff. They are guaranteed that five-sixths of their time can be devoted to professional work, with the rest being occupied by productive labour. Regular teachers are required constantly to undertake in-service education and professional development. Intensive in-service training programmes, based primarily on the principle of spare-time individual study, are conducted in various ways: for two afternoons a week, teachers are required to attend meetings in the school to study politics and engage in 'educational transformation' discussions to upgrade pedagogical effectiveness; they can attend either short-term courses or full-time one-year refresher courses organized by the teachers' colleges and normal universities; or they can take up correspondence courses or radio and TV lessons. Teachers who have not been professionally trained but have qualified through in-service training are to be recognized and therefore duly certified by the education bureau. The fact that *minban* teachers (locally hired teachers) are required to sit for a qualifying examination set by the education bureau as a condition for continued employment shows the determination of the authorities not only to upgrade the professional skills of teachers but also to keep the teaching profession under state control.

Higher Education

The demand that higher education must achieve objectives and functions defined in terms of manpower output and in terms of the political and ideological requirements imposed in the construction of a socialist state on the one hand, and the problem of working out how to allocate the means, financial and human, in the light of the country's real capacity on the other produce a constant strain on the Chinese leaders in their effort to follow a consistent policy for higher education. The tension was made acute during the 'mass line' struggle within the Party, causing setbacks which greatly hampered the development of higher education.

As part of the general programme of educational reform drawn up in October 1951, based on the principle of 'the unity of theory and practice', all higher educational institutions were given the task of educating qualified workers with modern scientific and technical capabilities. The university education system was reorganized into a system of specialized institutions in which more emphasis was laid on technical training than on basic theoretical studies. Measures were taken to increase the intake of students by making technical schools independent institutions, by reducing the duration of the courses to 3–4 years, and by lowering the entrance requirements to allow cadres and soldiers to be recruited. This resulted in a reduction in the number of universities and a large number of drop-outs (3·5 per cent of the total student population in 1954) who found themselves unable to assimilate the knowledge taught. It also resulted in a great demand for competent teachers for the basic courses. The system was based on the Soviet model, which turned out to be extremely costly and unpractical as it neither provided the required number of trained personnel nor provided them with the type of training that was relevant to the work of national construction.

During the Great Leap Forward movement (1957–60), attempts were made further to increase the number of students enrolled in other institutions so as to destroy the monopoly of the universities in training a ruling elite. To do so, parallel training instructions were established. Political commitment was made an important criterion of selection. Normal academic prerequisites could be waived, thus allowing students of worker and peasant origin to be enrolled. Individual examinations were replaced by collective exercises and group methods. Manual work became compulsory in all curricula, with students devoting at least two months per year to productive labour. The stress was laid on integration in society to produce 'red and expert' technicians. This resulted in the employment of members of the university community in factories, mines, and poeple's communes. The implementation of the policy of 'walking on two legs' encouraged other oganizations in society to set up institutions alongside the regular schools to train technical and scientific cadres. At the same time, two types of education were offered: the regular full-time education and the so-called 'spare-time' education which the Chinese call 'half-study, half-work' education on the one hand, or 'studies outside working hours' on the other. Other than those run by the local authorities, the so-called 'part-time universities' and vocational schools which offered crash courses were either sponsored by the regular higher educational establishments or run by industrial units. This reform of higher education was attacked by members of the academic community as having lowered the standard of studies considerably.

The economic crisis that accompanied the Great Leap Forward, however, led to a revision of education policy. Measures were adopted to focus on quality rather than quantity and on those specific aspects which would promote economic development. Unqualified worker and peasant students were sent home, which resulted in a great reduction of the student population. Many of the establishments which were opened during the Great Leap Forward were either closed down or amalgamated with other institutions. Specialization became a guideline for institutions and students were encouraged to become 'experts' in specific areas. Manual work was reduced to six weeks per year.

Within the establishments of higher education 'teaching and research groups' in different specialized areas were made the basic administrative unit – a significant step in reasserting the importance of 'expert' studies. Stricter admission requirements based on written examinations and intellectual attainment not only regulated the student population but also created a situation in which the young people from the best secondary schools in urban areas, especially those from the families of cadres who provided them with an incentive, became the advantaged group. Access to higher education was difficult for the children of workers and peasants. In higher education, priority was always given to scientific and technical training; agricultural skills were developed at the primary and secondary levels.

The education system as a whole was one of the main targets of the Cultural Revolution. Mounting criticism of higher education, of selection procedures, of curricula and methods, and of the system's overall orientation was turned into strong attacks on the system as being an essential instrument of discrimination against working-class children by creating an elite group which, benefiting from a higher educational status, was able to 'exploit' the working class. Mao's direction of 21 July 1968 restated his conception of all higher educational establishments as 'primarily scientific and technical institutions'. When he attacked the previous system of concentrating on 'expertness' to the neglect of 'redness', it should be noted that he used the term 'expert' to mean specialization in a particular field of study and not 'expert' in terms of high quality. Universities and higher educational establishments practically ceased to perform their regular functions except for political activities after June 1966. It was not until the latter half of 1968 that the reconstruction of higher education began.

During the so-called 'period of moderation' (1969–73) the administration of education in general was delegated to the provinces, which, in addition to their financial responsibilities, had the power to determine student enrolment and the appointment of teachers and to decide on the curriculum. Selection for most universities was conducted at provincial level. Within educational establishments, the duties of the workers' propaganda teams were taken over by revolutionary committees consisting mainly of teachers and cadres. Since the revolutionary committees were made up of the Party secretary and his deputies, in actual fact it was the Party committees that had effective control. The selection procedures relating to age limits and the criteria for admission, though based in theory on the same principles of 'democratization', varied from one year to the next and from one region to another. The major innovations after the

Cultural Revolution were the integration of manual and productive work into education and the more direct involvement of the school with society. Despite the political and moral implications of manual work as a fundamental issue, the 'open-door' school policy attempted to integrate practical production work with theoretical studies and to make use of in-plant training courses for experimental purposes. This was helped by the establishment of production units such as workshops, factories and farms by educational institutions and by the organization of regular contacts with other industrial plants, people's communes and economic units.

Higher education was then designed to run entirely on the 'half-work, half-study' system which provided accelerated training in various subjects through special classes at the university, through the dispatch of teaching teams to the units concerned and by radio and correspondence courses. Technicians and professional and research workers were called on to meet the need for large numbers of teaching staff to launch the new courses. Such a system sought to solve the problem of disseminating knowledge, particularly in rural areas, but the problem of the quality of this education remained in question.

Under the banner of 'modernization', which began in 1977, higher education was given a new meaning. Instead of training for middle-level cadres and skilled workers, the goal of higher education was to train senior professional workers and to develop science, culture and technology. Admission policies were officially announced in October 1977 and restored the national college entrance examination. Applicants were to be 26 years of age or younger and either graduates of the senior middle school or of an equivalent educational level. Students were to be admitted on the basis not only of their overall score but also of their achievement in particular subjects in the written examinations, which include six subjects: politics, Chinese language and literature, mathematics, a foreign language for all, and physics and chemistry for those intending to study science at the university, and history and geography for those who wanted to study liberal arts. Application has to be made to the basic unit for initial screening. The Ministry of Education allots quotas of college places to each province and sets the test papers. The provincial education bureaux then review the test results and the political report on each candidate prepared by the basic unit before selecting applicants for the physical examination. The revival of such a highly selective system is intended to standardize and raise the quality of higher education.

In 1979 there were 633 higher educational institutions – universities, colleges, institutes and higher professional schools. Among these 89 were key universities and institutions designated as centres of learning and scientific research. There are more than 800 specialities, among which more than 500 are science and engineering, which account for 65 per cent of the total curriculum offered. The period of higher education is from four to five years in the universities and institutes and from two to three years in the higher professional schools. Jobs are assigned to graduates essentially by the government.

Based on the 1958 principle of the 'three-in-one' combination of teaching, research and production, postgraduate education was given special attention after a period during the Cultural Revolution when it was suspended. Both the Chinese Academy of Sciences and the Chinese Academy of Social Sciences (which was established only in 1977) are engaged in basic research of major concern to the national economy. The period of postgraduate education lasts from two to four years. The Standing Committee of the National People's Congress announced regulations in February 1980 concerning academic degrees which were to become effective on 1 January, 1981. They represent a significant attempt to bring the higher education system up to international standards.

The new policies have not been received without protest. The rehabilitation of the intellectuals to participate in teaching and research brought about problems of organization, especially since the professionals held opinions in matters of curriculum design and management of educational and scientific resources different from those of the Party. It is apparent that a kind of meritocracy is being developed under the present selective system based on academic achievement. The Chinese leaders reject the notion that it will create an intellectual elite. Maybe meritocracy itself does not go against the principles of policy; it is the prevention of the possible emergence of a privileged 'new class' that calls for scrutiny.

General policy on higher education is one of gradual expansion. But, meanwhile, the demand for places is mounting – especially from the rural masses (the peasant population), who are being effectively excluded from higher education through lack of proper secondary schooling. A system of admitting commuter students has been introduced and a number of affiliated or branch colleges are being set up to help ease the tension. This is a temporary expedient, since the basic problem remains that the development of higher education should be the subject of a more consistent policy based on a more balanced development, both quantitatively and qualitatively.

Conclusion

The above discussion shows that the present education system in China is not without problems. Most of these problems are related to frequent changes in educational policy resulting from leadership controversies. The people are confused by the rhetoric of Party politics, let alone by proletarian politics which education is supposed to serve. Despite attempts made by their successors to remedy the damage done by the 'Gang of Four' attempts to achieve a revolution in education, fundamental contradictions in theory and practice both inside and outside the educational sector are still inherent. These inherent problems have been identified and interpreted differently at various periods by different people and have given rise to very different solutions. The rivalry among members of the leadership, the conflicts between groups of people holding traditional educational values and those adhering to socialist ideals, the challenge created by concepts of modernity, and the uneven development between rural and urban areas together constitute an immense developmental problem and create a complex and difficult situation in the process of socialist construction. Leaders prefer to view it as the challenge of backward productive forces to an advanced socialist system rather than as a continuous struggle between the proletariat and the bourgeoisie. Under such circumstances, it is vital that within the Party among the leaders some kind of compromise and co-operation is secured in matters concerning basic values, the definition of problems and the development strategy before educational policy initiatives have any chance of success. If leaders could adhere to the dialectical method of conscientiously drawing general conclusions from experience, exposing contradictions and analysing them, rather than resolving them through antithetical policy shifts, perhaps they could work out synthetic solutions to their problems.

High-speed economic development and the development of science and technology, which is necessary, is no doubt a great challenge to China's economy. But an answer to the question 'How can the new educational policies contribute substantially to the progress of modernization' depends largely on how soon the Party can win back the confidence of the people and on how soon it can overcome the problems of economic recession and inflation and the unemployment of 'educated youth' on the one hand, and maintain an intellectual community that is both 'red' and 'expert' on the other.

Notes: Chapter 5

1 The Yenan model is a system of education carried out in the old liberated areas in Yenan before 1949. It was based on the principles of self-sufficiency, self-reliance and local initiative. The major policies were to combine education with production and to promote popular education. In practice, various forms of part-time schools,

evening classes and other work-study programmes were implemented. The system then aimed at promoting basic literacy, imparting political consciousness, and providing practical technological knowledge that was directly relevant to the particular need of the local communities and production groups.

2 *Minpan* (people-operated) schools were the result of an overall concept of mobilizing the people at the grass roots to provide and operate their own schools in local communes or production brigades to promote culture and increase production. They were half-day schools, spare-time schools and factory-run schools, as well as seasonal schools.

3 The expression 'Three-in-one combination' appeared in 1958 during the Great Leap Forward movement as a slogan to raise the quality of both teaching and research by combining classroom instruction with productive labour as well as scientific research. But during the Cultural Revolution in 1968, it was used to describe the three-in-one combination of workers, PLA members (soldiers) and activists among students, teachers and university workers which formed the so-called revolutionary committee to run schools and universities.

4 Based on the principle of combining popularization with the raising of standards so as to ensure the quality of education, a number of key schools have been designated in all levels of education in all provinces, municipalities and autonomous regions. These schools have better administrators, teachers and equipment in order that they can play an exemplary role.

5 Ye Jianying in 1979 claimed that the work of the Communist Party was to shift to socialist modernization for the purposes of

1 training the necessary scientists, technologists and economic administrators,
2 raising the technical proficiency and scientific level of all workers, peasants and other working people,
3 stepping up economic construction, and
4 stepping up the development of science, education and culture.

These are known as the 'four modernization goals'.

6 The principles of the mass line are:

1 All correct leadership is necessarily 'from the masses, to the masses', that is, leaders must take the ideas of the masses and concentrate them and then go to the masses and propagate and explain these ideas until the masses embrace them as their own and translate them into action and test the correctness of these ideas in such action.
2 The authority of the non-party masses both to originate policy and to criticize the party for its incorrect implementation of that policy.
3 In education, the key concept is self-reliance, that is, relying on the resources and initiatives of the grass-roots people (the masses) using unprecedented methods and approaches to achieve the assigned goals.

7 Based on estimates provided by Reuters in April 1982, $1 US = *Rmb* $1·8132$ *yuan* or $1 HK = *Rmb* $0·3143$ *yuan*. (The currency was revalued with effect from 1 March 1955 on the basis of 10,000 old *yuan* for one new *yuan*, now termed *Renmimbi* – *Rmb* – *Yuan*.)

Further Reading

'Common Programme of the Chinese People's Political Consultative Conference' *Current Background*, no. 9, 21 September 1950.
The Constitution of the People's Republic of China (adopted on 5 March 1978),

Documents of the First Session of the Fifth National People's Congress of the People's Republic of China (Peking: Foreign Languages Press, 1978).

Theodore H. E. Chen, 'Changes in Chinese education', *Current History*, September 1978, pp. 73–6, 80–2.

Deng Xiaoping, 'Speech at the National Education Work Conference, April 1978', *Chinese Education*, vol. XII, nos 1–2 (1979), pp. 4–14.

Stewart E. Frazer (ed.), *Education and Communism in China: An Anthology of Commentary and Documents* (London: Pall Mall Press, 1971).

John N. Hawkins, *Educational Theory in the People's Republic of China: The Report of Ch'ien Chün-Jui* (Honolulu: University of Hawaii Press, 1971).

Hua Guofeng, Speech at the Second Session of the Fifth National People's Congress in June 1979, *Hongqi* (Red Flag), July 1979.

Chang-Tu Hu, *Chinese Education under Communism*, 2nd edn (New York: Columbia Teachers College Press, 1974).

Chang-Tu Hu (ed.), *Aspects of Chinese Education* (New York: Columbia Teachers College Press, 1969).

Hu Shi Ming and Seifman Eli (eds), *Towards a New World Outlook – A Documentary History of Education in the People's Republic of China, 1949–1976* (New York: AMS Press, 1976).

Clark Kerr (chairman), *Observations on the Relations Between Education and Work in the People's Republic of China: Report of a Study Group* (Berkeley, Calif.: Carnegie Council on Policy Studies in Higher Education, 1978).

Liu Xiyao, 'Report of the National Educational Work Conference, April 22, 1978', *Chinese Education*, vol. XII, nos 1–2 (1979), pp. 15–32.

The Ministry of Education, PRC, Peking, *A Survey of Chinese Education Report to the 37th Session of the International Conference on Education* (Geneva: Unesco/International Bureau of Education, July 1979).

National Committee on United States–China Relations, Report by the State Education Leaders' Delegation, *China's Schools in Flux* (White Plains, NY: Sharpe, 1979).

Organisation for Economic Co-operation and Development, *Science and Technology in the People's Republic of China* (Paris: OECD, 1977).

Suzanne Pepper, 'Chinese education after Mao: two steps forward, two steps back, and begin again', *China Quarterly*, no. 81 (March 1980) pp. 1–65.

R. F. Price, *Education in Modern China*, 2nd edn (London: Routledge & Kegan Paul, 1979).

Selected Works of Mao Tse-Tung, vols I–IV (1965) and vol. V (1977) (Peking: Foreign Languages Press).

State Statistical Bureau, 'Communiqué on fulfilment of China's 1979 National Economic Plan', *Beijing Review*, no. 20 (May 1980) pp. 20–24.

Chiu-Sam Tsang, *Society, Schools and Progress in China* (Oxford: Pergamon, 1968).

Organizational and Statistical Appendix

China

Agencies of Administration

NATIONAL   State Council.
Statutory   Ministry of Education.

Advisory   Planning Commission.

REGIONAL   Province.
Statutory   Department of Education (Provincial Education Bureau).

Advisory   Inspectors.

LOCAL   Municipality and Commune.
Statutory   County Education Office in Municipalities.
Commune Education Office.
(Both report to Education Bureau of Province.)

Advisory   Neighbourhood committees for municipalities and village committees.
Inspectors on municipal level.

The Structure and Organization of the Educational System (1979–80)

Age	Level and stage	Types of institution	Number of institutions	Enrolments
	Level 4	Universities Institutes Academies (sciences and social sciences)	319 2	17,728 (1980)
26	Level 3 Stages 1 and 2	Universities Colleges Institutes	675 (1980)	1,143,700
24	Stage 1	Teachers colleges Normal universities Higher professional schools	— 161	— 310,000
18	Level 2			
17	Stage 2	Upper middle school		Upper middle school 12,920,000
16				
15	Level		Junior middle 144	Junior middle Upper and junior middle 59,050,000

	Junior middle sch.(1) Agric. 2nd school	Vocational 2nd school	Sec. prof. school	Normal school		
Stage 1						
12	Elementary schools			(2) 3,033	(1) —	1,199,000 / 46,130,000
Level 1						
7				923,500		146,629,000
Pre-school	Kindergartens (some associated with primary schools).					
	Infant schools (boarding and day).			165,600		8,792,000
3	Infant classes.					

Note: Age limits are very flexible and differ between urban and rural areas.

The Progress of Pupils through the School System

Age and admission and transfer procedures

Pre-school   Parents apply. Schools admit. Multiple applications possible.

First Level   Parents apply to individual schools, frequently associated with kindergarten previously attended. School admits. Multiple applications possible.

Second level

Stage 1   Internal tests in first-level school results sent to various second level schools. Application normally by parents for lower middle school. Selection on basis of examination results and teachers' recommendations.

Stage 2   Internal tests at the end of each year decide promotion to next year. Failure means repetition of year or re-taking of examination.

Third level

Stage 1   National college entrance examination for universities. Colleges and institutes run by Ministry of Education. Selection made by individual institutions based on strict quota system.

Stage 2   Internal tests determine progress.

Fourth level   Recommendation by teacher or tutor at university, college or institute.

Curricula

Pre-school   No specific subjects – introduction to reading and writing, arithmetic and organized activities to acquaint children with predictive labour.

First level

Stage 1   *First to third grades*   Chinese language, mathematics, physical education, music, drawing and painting.

Stage 2   *Third grade onwards*   As above, plus foreign language (English, political education).

Stage 2   *Fourth and fifth grades*   As above, plus general knowledge of history, geography, natural science and labour education (half a month each year).

Second level

Stage 1   *General Secondary School*   Political education, Chinese language, mathematics, physics, chemistry, biology, foreign languages, history, geography, fundamental knowledge of agriculture, physiological hygiene, physical education, music and art.

Stage 2   *Secondary Professional Schools*   A total of 347 specialities classified as follows: Engineering 242, finance and economics 34, agriculture 25, arts 20, medicine 12, forestry 11, teacher training 2, physical education 1.

	The curriculum consists of 4 basic areas: (a) politics, (b) courses in literature, (c) basic courses in a field of specialized study, (d) specialized courses.
Third level	
Stage 1	*Universities, colleges, institutes, teacher training colleges, higher professional and higher training schools* Curricula are based on the principle of the three-in-one combination of teaching, research and production.
Stage 2	More than 800 specialities are on offer with over 500 in science and engineering.
Fourth level	Curricula are based on the principle of combining knowledge with practice. The following areas of research are covered: (a) technology, (b) agriculture, (c) forestry, (d) economics, (e) politics, (f) art, (g) science, (h) arts, (i) medicine, (j) teacher training, (k) physical education.

Teacher Education and Training

Type of Institution	Qualification awarded	Level of school in which teacher can teach
Normal schools for kindergarten and elementary teachers	Transcript certifying completion of course	Kindergarten or elementary school, according to course taken.
Secondary teacher training schools	Transcript certifying completion of course	Lower middle schools
Universities and Higher teacher training institutes and colleges	Degree Transcript certifying completion of course	Upper middle schools

Note: Curricula in all teacher training institutions include:
1 Political theories,
2 Fundamental courses,
  (a) pedagogical studies (including pedagogy, psychology, teaching methods),
  (b) courses in specialized subject areas,
  (c) teaching practice.

UNESCO Statistical Information: China

UNESCO date of entry: 13 Sept. 1946
Surface area (km²): 9,596,961
Population 1980 (millions): 956·85
Persons/km² 1980: 100
Rural population (%) 1980: 74·6
Births per 1,000 pop. 1975–80: 21·3
Deaths per 1,000 pop. 1975–80: 7·4
Infant deaths per 1,000 live births: —
Life expect. at birth 1979: 47 years
Pop. growth rate (% p.a.) 1975–80: 1·4

Est. illiteracy rate 15+ (%)
  M: — F: — MF: —
National currency: yuan
National currency per US $ 1980: 1·53
GNP per capita in US $ 1979: 260
GNP per capita real growth rate
  (% per annum): —
% agriculture in GDP 1979: 31
% industry in GDP 1979: 47
of which manufacturing: —

Data Series	1975	1977	1978	1979
Education				
Education Preceding First Level				
1 pupils enrolled	—	—	7,870,000	8,792,300
2 of which female (%)	—	—	—	—
3 teaching staff	—	—	—	294,500
4 of which female (%)	—	—	—	—
Education at First Level				
5 duration (years)[a]	—	—	—	6
6 official age range[a]	—	—	—	7–12
7 gross enrolment ratio (%)	—	—	—	103
8 pupils enrolled	—	140,000,000	146,240,000	146,629,400
9 of which female (%)	—	50	—	45
10 teaching staff	—	—	—	5,381,800

11 of which female (%)	—	—	—	37
12 pupils repeaters (%)	—	—	—	—
13 pupil/teacher ratio	—	—	—	27
Education at Second Level				
14 duration gen. educ. (years)[a]	—	—	—	5
15 official age range gen. educ.[a]	—	—	—	13–17
16 gross enrolment ratio (%)	—	—	—	—
17 pupils enrolled	—	60,000,000	65,483,000	60,248,676
18 of which female (%)	—	40	41	41
19 teaching staff	—	—	—	3,190,884
20 of which female (%)	—	—	—	25
21 pupils repeaters gen. ed. (%)	—	—	—	—
Education at Third Level				
22 students per 100,000 inhabit.	—	65	92	108
23 students enrolled	—	600,000	856,322	1,019,500
24 of which female (%)	—	30	—	24
25 students scient./tech. fields (%)	—	—	32	—
26 foreign students	—	—	—	—
27 teaching staff	—	—	—	236,637
Public Expenditure on Education				
28 total in nat. currency (000)	—	—	—	—
29 of which current expend. (000)	—	—	—	—
30 total as % of GNP	—	—	—	—
31 current expendit. as % current government expenditure	—	—	—	—

continued

Data Series	1975	1977	1978	1979
Science and Technology				
32 stock of university graduates per million inhabitants	—	—	—	—
33 stock of persons with complete second educ. per million inh.	—	—	—	—
34 scientists and engineers in R&D per million inh.	—	—	—	—
35 technicians in R&D per million inh.	—	—	—	—
36 expend. on R&D as % of GNP	—	—	—	—
Culture and Communication				
37 book titles published	—	—	12,493	14,738
38 circulation daily newspapers per 1,000 inh.	—	—	—	—
39 consumption (kg) newsprint per 1,000 inh.	1,263	1,355	1,410	1,392
40 consumption (kg) printing and writing paper per 1,000 inh.	2,162	2,282	2,405	2,375
41 cinema seats per 1,000 inh.	—	—	—	—
42 radio receivers per 1,000 inh. [b]	1·7	—	—	—
43 TV receivers per 1,000 inh. [b]	1·0	1·4	2·7	3·4
44 volumes in public libraries per 1,000 inh.	—	—	—	—

Notes:
[a] The educational structure allows also for other alternatives.
[b] For 1975, number of licences.
Source: Statistical Digest 1981 (Paris: UNESCO, 1981).

6
Education in Japan
Competition in a Mass System

BRIAN HOLMES

The surrender of Japan to the allied powers in September 1945 marked a major turning point in the history of Japan. Against a background of the horrors of Nagasaki and Hiroshima and a devastated school and university system, General Douglas MacArthur and President Harry Truman, as spokesmen of the victorious allies, set out to ensure that a peacful democratic and responsible government would be established in Japan. The re-education of the Japanese people in accordance with acceptable aims was vitally important for the Supreme Commander of the Allied Powers.

Aims

The view of the Americans was that prewar system of education had contributed to ultramilitarism and totalitarianism. Its aims were embodied in the Imperial Rescript on Education proclaimed in 1890, which stated:

Know ye, Our subjects,
Our Imperial Ancestors have founded Our Empire on a basis broad and everlasting and have deeply and firmly implanted virtue; Our subjects ever united in loyalty and filial piety have from generation to generation illustrated the beauty thereof. This is the glory of the fundamental character of our Empire, and herein also lies the source of Our education. Ye, Our subjects, be filial to your parents, affectionate to your brothers and sisters; as husbands and wives be harmonious, as friends true; bear yourselves in modesty and moderation; extend your benevolence to all, pursue learning and cultivate arts, and thereby develop intellectual faculties and perfect moral powers; furthermore advance public good and

209

promote common interest; always respect the Constitution and observe the laws; should emergency arise, arise courageously to the State; and thus guard and maintain the prosperity of Our Imperial Throne coeval with heaven and earth. So shall ye not only be Our good and faithful subjects, but render illustrious the best traditions of your forefathers.

The Way here set forth is indeed the teaching bequeathed by Our Imperial Ancestors, to be observed alike by their Descendants and the subjects infallible for all ages and true in all places. It is Our wish to lay it to heart in all reverence, in common with you, Our subjects, that we may all thus attain to the same virtue.

Before the Second World War filiality, affectionateness, friendliness, modesty, moderation and benevolence were personality traits which were to be developed through education. Further aims included the cultivation of arts, the development of the intellect and the perfection of moral powers. In short, the schools were to ensure the all-round – intellectual, moral and aesthetic – development of individuals. The contexts were first loyalty to elders in the immediate family and then to the state represented by a divine father figure, the emperor. Faith, obedience to the constitution and commitment to the prosperity of the nation were qualities designed to promote the welfare of Japanese society.

These child- and society-centred aims are unexceptional. In most countries both the personal qualities emphasized and the contribution education should make to society would be accepted, indeed applauded. What the allied powers objected to was the way, as they saw it, in which for more than half a century these aims had been interpreted and realized in practice during the extraordinary growth of the Japanese education system since the Meiji Restoration in 1868. For American observers, national well-being had been stressed at the expense of individual development. Obedience rather than freedom of choice had been inculcated.

The postwar period can therefore be seen as one during which new aims have been proposed for education or new interpretations of longstanding aims have been advocated. Central to American thinking was the view that prewar Japan was not democratic and should therefore be democratized and that the divinity of the emperor which legitimized the demand for obedience in hierarchical status and power structures should be denied, making the 'Way of the Emperor' far less important than had previously been the case.

For some years the different interpretations given to the aims of education might be seen as a conflict between American and traditional Japanese views. Certainly US advisers regarded the principles of Japanese moral education (*Shushin*) and even more the Cardinal Principles of the Entity of Japan as abhorrent to their way of life.

Even this broad distinction is too simplistic because before the war the 'liberals' in Japan were not entirely eliminated by the ultramilitarists. Moreover, a distinction should be drawn between the views and policies of prewar army hard-liners and navy leaders. At the same time the normal schools in which most of the elementary teachers were trained were hotbeds of nationalistic fervour and militarism. University teachers were on the whole less militant. In short the American liberalism which had informed institutional proposals made immediately after the 1868 Meiji Restoration was not entirely absent in Japan when the allies occupied the country in 1945 and there were certainly differences of opinion.

Nevertheless, there can be little doubt that the occupying powers influenced the content of the new Japanese constitution and related legislation. They were not, for example, satisfied with the initiatives taken by the Ministry of Education in its Educational Plan for Building the New Japan announced on 15 September 1945, issued a number of directives and clearly had some say in major features of the Fundamental Law of Education 1947 (Law No. 25). The aim of education in the new Japan was stated in Article 1 as:

Education shall aim at the full development of personality, striving for the rearing of the people, sound in mind and body, who shall love truth and justice, esteem individual value, respect labour and have a deep sense of responsibility, and be imbued with the independent spirit, as builders of the peaceful state and society.

Independence of spirit suggests that those who framed this law had in mind concepts of individualism and liberty not vastly different from those held dear by many Americans. It contrasted sharply with Japanese concepts of obedience.

The principle of equal opportunity in education was also stated. Article 3 reads:

The people shall be given equal opportunities of receiving education according to their ability, and they shall not be subject to educational discrimination on account of race, creed, sex, social status, economic postition, or family origin.

Criteria on which previous inequalities of treatment in Japan had been legitimated – sex, social status and family origin – were rejected in the article, which clearly reflected American concepts of equality.

This article left open the question of inequalities in individual learning abilities, thus making it possible for traditional attitudes to prevail in the organization of schools and the promotion of pupils through the system. These attitudes probably allow for intense competition among pupils at all levels in a mass system of education. Debates about the innate abilities of children have not, however, dominated the postwar scene. At the time, American and Japanese beliefs were perhaps not vastly different.

The position of girls and women in Japan has been more controversial but Article 5 of the law stated that:

Men and women shall esteem and co-operate with each other. Coeducation, therefore, shall be recognized in education.

This represents a change in attitude which was also applied more widely. The different position of women in many spheres of Japanese life was abhorrent to the allies, whose aim in the new Japan was to improve the lot of women in accordance with Western criteria of equality. For example, it was held that women should be permitted to seek a divorce and that economically they should enjoy the same rights as men. These and other views were contrary to Japanese traditions, in which women had honourable roles to perform but which, were however, vastly different from occidental rhetoric.

In retrospect it seems that after the war a majority, a high proportion, or some of the Japanese people were able to accept some but not all the principles on the basis of which the allies proposed to create a new Japan. It is impossible of course for anyone, let alone an outsider, to say how many traditional Japanese values were retained and the extent to which overt changes in attitude really modified behaviour patterns.

There is certainly some evidence to show how attitudes in Japan have changed since 1945. Surveys of the Japanese national character have been carried out every five years by a research committee of the Institute of Statistical Mathematics. A nationwide survey in 1975 conducted by the Research Institute for Broadcasting and Public Opinion confirmed the results of the fifth national survey of 1973. Both showed that in the 1970s health, home life and happiness had replaced an earlier emphasis on material success and wealth in the order of priorities. Democracy and liberalism remained the favoured political ideologies. Socialism, communism and Fascism were poor runners up. A pragmatic view that whether a political system was good or bad depended on circumstances represented a move away from dogmatism and an earlier willingness of many Japanese to accept unconditionally the authority of an older, higher-status person.

Against these indicators of change, however, can be placed evidence suggesting that some traditions die hard. Examples have been given of how the behaviour of young radicals is still held to be the responsibility of their parents. Even today individuals may be treated as less than independent agents and their families may be held responsible for their crimes. Failure in an examination shames the candidate and his or her family.

The zeal for education is, however, universal. The aim of parents that their children shall succeed finds practical expression in the many sacrifices they are prepared to make to ensure that their children get into a high-status secondary school or a chosen university. The competitiveness which informs parental (and pupil) behaviour represents a marked change since Jean Stoetzel reported in 1955 on the attitudes of youth in postwar Japan. Such studies of attitudes are revealing but they do not conclusively demonstrate which of the values introduced into Japan after the war have been thoroughly internalized. Certainly there is evidence to show that Japanese children accompanying their parents working abroad who receive some education in a foreign country face considerable problems of readjustment when they return to Japan and seek to re-enter and settle down in the educational system there.

What can be said with more certainty is that the aims of members of the occupying forces were made clear in the directives issued by the Supreme Command Allied Powers (SCAP) between October 1945 and January 1946. They were designed to destroy militarism, the authority of the emperor, and state Shintoism. In particular the aim was to prevent the teaching of Shintoism and moral education (*Shushin*) in schools and to eradicate, through the censorship of textbooks and the screening of teachers, all aspects of ultranationalism. Many Japanese educators, however, aimed at the preservation of the Imperial Rescript on Education, which prewar had been committed to memory by millions of schoolchildren. It was not banned by the allies although its ceremonial reading was not allowed.

It is also clear that some of the educational practices introduced in the light of 'the aims of education' proposed by the United States education mission in March 1946 have survived. Based on respect for the worth and dignity of individuals, the need to provide equality of opportunity in accordance with ability and the requirement that young people should become responsible members of society, the mission made specific proposals about the administration of education, the organization of the school system, curricula and the expansion of adult and university education. Early allied attempts to restructure the school system along US lines, expand higher education and reform teacher education were accepted and built permanently into the system.

Hence some allied initiatives have been carried forward by some Japanese educationists, perhaps in different ways from those proposed immediately after the defeat and more in accordance with deep-rooted Japanese traditions. There has, for example, been a shift from an emphasis on society-centred to child-centred aims and from national Shintoism (a family and state religion) to a belief in and acceptance of the principles of Western democracy. These changes have, to be sure, been opposed and at the same time more radical positions including communism have been advanced by some Japanese themselves as the basis of educational aims.

The context in which educational aims have been debated and interpreted has undergone remarkable material change. Economically Japan has been transformed since around 1951 and now in terms of wealth, industrial output, the magnificence of its modern hotels, the availability of consumer goods and the expansion of its educational system matches the USA and has surpassed many European countries. Not everything has changed. Cheek by jowl with the elegant stores in the Ginza in which the best products of every nation can be bought, there are theatres where Noh and Kabuki plays are performed by actors in traditional garb and watched by women dressed in beautiful kimonos. The obvious differences between old and new institutions and between the cities and villages are staggering. It is against this background that the successes and persisting problems found in the educational system should be assessed.

The two big issues on which the practicalities of educational reform along American lines have turned have been administration and the curriculum. The balance of power between the central, regional and local authorities has been a matter of contention ever since SCAP set out to democratize the system in the belief that local participation and control would promote freedom and independence. Just as contentious has been the content of education, which was seen, in its prewar guise, as denying the inculcation of concepts of liberty and equality. In particular the content and methods of teaching moral education (formerly *Shushin*) became the subjects of violent debate and political conflict. Once USA policy towards Japan changed both these issues became central to the internal politics of education in Japan and reflected the extent to which Japanese educators disagreed among themselves.

At first teachers associated with the Japan Teachers' Union supported American initiatives. Many of them, no doubt disillusioned by the war, were communist sympathizers. Their protest was as much against their former leaders and their support as much for their new masters as ideological. Their objective was to increase the power of the union and weaken or destroy the power of the Ministry of Education

(*Mombushō*). They had the support of SCAP and they went along with American proposals in spite of their political sympathies.

The situation changed when in response to the Soviet threat, as the Americans saw it, Japan as a defeated enemy was transformed into an ally whose economy had to be made viable. At the same time US policy was designed to make Japan an independent bulwark against Soviet aggression. In pursuit of their policies Americans supported the reassertion of central government and power and identified communist 'fellow travellers' as potential enemies, while ostensibly withdrawing from involvement in Japanese domestic affairs. Debate about the aims of education and how they should be realized became increasingly Japanese-centred. On the two issues mentioned, immediate postwar American policies made inevitable a polarization of opinion and a fight for power between conservative (traditional Japanese with its many positions) and radical (communist with Japanese accretions) protagonists.

Administration

Prewar, the administration of the Japanese education replicated that of France in many respects. The post-1868 Meiji government wished to unify both the nation, choosing national Shintoism as an appropriate ideology, and the education system as central to the achievement of this aim. It chose as its administrative model the centralized educational system of France. In the Educational Code of 1872 is found a systematic body of laws regulating all details of organization, finance and administration. Probably the most important feature of the code was the power given, at least by implication, to *Mombushō*, or National Department of Education, later the Ministry of Education. The constitution of *Mombushō* was established in 1871 and revised in 1876. In one category of business the ministry had the power to establish systems of education, draw up regulations raise taxes for the schools and to distribute grants to local districts. At another level the ministry had power to confer degrees, disburse funds, collect and disseminate education and summon conventions of inspectors, school directors and schoolteachers.

An Imperial Ordinance of 1891 gave the Minister of State for Education power to licence, appoint, promote, dismiss and pension school officials. It also regulated the production, supply and content of textbooks and examinations.

As in France, the country was divided into university districts, in each of which was established an imperial university. The power to establish and run elementary schools was delegated to local officials.

Nevertheless, in a highly structured national system of education a great deal of power was placed in the hands of members of the bureaux or directorates in the ministry. The number and functions of these bureaux changed over the period in which the Meiji Constitution of the Empire of Japan was in force, namely from 1889 until a new Constitution was promulgated in 1946 and made effective in 1947. These prewar changes in the organization of the ministry were not intended to affect its power, which remained supreme under the divine and external authority of the emperor and was expressed in detailed imperial ordinances.

This degree of centralized power offended American officials and educationists. A US education mission to Japan under the leadership of Dr George D. Stoddard, which included Professor Isaac L. Kandel as one of its members, reported that it was necessary to clarify the bases of a philosophy of education in a democracy and to 'clothe' the word 'democracy' with 'content'. An appeal was made to the spirit of inquiry embodied in the Charter of the United Nations and in the Constitution of Unesco. In practice the mission recommended that the central ministry should not prescribe textbooks or the content of education and should not lay down methods of teaching. Paradoxically, in a policy statement on the revision of the Japanese education system approved by the Far Eastern Commission in 1947 new objectives and content were prescribed, aspects of prewar content eliminated, the martial arts totally abandoned and the Imperial Rescript was not to be used as a basis of studies or ceremonies in the schools. More important, the Japanese government was to exercise such control over the educational system as to ensure that the objectives of the occupation were achieved. Subject to this overriding requirement the Japanese system was to be decentralized so that parents and citizens could feel responsibility for the achievement of these new objectives.

Democracy apparently depended on the devolution of power and could be realized by the centralized edicts of the occupying powers! Not surprisingly, the policy did not work and gave rise to long, acrimonious and at times vicious battles between the supporters of *Mombushō* and those who, claiming to be democrats, wished to reduce its authority very drastically. In political terms conservative-liberals fought to restore the position of *Mombushō*. The radical-communists, through the Japan Teachers' Union, struggled to ensure that the process of decentralization initiated by SCAP was sustained. Benjamin Duke has described and carefully documented the long-drawn-out conflict in *Japan's Militant Teachers*. Duke prefaces his account by describing the extent to which teachers became involved in the postwar ultramilitarist movement through their training and the growth of Marxist-inspired teacher groups. The latter were in a position in 1946 to establish a lasting teachers' movement before the occupying powers and the Ministry of Education were able to prevent it.

Teachers' union representatives argued that the democratization of education depended on the activities of teachers and not on a ministry which was being asked to reduce its own powers. The American mission was inclined to agree and recommended that teachers, school principals and local heads of schools should be freed from the domination of high-ranking school officials. It reflected SCAP's support of the labour union movement in general. This was soon to change and after 1947, when a unified Japan Teachers' Union was formed, its right to strike was repealed on the ground that teachers were public and indeed civil servants.

At the same time SCAP wanted to extend to towns and villages a school board system. The ministry proposed that school boards should operate only at the prefectural and big city level. SCAP compromised but the teachers actively campaigned to have their representatives elected to school boards and at first supported the view that there should be town and village school boards, but soon, realizing that elections to such boards would be dominated by conservative landlords, went along with a policy of prefectural boards. But American notions about elected school boards were not shared by the communist-influenced Teachers' Union. Although teachers supported by the union won a majority of the seats to which they could be elected, the Ministry of Education never quite lost its power in these early days after the end of the war. The threat of communism and the outbreak of war in Korea in 1950 marked a radical reversal of US and SCAP policies.

Teachers purged in 1946 were rehabilitated. Many others were eliminated during the Red Purge of 1949–50. The reforms introduced by the occupation were re-evaluated. A committee of businessmen and educationists recommended that the power to prepare textbooks and control educational matters should revert to the Ministry of Education. It also recommended that each prefecture and city with more than 150,000 inhabitants should have an appointed school board to supervise local education. A Central Advisory Council was to advise the ministry. Throughout the 1950s most of the recommendations were incorporated into national policy, thus strengthening the power of *Mombushō* and antagonizing members of the Japanese left wing, who rejected most of the recommendations or made proposals designed to ensure that members of the Central Advisory Council and the prefectural and city school boards were elected rather than nominated.

Issues, including the election of members of school boards, became highly politicized and it is difficult simply to identify policies ascribing to members of the ministry one set and to members of the union a different set. In short, whatever was proposed by one side was opposed by the other side. Clearly the power of the central authority was at the root of the conflict and reflected the general politics of post-occupation Japan. Among the weapons used by the teachers were strikes, demonstrations and violence.

Slowly *Mombushō* powers were restored. In 1952 the ministry was given responsibility for educational matters but could not compel boards of education to obey ministerial wishes. Next it was proposed that school board members should not be elected but appointed and boards should be required to obey ministry directives. The School Board Act was passed in 1956. Violence followed.

Student violence in Japan reflected not only an attack on university practices but a protest against a range of government policies. Much of the violence between the teachers and officials was occasioned by government policies which had little to do with the working conditions of teachers but much with party politics. Towards the end of the 1960s, however, the economic position of teachers and their conditions of service increasingly occupied the attention of the leaders of the Japan Teachers' Union, thus reducing the attention paid to highly political issues. Moreover, in 1975 the Japan Communist Party and the Value Creating Society (which formed the Clean Government Association) announced a ten-year accord on 'agreement of views'.

No decisive conclusion to the tension between *Mombushō* and the Teachers' Union over the question of how power should be distributed in the education system has been reached, although a decline from 86 per cent in 1958 to 55 per cent in 1977 of teachers in membership of the Japan Teachers' Union gives some indication of a trend. Suffice it to say that *Mombushō* has regained a great deal of the power it possessed before the Allies nudged the Japanese towards a more decentralized system of educational administration soon after the end of the Second World War, but a more balanced allocation of responsibilities has been achieved.

Today 'on behalf of the people' the administration of education is shared between the national government and local government at prefectural and municipal levels. The Ministry of Education's tasks are to integrate the administrative services at the national level, to promote education at *all* levels and to manage some national educational institutions. The Ministry advises and indeed supervises local authorities and reserves the right to require regular reports, to conduct inquiries and where necessary to insist on changes.

Under a minister, the ministry is responsible to the Prime Minister and ministers of state, who form a Cabinet nominated by the National

Diet. Within the ministry there is a parliamentary vice-minister and a permanent vice-minister. Councils and internal subdivisions of the ministry are responsible to the minister who has links with prefectural boards of education through supervisors and subject specialists who keep the boards informed, offer advice and undertake supervisory duties. In addition these supervisors organize conferences and workshops attended by teachers and prefectural supervisors and are responsible for the publication of guides, manuals and handbooks for teachers. The Agency for Cultural Affairs and its auxiliary organs and the national universities and other educational institutions are responsible to the ministry.

Within the ministry there are a number of directorates which deal with defined aspects of education. During the occupation the ministry was reorganized many times. In 1978 it comprised the following bureaux, departments or directorates:

1 *The Minister's Secretariat* is responsible for personnel, general affairs, the budget, planning and research and statistics.
2 *The Higher Education Bureau* looks after planning, university, technical, medical and teacher education and student affairs.
3 *The Social Education Bureau* is responsible for social, youth, women's and audio-visual education.
4 *The Elementary and Secondary Education Bureau* is responsible for a wide range of activities, including financial and local affairs, kindergarten, elementary, lower, upper secondary, vocational and special education, and for textbooks.
5 *The Science and International Affairs Department* takes care of science, research, libraries, relations with international agencies and foreign exchanges.
6 *The Physical Education Bureau* has under its administration sports, physical education, school health and school lunches.
7 *The Administrative Bureau* has responsibility for private schools, welfare and construction.

The ministry establishes standards and supervisory services, gives advice and makes grants in aid and passes these on to prefecture and municipal boards of education.

Attached to the ministry are fourteen advisory councils. There is a central council for education and councils which advise on individual aspects of education, for example, the curriculum, science, universities, and technical education. The ministry also has links with an agency of cultural affairs which under a commissioner has a wider remit, including the fine arts, religious affairs and the Japanese language.

Prefectures have assemblies and governors. All the members of each prefectural board of education (a superintendent and four other members) are appointed by the governor and the prefectural assembly – a resolution of a controversial issue in favour of appointment rather than election. Each board of education appoints supervisors and social education officers and can establish and manage educational institutions in the prefecture, especially upper second-level schools and special schools. The board supervises municipal and local level school boards, issues certificates to teach, appoints teachers and pays salaries. Prefectural governors have some responsibility for local (prefectural) universities (not the imperial universities), for private first- and second-level schools and for educational property in the prefectures.

The distribution of population in Japan is largely determined by the topography, which has forced people either to crowd together in narrow coastal plains or to live in small isolated areas. As a consequence, in 1977 of the 3,229 municipal boards of education only 21 served populations of over half a million. More than 1,000 boards of education serve populations of less than 8,000 people and a further 1,500 boards serve populations of between 8,000 and 30,000 people. It is not surprising that a major concern among Japanese educators is that children in small isolated rural comunities should receive the same quality of education and reach the same standards of achievement as pupils in the densely populated urban areas.

Each municipality has a mayor and an assembly. The municipal boards have chairmen and some 12 per cent of them appoint supervisors, although very few of the municipalities with less than 30,000 inhabitants have them. The municipal boards perform similar functions at the local level to the prefectural boards, principally in relation to first- and second-level schools and community educational projects. Municipalities may have some responsibility for municipal universities through the mayor's office. Municipal supervisors visit schools and participate in conferences.

Thus the administration of education resembles to a considerable extent the system set up early in the nineteenth century by Napoleon and his advisers. It is of course not significantly different from the systems which are found in many European countries. What makes for interesting and useful comparisons is the degree of power enjoyed by ministers of education in a national government and the power exercised by personnel appointed to positions in the national bureaucracy. What is of particular interest in Japan is, on the basis of deeply ingrained beliefs about the authority of people in terms of their age, seniority and position in the hierarchy, how individuals behave in their day-to-day work. It is not easy, even if they wished to do so, for

Japanese scholars and administrators to be as independent as the Americans hoped they would become. This is particularly the case if independence involves challenging the authority of an older person to whom filial piety and obedience are due or the pronouncements of a person in a senior position. On these grounds it may be supposed that national figures in the administration wield a great deal of authority and can if they desire ensure a uniformity throughout the system which is remarkable if not unique.

For this reason it is possible to see the conflict between the Japan Teachers' Union and *Mombushō* as a clash between personalities each of whom had supporters whose commitment was to a person rather than an abstract ideal or principle. It also helps to explain how, in the event, members of the Ministry of Education and its associated agencies regained power and are able, through the system, to control a great many aspects of education. The structure and organization of schools, for example, is the same throughout the country. Curricula at all levels are laid down nationally, leaving local teachers little freedom to choose what they teach, to experiment with methods of teaching, or to select from a wide range the textbooks they use. The continued expansion of Japanese education, in accordance with national policy, the proportion of the budget and GNP spent on education and the uniformities found in the system suggest that the minister and his staff possess very considerable power and that the status of the minister among his Cabinet colleagues is high.

Finance

In terms of finance, for example, an issue on which all ministers of education have to compete with their colleagues, according to many Japanese and foreign assessments an unusually high proportion of the nation's resources has been made available for education since the Meiji Restoration in 1868. Many observers would attribute to this policy the reason for the transformation of the Japanese economy after 1868 and its rapid growth after 1957. Massive investment in education enabled the nation to build up a reservoir of highly skilled personnel who, in the first instance, were quickly able to rebuild shattered industries when US policy changed. Subsequently the high level of education of the population as a whole helped Japan to challenge the economic dominance of Western industrialized nations and to surpass, on many economic indicators, a high proportion of them.

Investment in education has resulted in the expansion of education at first and second levels so that by 1970 the rates of men and women between the ages of 15 and 64 years of age in receipt of secondary and higher education came close to 50 per cent. The massive growth of higher education has resulted in a well structured and technological labour force. (Parenthetically it should be said that the way in which the workforce is organized and managed in the light of traditional and modern methods has a great deal to do with Japan's successful economic growth.) In 1970, for example, less than 20 per cent of those entering the labour market had no more than a compulsory or lower secondary school education.

The successful investment of resources depends not only on how they are raised but on how they are allocated. Policies determined at the centre may well improve the equality of provision but raise resentment among people who, bearing a substantial proportion of the costs of education, are unwilling, in effect, to subsidize the schools serving less affluent members of the nation. Only a strong sense of nationalism or a powerful central government makes it possible to equalize the allocation of capital, personnel and equipment. As in many other countries the finance of education in Japan is complex and is designed to equalize provision as far as possible while allowing parents to make a direct contribution to the costs of educating their children in accordance with their wishes.

It is a basic legal principle that compulsory education is provided free to pupils. However, parents actually pay something for their children to attend public schools, amounting to about £70 per annum in public elementary, over £100 in lower secondary and nearly £240 in upper secondary schools. About 11 per cent of the total expenditure on elementary schools is met by parents; parents pay around 15 per cent of lower secondary school expenditure and about 23·5 per cent of full-time upper-secondary-school expenditure. Tuition in elementary and lower secondary schools is however free – other costs involve transportation, extracurricular activities and other attendance expenses. Tuition fees are charged for students attending national and local public upper secondary schools which for national schools are the same throughout the country. Fees for prefectural and municipal public schools are not uniform and are fixed by the local authorities. In 1978 the tuition fee in national schools was fixed at 36,000 yen ($177). In local public schools fees varied from 14,000 to 38,400 yen ($56–150), while for private schools the fees charged varies enormously but an *average* figure in 1978 was 151,000 yen ($589) – a vastly greater sum than for public schools. Parental contributions are bound to induce a measure of inequality into educational provision in spite of the uniform curricula which prevail.

Revenue is raised through taxes, loans and receipts from properties by the national, prefectural and municipal authorities. In 1976 the proportions of revenues raised were 47·4 per cent national and 52·6 per cent prefectural and municipal so that roughly half the nation's total expenditure on education comes from national funds. This is in sharp contrast to the situation in the USA where less than 10 per cent of educational expenditure is federal. This difference draws attention to the relative power of the purse and the central government in the two countries.

There are in Japan as elsewhere differences between the ways in which first-, second- and third-level institutions are financed. It is common for elementary schools to be financed locally and for secondary and higher education to be financed from national or federal funds. In Japan nearly all the national government's expenditure is on compulsory and higher education through grants to the prefectures and the universities but a proportion goes to national museums, art galleries and research institutes and as subsidies to private schools. National grants to local authorities are spent on salaries, school buildings, equipment for kindergartens, social education, and to help needy children and children in isolated areas by providing special facilities and part-time and correspondence upper secondary schools. Through a local allocation tax – derived from income tax, corporation tax and liquor tax – the national government distributes grants to local authorities to reduce inequalities. Part of this money is spent on education.

Prefectural funds, including government subsidies, are spent on libraries, prefectural upper secondary schools and schools for blind, deaf and otherwise handicapped children and on municipal schools from kindergartens up through lower secondary schools. Prefectures finance teachers' salaries and with the municipal authorities meet a high proportion of the costs of compulsory and upper secondary school education. Together the local authorities meet two-thirds of the cost of providing facilities and equipment for vocational education. Municipal goverments finance non-salary expenditure and pay for municipal schools, for special education facilities and such services as citizens' public halls.

In general, as might be expected, more than two-thirds of the money spent on education goes into compulsory education; about a fifth is spent on special education, although the cost per pupil in special schools is second only to the *per capita* cost of providing education in technical colleges. About one-fifth of the total national expenditure is spent on private schools. Finally, since 1965 the proportion of national government expenditure has declined in spite of the fact that the power of the Ministry of Education has increased. Basically local government meets more than half the nation's total expenditure on education. Municipal governments finance non-salary expenditure and pay for municipal schools and for special education facilities.

Structure and Organization

The problems created by the reorganization of the school system under the influence of SCAP did not provide serious conflict between the Japan Teachers' Union and the Ministry of Education. The aim of SCAP to democratize the system by massively expanding educational provision was in line with the trends which were initiated after the introduction of a modern education system shortly after the Meiji Restoration in 1868.

In 1875 some 2 million pupils were in elementary schools, 35·2 per cent of the appropriate age group; by 1935 the figures were 10 million and 99·6 per cent and in 1978 there were 11,148,859 pupils in elementary schools, or 99·9 per cent of the age group. Until the postwar expansion the numbers of young people in second-level schools and in higher education were much less. In 1870 there were, in fact, more students in higher than in secondary education, but by 1880 secondary school enrolments had risen sharply to 45,000 while higher education numbers had remained more or less steady at around 8,000. There was no pre-school provision. Some idea of the growth can be gained from the facts that in 1875 only 0·7 per cent of the age cohort was attending secondary education, and 0·4 per cent of the appropriate age group was in universities. By 1935 comparable percentages were 39·7 and 3·0 per cent. The enormous expansion of postwar education is reflected in percentages of 96·2 (10 million in all) and 34·0 (2,260,000) in 1978. By that date almost $2\frac{1}{2}$ million young children were attending pre-school institutions.

During this period of steady expansion the structure and organization of the system emerged. It was more or less on European lines. In 1872 the government made an order organizing the school system in three progressive stages. Elementary schools lasted three years (in 1881), middle schools lasted three years, after which pupils remaining in school moved into one or other of the institutions which constituted the stage of secondary and university education. As in most countries the period of elementary education was lengthened and post-elementary institutions expanded and became more differentiated. Thus by 1900 there were kindergartens, a four-year ordinary elementary school followed by a two-year upper elementary school for a high proportion but not all pupils, and middle schools, girls' high schools, vocational schools, higher schools, colleges, higher normal schools, higher normal schools for women and, of course, at the apex of the structure, Tokyo Imperial University. By 1941 the elementary schools (now national schools) lasted six years and enrolled virtually every child. Higher divisions of the elementary school and a range of middle schools had been created so that there was a wide choice of institutions based on a six-year period of compulsory elementary schooling. Subsequent education was based on selection in which sex, social class origin and achievement played their parts.

The allied occupation brought about major changes. They were designed to expand provision and reduce selection. Soon after the war the period of compulsory attendance was raised from six to nine years. In 1947 the Americans influenced the introduction of a 6–3–3–4 system similar to that which prevails in the USA. The system survived so that now six-year primary (or elementary) schools are followed by three-year junior high schools, which together constitute compulsory education, then three-year senior high schools and colleges and universities which offer four-year undergraduate courses. Into this structure were introduced junior colleges, which provide two- or three-year post-upper-secondary school courses and technical colleges which recruit, into five-year courses, graduates from lower secondary schools. Within this structure well over 90 per cent of children and young adults between the ages of 6 and 17 or 18 are attending some kind of school. Moreover, the fact that in 1978 some 34 per cent of the age group was in higher education suggests that in Japan there is virtually a mass system of education.

From their perspective, however, the Americans regard selection within education, particularly if it is based on social origins, wealth or sex, as perpetuating inequalities. Undoubtedly in the prewar Japanese system transfer from the elementary stage to one of several second-level institutions reflected traditional attitudes towards men and women and the position parents held in society. The prestige schools were, of course, those which prepared boys for university entrance. The existence, in 1941, of girls' high schools, youth schools for girls, and higher normal schools for women suggests that in terms of access to prestige education girls were at a disadvantage. Along with pressure from the allies to equalize their rights in general, more equal access to education for girls was advocated and realized in practice. By 1978 the enrolment by sex was almost fifty-fifty up to the upper secondary school level. Of the age cohort 3–21 the proportions of males and females enrolled in schools was roughly in line with the male–female distribution of the population as a whole. However, while women represented almost 90 per cent of the total enrolment in junior colleges the proportion of women students in universities was just over 20 per cent. Undoubtedly, junior colleges are regarded as 'finishing schools' for women, the universities still to some extent the preserve of men. These figures suggest that the role of women in modern Japanese society is still rather ambiguous and the education they should receive to perform that role is regarded as being somewhat different from that needed by men to prepare them for society.

After the war the second-level vocational schools were abolished, coeducation (as mentioned) was introduced, the normal schools for teachers were converted into universities and in theory selection at the point of transfer from one level to the next was abolished, as in the USA, so that by intention all pupils would move smoothly from one level to the next without facing selective tests.

The status of institutions within the prewar structure could not, however, be equalized by fiat. Prestige universities survived. For many years graduates of the national imperial universities (particularly from the Tokyo law schools) had taken up positions of power in government, the bureaucracy and industry. These graduates constituted, in terms of status and power, a powerful group of leaders. As such they were responsible for many notable achievements between 1868 and 1930. In the 1930s, on the other hand, the normal schools responsible for the training of large numbers of teachers became a source of recruits to the ultramilitarists, who in a successful *coup* brought down the elected government. The distribution of prewar university and normal school graduates among the groups which competed for power in the early postwar period is something which warrants a fuller analysis than is possible in this chapter.

Suffice is to say that postwar attempts to democratize the system of education by extending and equalizing access to it did little to alter the status and position in the hierarchy of the former imperial universities – Tokyo, Kyoto, Kyushu, which either have recently celebrated or are about to celebrate their centenaries. The municipal universities and upgraded normal schools which were able to attract, in a rapidly expanding system, large numbers of students (in the late 1970s some of them were enrolling over 40,000) were never able to challenge the high regard in which the older universities were held. Competition to gain admission to these became, and is, fierce. Overtly success depends upon academic achievement but it should be noted that ability to pay is an important basis of admission to several prestige universities which are private. In Tokyo, for example, Waseda and Keo universities are outstanding private institutions which compete at least in some respects with Tokyo University. Tuition fees in these and in many other less prestigious private universities are, as mentioned, very high in relation to the contribution parents are expected to make to the education of their sons and daughters in public universities.

Since education and qualifications, rather than patronage, are the keys to political and economic success, parents, and particularly mothers, are willing to sacrifice a great deal to give their children a good education. At a very early age children are coached at home so that they may enter a 'good' nursery school. Coaching for examinations on the basis of which admission to a favoured senior high school or university may be achieved is widespread. The fact that parents pay modest fees while their children are in publicly maintained schools also plays a part in selection processes. In spite of postwar intentions these remain extremely competitive and covertly allow traditional influences to operate.

Admission to elementary schools is apparently straightforward. Municipal boards prepare a list of children who can enter school at the age of 6. On the basis of medical examinations some children go to schools for delicate children, others such as the blind, the deaf and the severely handicapped (physically and mentally) are recommended by municipal committees to prefectural boards as in need of special schools. All pupils enter lower secondary schools, spend three years there, and thus complete a nine-year period of compulsory schooling.

Admission to upper secondary schools is rather competitive. It is based on the expressed desire of a pupil and the advice of a school counsellor. Selected pupils sit an entrance examination for the desired schools and lower secondary schools submit reports on individual pupils to the principal of the upper secondary schools for which they have applied. Selection is made therefore on a range of criteria. Success is very important and accepted joyfully by pupils and parents.

Admission to a chosen third-level institution is even more competitive. Again it is based on a student's desire and the guidance of teachers. Applications are made to any number of public and private institutions. Credentials are prepared for each student which include a record of scholastic performance, a statement of behaviour, a profile of health and physical condition, and a record of attendance. Applications are sent from the upper secondary school to the entrance examination boards, which administer a joint achievement test and a second-stage entrance examination. Credentials are also sent to the universities and colleges to which candidates have applied and successful candidates are accepted on the results of the entrance examination by a committee established in each institution. In 1978 nearly half the universities and 67 per cent of the junior colleges did not require an entrance examination for a certain number of applicants recommended by the upper secondary schools.

This system gave rise to multiple applications to favoured colleges and universities and made it necessary for candidates to sit an entrance examination for each application. Within a period of weeks a student may take up to five competitive entrance examinations. In an attempt to reduce the pressure on upper secondary school leavers a national entrance examination was introduced in 1979. The intention was that the number of examinations taken by a student would be radically reduced, hopefully to one national test. Early indications suggested that far from reducing the number of examinations taken the national examination was simply added to those already taken. To be sure, junior colleges have helped to reduce the tremendous pressure on the part of pupils anxious to receive some form of third-level education but their status is much lower than that of major universities. Nevertheless, much is at stake in terms of family honour and indeed in terms of future life chances as students compete to enter a college or university of their choice. Reported suicides as a consequence of strain or failure are frequent. No wonder the situation throughout the system has been described as the 'examination hell'!

There is some reason to believe that girls and women are less involved in it than boys and men. The low proportion of women university students and the types of course they follow in junior colleges suggest that Japanese women are still expected to be good wives and mothers and not to compete for professional, commercial, or industrial jobs. Recent trends indicate, however, that more women are entering teaching, particularly in elementary schools. Teaching was, of course, a largely male and high-status occupation.

Thus while the structure of the educational system is similar to that found in the USA it is operated in somewhat different ways. To be sure, Harvard, Yale, Princeton, Columbia, William and Mary, Chicago and other Ivy League universities enjoy in the USA the same kind of prestige as the national (imperial) universities in Japan. Competition to enter such universities is high but the mass of American youngsters are absorbed into a flexible system of higher education without having to pass rigorous entrance tests. Status remains more important to the Japanese, standards are less variable than in the USA and while there is no doubt that expansion has extended opportunities it is unlikely that the proportion of students from working-class backgrounds has been radically increased.

In both countries the expansion of third-level education has given rise to problems of accommodating graduates in the economy. Japan's revitalized economy could and did absorb more and more highly qualified graduates but eventually in this highly educated society as automation in industry has become a norm rather than an innovation not every graduate is able to find the kind of job he would traditionally have been led to expect. Policy in Japan is, however, based on the premiss that education *per se* rather than specific training benefits the economy. As Japanese commercialism grows it is likely that well educated graduates can be absorbed but it is nevertheless surprising that so many Japanese graduates are willing to work in jobs which previously would have been regarded as unworthy of them.

Curriculum

The ebb and flow of curriculum debate in Japan since 1945 has followed a similar pattern to conflicts over administration. Some members of SCAP held that curriculum reform was vital to the democratization of the country since behind the ultramilitarism of the 1930s could be detected major curriculum defects. In particular they pointed to the position and content of 'moral' education (*Shushin*) – a weekly subject in the curriculum of every school – which through traditional stories and examples was intended to promote loyalty to emperor and nation. Even more offensive to the Americans was the policy statement *Kokutoi no Hongi* (Cardinal Principles of the Entity of Japan), published in 1937, which offered an ultramilitaristic interpretation of traditional codes of behaviour. It was held accountable for the absence of democracy in Japan and for the atrocities which were undoubtedly committed during the Second World War. Certainly they made clear the differences between Western parliamentary democracies and the Imperial Diet and stated that the mission of the Japanese people was to build up a new culture by adopting and sublimating Western cultures so as to sustain nationalism and bring the benefits of the Japanese way to countries in east Asia.

This analysis was not acceptable to all shades of opinion in Japan. One school of thought held that the ultramilitarism of the 1930s had distorted soundly based concepts developed in the Meiji and Taisho periods. These liberal and democratic traditions should be revived and retained as a way of preserving the identity and unique way of life of the Japanese people. Opponents of this view held that the prewar policies pursued by military men had been wrong; they were not willing to accept the legitimacy of the war or their responsibility for Japan's defeat and were relieved when the war ended. Among teachers, as mentioned, there were many who had been educated under the harsh regime of prewar normal schools for teachers where they had been indoctrinated with militaristic ideas. They had not been members of the prewar elite and consequently had little chance to share the more liberal ideals of the Meiji and Taisho democracies. The war and its aftermath persuaded many such teachers that they had been wrong. Guilt and anger drove them to support either the Socialist Party or the Communist Party. They were prepared to give unqualified support to SCAP's 1945 directives, which proscribed *Shushin*, censored textbooks, and dismissed teachers suspected of militarism, and to the American mission's recommendations in 1946. With the help of a Japanese committee the mission recommended that a central authority should not prescribe content, methods of teaching, or textbooks. On the contrary, teachers should be free to develop their own methods and adapt them to the needs of individual pupils. Methods of free inquiry were advocated and examinations which stifled inquiry and created conformity were condemned.

Paradoxically, in view of this recommendation, SCAP effectively replaced *Shushin* in the curriculum by social studies as a way of inculcating civic values and virtues. The Teachers' Union accepted this major change without necessarily understanding what social studies involved or how to teach it. Less radical Japanese educators, while accepting that the values of ultramilitarism were false, maintained that to accept American concepts of democracy would destroy those valuable traditions which gave the Japanese people their identity and unique way of life. The scene was set for a prolonged political conflict between ministry supporters and Teachers' Union leaders over the teaching of morals or civic virtues, the power of the ministry to lay down curricula and the freedom of teachers to devise their own curricula. It should be said, however, that while 'social studies' might make sense to American teachers it represented an innovation with which by training and temperament few Japanese teachers were able to cope. The latter, moreover, were accustomed to following a prescribed syllabus. Both innovations created practical problems as well as promoting politically motivated violence.

Curriculum reform in general became very controversial when in 1951 the Japanese government appointed a committee to evaluate the American inspired occupation reforms and recommended that while the 6–3–3–4 system should be retained more emphasis should be given to vocational studies at the upper secondary stage. This reversion to greater differentiation of content is reflected in the three categories of upper secondary schools which now exist. In the first of these only a general secondary course is provided, in other schools general and specialized vocational courses are offered and in the third type of school training in one or more areas is given.

The reintroduction of vocational courses has been controversial. The differentiated prewar system had been admirably geared to the production of skilled technically trained personnel for Japanese industry. The single line – USA-style – system was criticized by industrialists in the 1950s as failing to supply the trained manpower needed. A ministry survey published in 1957 forecast an over-supply of graduates in law and the liberal arts and a shortage of those graduating from engineering and natural science departments. In 1962, in an education White Paper, a commitment was made to the view that investment in education was fundamentally important to the growth of the economy. From then on priority was given to the training of scientists and technicians. This policy had its most obvious

effects at the level of higher education, so that by 1978 more than 40
per cent of students enrolled in the universities were following courses
other than in literature and the social sciences and nearly 25 per cent
of the students in junior colleges were following teacher training
courses and 27 per cent home economics. At the same time, however,
nearly 70 per cent of the pupils in upper secondary schools were still
following general courses, only 10 per cent were on technical courses
and less than 5 per cent were on agriculture and fisheries courses.

Attempts on the part of the Ministry of Education to reintroduce
'moral' education was even more fiercely resisted by leaders of the
Japan Teachers' Union. By 1956 social studies could occupy more
yearly hours on instruction in the seventh grade than mathematics and
science and in the third grade the yearly allocation could be twice that
for mathematics and science. In their successful attempts to moderate
the position held by the union nothing illustrates better the care
Japanese educators have taken to retain what was well understood and
revered in the prewar system while adapting it to postwar aspirations
and conditions than the reintroduction of moral education based on a
new concept of the ideal person.

Towards the end of the 1950s the late Professor M. Hiratsuka, then
at Kyushu University, devised a comparative education research
project in which he and several senior colleagues actively participated.
An interdisciplinary team – a psychologist, a sociologist, a philosopher,
a historian and a curriculum studies administrator – drew up attitude
tests and a schedule of interview questions for teachers in Japan,
Germany, England and France. Their intention was to compare
systems of moral education in the four countries in order to improve
their own system. In the event they decided that in the prewar system
of Japanese moral education too much attention had been paid to
belief in, and behaviour in accordance with, the status of persons and
not enough attention had been paid to the legitimizing power of
'principles' which could be internalized.

Doubltess this research had some influence on the establishment by
the Central Advisory Council on Education in 1966 of a new moral
code to be taught in schools. A comparison of this new code, *Dotoku*
and *Shushin*, based on the Imperial Rescript of 1890, is very
instructive. The aims of *Dotoku* were to foster a respect for humanity,
a desire to create a unique democratic society and the will to
contribute to world peace. The content of courses designed to create
this 'new man' and promote this ideal image were spelled out in some
detail. The order in which items appeared is in sharp contrast to that
established in *Shushin*. In that document filial piety and family
obligations came first, followed by virtues such as thrift, trust,
generosity, and hard work. Finally *Shushin* was expected to develop

respect for the law and to promote a wish to contribute to society. First on the *Dotoku* list of attitudes appropriate to the ideal human being were the values of life, health and safety, followed by principles relating to appearance, language, respect for property, punctuality, freedom and justice. Family relations and love of country came low in the hierarchy of desirable attitudes. There is nevertheless a blend of the old and new in this fundamental document, the basis of courses in 'moral' education which are now compulsory in elementary and junior secondary schools.

At the same time social studies is retained as a subject in the elementary and lower secondary schools and modern society, Japanese history, world history, geography, ethics, political science and economics are grouped together in the upper secondary school curriculum as 'social studies'. This solution to a problem raised by American initiatives immediately after the war reflects the outcome of a battle between the Teachers' Union and the ministry which was as fierce as that over the distribution of administrative power. It shows the extent to which the ministry's view has prevailed but at the same time illustrates how far American innovations have been incorporated into a traditional system.

Revisions in the content of moral education and particularly in the emphasis placed on the principles which inform it reveal the extent to which suporters of the ministry took the criticisms made by SCAP seriously, and in the light of international trends, adapted traditional Japanese values to meet postwar circumstances.

Another issue has been debated among educators interested in the content of Japanese schools. SCAP officials and members of the American mission were not used in the USA to curricula being prescribed by an agency of the federal government. State laws in the USA may lay down that some subjects must be taught and court decisions have prevented the teaching of other subjects but, while textbooks may to a large extent determine what is taught, in principle curricula are drawn up by schoolteachers in individual schools. Progressive curriculum theory justifies a core of subjects based on the problems young people are likely to meet and a choice from among a small or large number of options or electives. As a result of American pressure more flexible timetables were introduced into the Japanese system.

For example, in 1956 subjects in the elementary schools were grouped as Japanese language and mathematics, on which about 40 per cent of the time was spent; social studies and science occupied between 20 and 35 per cent of the time; music, drawing and homemaking between 20 and 25 per cent; and physical training 10 per cent. Minimum and maximum yearly school hours were laid down for the required and optional subjects in the lower secondary school. The variation was considerable. Between 175 and 280 hours of Japanese could be taught in the seventh grade (first year of lower secondary school); the ranges for mathematics and science in the same grade were 140–75 and 105–75 respectively. As stated, social studies could occupy as many as 315 hours in the third grade, or twice as many hours as for mathematics or science. Moral education as a separate subject was proscribed.

Less choice, a greater emphasis on so-called traditional basic subjects and the reintroduction of a special course of lessons in moral education characterized the revision of curricula at all levels under the influence of liberal-minded Japanese educators who perhaps retained a deep-rooted nostalgia for some aspects of a prewar system which had been built up over more than half a century. They set out to correct some of the excesses introduced when control gave way to freedom, centralization to decentralization and uniformity to diversity. The present system is neither prewar nor yet immediately postwar in its characteristics, nor is it simply a compromise of the two.

On the whole curricula are laid down by the Ministry of Education. They are based on respect for independent initiatives made by schools and recognition of the differing abilities and aptitudes of individual students. The curriculum in an individual school must comply with ministry standards, however. Thus in the elementary school 70 class periods per year are set aside for special activities, which include class assemblies, club activities and classroom guidance and such others as may be fixed by each school. In the lower secondary school between 105 and 140 periods are allocated to elective subjects and 70 to special activities. A standard number of 35 hours is allotted to music, fine arts, health and physical education in the third grade of the lower secondary school and 105 hours are given over to a foreign language in each of the other grades. Most schools offer instruction in the English language.

The same principle applies in the case of upper secondary school curricula, which are based on the course of study issued by the Ministry of Education, Science and Culture. The 'Course of Study for Upper Secondary Schools' was revised in August 1978 and put into effect in April 1982.

It is possible, within these principles of curriculum determination, to describe the content of education at each level of schooling. Lower down the system less choice is available. So in kindergartens the prescribed content of education includes health, social life, nature, language, music and rhythm and art and craft in classes which last four hours a day for 220 days of the year. Although in elementary schools each school organizes its own curriculum in the light of local conditions, it is based on a ministry-issued course of study, which prescribes the subjects to be taken and the number of hours each of them has to be studied. The regular subjects in the elementary school curriculum are: Japanese language, social studies,arithmetic, science, music, art and handcraft, homemaking and physical education. Moral education again occupies a special place. Each year 35 lessons are provided in the subject – about one a week. Special activities, such as school and class assemblies, club activities, ceremonies, cultural performances, school excursions and so on occupy 35 lessons a year for the first three years and then rise to 70 per year. The emphasis in the curriculum is heavily on Japanese language, arithmetic and physical education. As the number of lessons increases in the upper grades the same balance is maintained.

In all three grades of the lower secondary school, Japanese language, mathematics, social studies, science, industrial arts or homemaking, health and physical education receive greatest attention, although music and the fine arts are included in the required subjects. Moral education continues to be a required subject.

A compulsory core of subjects has to be studied by all upper secondary school pupils: Japanese language, social studies, mathematics, science, health and physical education and art. In addition young women must study general homemaking and students in specialized vocational courses must study their specialized subject for some 37 per cent of the time. Home rooms and club activities must also be provided. Outside the compulsory subjects a choice can be made from subjects grouped under Japanese language, social studies, mathematics, science, arts and foreign languages. Each course is allocated a number of credits in the light of the number of 50-minute lessons taken in that subject over the three-year courses. Hence a degree of specialization is possible at this level of schooling. The distinction drawn between males and females is, however, worthy of note. The range of specialized vocational courses is also impressive. It includes commercial, technical, agricultural, fishing, domestic arts, fine arts, science, mathematics and others.

The US credit system operates in upper secondary schools (and indeed in higher education). Thirty-five units of school hours, approximately a lesson per week, yield one credit. Each of these class periods last 50 minutes. Four credits are the maximum allocated to any subject in the upper secondary school course. Some indication of the emphasis placed on subjects is given by the allocation of 4 credits to Japanese language I and 4 to Japanese language II, 4 to classics, 3 to modern Japanese and 2 to Japanese expression. Altogether 19 credits of mathematics (including algebra, basic analysis, differentiation and integration, probability and statistics) can be acquired and

26 in the natural sciences. In each area, however, only 4 credits in Japanese language I, mathematics I and science I are required. A minimum of 80 credits is required for graduation from upper secondary school.

In elementary and lower secondary schools a similar system operates but with less choice and specialization. More than 90 per cent of the elementary school course is laid down and about 80 per cent of the lower secondary school curriculum is prescribed in school hour units. One unit school hour in the elementary school is a class period of 45 minutes; in the lower secondary school it lasts 50 minutes.

To many observers the re-establishment of 'moral' education, the reintroduction of vocational courses and the re-emphasis on laid-down curricula in basic subjects might suggest that the problems created by curriculum proposals made by SCAP and the American mission have been solved in Japan simply by a reversion to type and to forms of control similar to those which existed before the Second World War. There is, of course, evidence to suggest that this has indeed happened and that curriculum content and control is more Japanese than American. On closer examination, however, it is apparent that in the face of problems created by postwar proposals Japanese educators, as in the past, have adopted and adapted principles from outside their country and, blending them with their own traditions, devised uniquely Japanese solutions.

Teacher Education and Higher Education

The status of a teacher has always been high in Japan. *Sensei* (teacher) is still a greatly respected term but in real economic and social terms the position of teachers has changed considerably in the past hundred years. Between 1878 and 1887 some 80 per cent of the students attending teacher training schools came from *Samurai* families. By the end of the Meiji period in 1912 and thereafter a majority of students in normal schools was from non-*Samurai* families.

In the 1930s these potential teachers, who strongly supported the ultranationalists, claimed that teaching was a holy profession. Teachers were indoctrinated with nationalistic and semireligious beliefs and as students in normal schools participated in military exercises as part of their training. A series of economic depressions made teaching in the 1930s an occupation which offered security, so that provided teachers were loyal to emperor and state they were, in comparison with others, well looked after. At the same time some teachers were critical of contemporary Japanese education but did not criticize the ministry. Out of these two minority movements emerged after 1945 a powerful Marxist-oriented Japan Teachers' Union and a group of liberal teacher-educators joined by university graduates who had never succumbed to the same extent to the ultramilitarists.

The postwar conflicts between the Japan Teachers' Union and the Ministry of Education have been discussed in the sections on administration and curricula. They undoubtedly affected the status of teachers as a group. Until leaders of the union turned their attention to salaries, pensions and conditions of work, teachers' salaries were modest. In six years between 1972 and 1978, however, teachers' salaries were increased by 30 per cent. The differentials between university, upper secondary school and lower secondary school and elementary school teachers are between 10 and 15 per cent on national scales. These take into account the grade and length of service of teachers and are formulated in the Law Concerning Compensation of Employees in the Regular Governmental Service.

Welfare benefits include medical care, childbirth expenses, sick allowance and funeral expenses. Retirement annuities and lump-sum retirement allowances are part of the long term benefits. Up to 70 per cent of the final teaching salary can be made available as a pension.

Thus conditions compare favourably with those enjoyed by teachers in most industrialized countries. Indeed, as in some countries teachers in the many very isolated areas receive special allowances if they teach multigrade classes. They also receive accommodation to encourage them to serve in the 22 per cent of elementary schools and the 17 per cent of lower secondary schools which are designated as in isolated areas.

Elsewhere class sizes are relatively high, as in most countries, reducing in size as children move up through the system. Again class size is regarded as an important criterion of quality and is in the process of being reduced.

At the same time the training of teachers for all types of school has been unified, the period of training increased and the provision of in-service education expanded. Certification requirements vary, however, with school level. For example, teachers receive a certificate to teach all subjects in elementary schools but are authorized to teach specified subjects in the lower and upper secondary schools. Regular certificates are either first- or second-class. Holders of the latter can teach only as assistants and the legal and economic differences between the two classes are great. Temporary certificates, for example, are for three years; regular certificates are for life. Although certificates are issued by prefectural boards of education, regular certificates are valid in all prefectures while temporary certificates are valid only in the issuing prefecture.

The pattern of courses available to intending teachers are rather similar to those in the USA. First-class certificates for kindergarten, elementary and lower secondary schoolteachers and temporary certificates for upper secondary schoolteachers are granted to university graduates who have completed a university bachelor's degree in which a prescribed number of credits in teaching subjects and professional subjects has been obtained. The number of teaching subject credits is high for upper and lower secondary schoolteachers' certificates – amounting to nearly 90 per cent of the course. For elementary and kindergarten teachers the balance is different – rather more than 30 per cent of the credits must be in teaching subjects, the rest in professional subjects. This position is similar to requirements in many industrialized societies but the emphasis on teaching subjects for lower second-level teachers is probably greater than for some teachers in England or the USA.

First-class certificates for teachers in upper secondary schools are granted only to teachers with a master's degree gained on the basis of credits in which teaching subjects overwhelmingly predominate in the requirements.

Teachers with second-class certificates in schools other than the upper secondary schools have followed a two-year post-upper-secondary school course. Such courses lead to temporary certificates for upper secondary schoolteachers. Thus for the most part teachers in Japan are graduates – a situation desired in many countries and most obviously exemplified by the USA.

Higher-level certificates are obtained on the basis of additional coursework leading to more credits and a period of teaching. In-service training is provided in universities and enterprises. Prefectural boards of education offer courses in educational centres and in workshops and study meetings; grants in aid are made by the Ministry of Education, Science and Culture to support these in-service facilities.

Teachers are appointed to municipal schools as an outcome of the results of examinations administered by the prefecture. They apply to the municipal board of education, which calls for references. Applicants for jobs in prefectural schools apply to the prefecture board of education which calls for references and administers admission examinations before appointing successful applicants.

As stated, no more than 55 per cent of teachers were members of the Japan Teachers' Union in 1977 compared with 86 per cent in 1958. More than a quarter are not members of any union in spite of the fact that the unionization of teaching has helped teachers to recover economically and regain some of the prestige and status they enjoyed when they were principally drawn from the *Samurai* class. In a country where age, sex and status remain important the overt success of the educational system depends, perhaps more than elsewhere, on the public image of members of the teaching profession. In terms of this worldwide problem the Japanese system has succeeded as well as most and better than many in maintaining, in a mass system of education, a high status for its teachers.

The growth of higher education in Japan has kept up with most, and outpaced many, rates of expansion throughout the world since 1945. In 1978, if the two junior colleges are added to designated universities, there were almost a thousand institutions enrolling almost 2^14 million students. As stated, a high proportion of students in junior colleges are women. The distribution of students in terms of enrolments in universities by field of study shows that as in many countries expansion has been most obvious in the social sciences. Forty-one per cent of university undergraduates were enrolled in the social sciences in 1978, followed by engineering with just less than 20 per cent and 13 per cent in the humanities.

In contrast only 9 per cent of the students in junior colleges were studying social sciences; 27 per cent, however, were enrolled in home economics and more than 24 per cent in education and teacher training. The last figure should be compared with the 10 per cent enrolment in education and teacher training at universities. The comparison suggests that while many more teachers are trained in the universities a high proportion receive their training in junior colleges. The balance of studies in universities and junior colleges suggests that while the vocational orientation of the junior colleges is more pronounced neither type of institution prepares personnel for the labour market.

Technical colleges offer five-year courses which include a general education component (humanities, natural science, social science, foreign languages and health and physical education) and a professional education component which occupies more than half the total credits required. These institutions play an important role in the preparation of skilled personnel but a widely held view in Japan is that the generally high level of education acquired by a very high proportion of the population has been most important in the economic development of the country.

In terms of the internal organization and management of universities the earlier models were drawn from Europe. They persist, so that in spite of the *de jure* position of the Ministry of Education Japanese academics enjoy a good deal of academic freedom and autonomy. Traditions, however, die hard and age overtly plays a very important role in the respect accorded to academics within institutions and by laymen outside them. Academic affairs, consequently, more than in many countries, are dominated by the revered elder professor who, frequently, after retiring from the national university is invited to become president of one of the many private universities. The success of the system depends on the care with which young academics are chosen and trained by senior professors. Dangers lie in the extent to which a 'person' rather than a principle is the source of knowledge and legitimizes it. Clearly the two approaches can be reconciled but disagreement may lead to violent personality clashes; agreement may lead to a lack of criticism of positions advanced by persons in authority. The resolution of the dilemma posed by the tension between moral obligation, in traditional Japanese terms, and international concepts has been more difficult in the political than in the economic spheres of activity. In higher education in Japan as elsewhere student unrest in the late 1960s made clear that it is by no means certain that in future conflicts in higher education will be resolved along traditional lines.

Some Concluding Thoughts

The case of Japan is an excellent example of how, from a recent historical perspective, the problem-solving approach in comparative education can be applied. The surrender of the Japanese forces in 1945 was dramatic. The changes introduced by SCAP were less obvious but nevertheless profound. The surrender and its legislative aftermath did not transform the profoundly held beliefs of the Japanese people, who were for some time expected to operate political and educational systems with which they were not familiar. Two examples have been mentioned to illustrate how attempts were made to introduce in practice Western ideals against a background of deeply held Japanese beliefs and practices.

The Americans proposed to introduce coeducation in spite of the long-held attitudes of the Japanese that a women's main duty was to be a good wife and mother. The desire among some Japanese to send their children to single-sex schools lingers on and is reflected in the desire among young Japanese women to learn those traditional domestic arts for which they are famous. The popularity of tea ceremony training in private schools and homemaking courses in junior colleges and the persistence of flower arranging as a feminine accomplishment are examples of this desire.

A second example is found in the traditional dilemma which faces individuals in Japan. Should they obey their conscience or an older high-status person? Much of the conflict observed in the internal affairs of Japan between supporters of the Ministry of Education and supporters of the Japan Teachers' Union can be simply (perhaps too simply) explained by examining the extent to which both groups were willing to follow respected leaders who could not compromise.

The resolution or partial resolution of conflict situations in Japan over the past thirty years provides evidence of great value to comparative educationists who are interested in the success of policies to identified problems in a very specific national setting. Japan is still a nation in which the people are intensely conscious of their national origins and justly proud of their aesthetic, intellectual, moral and economic achievements. They are also determined to avoid the mistakes of the past and to become accepted members of a world community. The development of education under the influence of Japanese educationists illustrates the extent to which the problems they faced, while common to many countries, had a very Japanese flavour and the solutions they proposed have been uniquely Japanese. The outcomes of these attempts cannot be predicted but it is to be hoped that they will not include a revival of the ultramilitarism which came as a culmination of developments which followed the Meiji Restoration.

Further Reading

Don Adams, *Education and Modernisation in Asia* (Reading, Mass., and London: Addison-Wesley, 1970).

R. Adey, *Innovation in Science Education* 2nd UK/Japan Science Education Seminar, 1980, London (London: British Council, 1981).

R. S. Anderson, *Japan: Three Epochs of Modern Education*, Bulletin No. 11 (Washington, DC: US Office of Education, 1959).

H. Azuma in collaboration with the Japanese Ministry of Education, *Innovation in Inservice Education and Training of Teachers: Japan* (Paris: OECD, Centre for Educational Research and Innovations, 1976).

E. R. Beauchamp, *Learning to be Japanese* (Hamden, Conn.: Linnet Books, 1978).

J. M. Bowman, I. Hideo and T. Yasumasa, *Educational Choice and Labour Markets in Japan* (London: University of Chicago Press, 1981).

T. Brameld, *Culture, Education and Change in Two Communities* (London: Holt, Rinehart & Winston, 1968).

W. K. Cummings, *Education and Equality in Japan* (Princeton, NJ: Princeton University Press, 1980).

W. K. Cummings, 'The problems and prospects for Japanese higher education' offprint from Lewis Austin (ed.), *Japan the Paradox of Progress* (New Haven, Conn., and London: Yale University Press, 1976), pp. 57–87.

W. K. Cummings, I. Amano and K. Kitamura, *Changes in the Japanese University* (New York: Praeger, 1979).

R. P. Dore, *Education in Tokugawa Japan* (London: Routledge & Kegan Paul, 1965).

B. C. Duke, *Japan's Militant Teachers* (Honolulu: University Press of Hawaii, 1973).

B. Groombridge, *Adult Education and Television (Canada, Czechoslovakia and Japan)* (London: National Institute of Adult Education with Unesco, 1966).

R. K. Hall, *Education for a New Japan* (New Haven, Conn.: Yale University Press, 1949).

Hiroshima International Seminar on Higher Education, *Perspectives for the Future System of Higher Education* (Hiroshima: Hiroshima University, 1977).

B. Holmes, *Problems in Education* (London: Routledge & Kegan Paul, 1965).

B. Holmes, 'Education in Japan' (London: Stevens, 1979), reprinted from the *Year Book of World Affairs*, vol. 33, pp. 126–47.

B. Holmes, 'Education in the Soviet Union', in E. Ignas and R. J. Corsini (eds), *Comparative Educational Systems* (Itasca, Ill.: Peacock, 1981), pp. 235–83.

Japan Ministry of Education, *Japan's Growth and Education*, the 1962 White Paper on Education (Tokyo: Ministry of Education, 1963).

Japan Ministry of Education, *Educational Standards in Japan*, the 1964 White Paper on Education (Tokyo: Ministry of Education, 1965).

Japan Ministry of Education, *Educational Policy and Planning: Japan*, reports prepared by the department with recomendations of the Central Council for Education (Paris: OECD, Directorate of Scientific Affairs, 1973).

Japan Ministry of Education, *Education in Japan* (Tokyo: Ministry of Education, 1971).

Japan Ministry of Education, *Outline in Education in Japan* (Tokyo: The Bureau, 1977).

Japanese National Commission for Unesco, *The Role of Education in the Social and Economic Development of Japan* (Tokyo: Ministry of Education, 1966).

H. Kato, *Education and Youth Employment in Japan* (Berkeley, Calif.: Carnegie Council on Policy Studies in Higher Education, 1978).

A. Kloskowska, G. Martinotti and W. K. Cummings, *Education in a Changing Society* (London: Sage, 1977).

T. Kobayashi, *Society, Schools and Progress in Japan* (Oxford: Pergamon, 1976).

K. Moro-Oka, *Policy and Development in OECD Member Countries: Japan (Recurrent Education)* (Paris: OECD, 1976).

M. Nagai, *Higher Education in Japan*, trans. J. Dusenbury (Tokyo: University of Tokyo Press, 1971).

K. Narita, *Systems of Higher Education: Japan* (New York: International Council for Educational Development, 1978).

OECD, *Reviews of National Policies for Education* (Paris: OECD, 1971).

H. Passin, *Society and Education Japan* (New York: Columbia Teachers College Press, 1965).

D. T. Roden, *Schooldays in Imperial Japan* (London and Berkeley, Calif.: University of California Press, 1980).

N. Shimahara, *Adaptation and Education Japan* (New York: Praeger, 1979).

N. Shimahara, *A Japanese Minority and Education* (The Hague: Nijhoff, 1971).

J. Singleton, *Nichu, A Japanese School* (New York: Holt, Rienhart & Winston, 1962).

R. Tames, *The Japan Handbook (A Guide for Teachers)* (Tenderden, Kent: Paul Norbury, 1978).

E. F. Thurley, *Understanding and Perceptions of London School Children of Japanese Society* (London: Japan Foundation Research Project, 1978).

D. R. Thurston, *Teachers and Politics in Japan* (Princeton, NJ: Princeton University Press, 1973).

E. F. Vogel, *Japan as Number One* (London: Harvard University Press, 1979).

D. F. Wheeler, *The Structure of Academic Government in Japan* (New Haven, Conn.: Yale University Press, 1976).

Organizational and Statistical Appendix

Japan

Agencies of Administration

NATIONAL Nation.

Statutory National Diet, Ministry of Education, Science and Culture, Minister, Parliamentary Vice-Minister.

Advisory Councils, auxiliary organs, quasi-governmental organizations.
National Research Institutes.
International Education Activities.
Supervisors, subject specialists.

REGIONAL Prefecture.

Statutory Prefectural assembly and governor's office (governor).
Board of Education (chairman, members, superintendent, Secretariat).

Advisory Supervisors.

LOCAL Municipality.

Statutory Municipal assembly, municipal mayor's office (mayor).
Municipal Board of Education (chairman, members, superintendent, secretariat).

Advisory Supervisors.
Teachers.

The Structure and Organization of the Educational System (1978)

Age	Level and stage	Types of institution	Number of institutions	Enrolments
	Level 4	Private and national universities offering 2 or more years for master degrees and 5 or more years for doctorate	(Included in level 3)	
22	Level 3 Stage 2	1 Private and national universities offering bachelor degree courses covering Stages 1 and 2 lasting 2–4 years.	433, nearly a half private	1,862,262, over three-quarters private
	Stage 1	1 Junior colleges – 2, 3, 4 or more year courses. 2 Technical colleges offering 5 year courses from 15 years of age	519, mostly private See Level 1, Stage 1.	380,299
18+	Level 2 Stage 2	1 Prefectural, private and municipal upper secondary schools. Full-time, part-time, and correspondence courses lasting 3, 4 or more years.	5,098, mostly local	4,415,074, almost 80% local

Age	Level	Description	Schools	Students
15	Level 2 Stage 1	2 National and private technical colleges offering 5-year courses.	64, mostly national	46,636
		Municipal lower secondary schools offering a 3-year course. A small number of private and national schools exist. (Entry to technical colleges level 3 stage 1 possible after completion.)	10,777	5,048,293
12	Level 1	Municipal elementary schools. Admissions at the age of 6, providing a 6-year course. A small number of private and national schools exist.	24,826	11,146,859
6 5				
3	Pre-school	Private and municipal kindergartens. Courses last 1, 2 or 3 years. Age of admission 3, 4 or 5.	National 500 Local 4,500 Private 8,500 Total 16,227	2,497,730

The Progress of Pupils through the School System

Age and admission and transfer procedures

Pre-school   Application by parents. School admits.

First level   *Elementary school* Municipal boards prepare a list of schools, children undergo medical examinations, municipal board notifies parent which school child should attend, parents apply to national or private school or schools, after admission the name of the school is reported to the municipal board. Advisory board may recommend school or refer child to a school for delicate or handicapped children.

Second level

Stage 1   *Lower Secondary School* Procedures as for elementary school.

Stage 2   *Upper Secondary School* Parental and pupil wishes taken into account. Principal of lower secondary school prepares pupil record and submits credentials to principal of upper secondary school applied for. Pupils sit entrance examination appropriate to desired school. Selection made by upper secondary school.

Third level   *Junior Colleges, National and Private Universities*

Stage 1
1   Student wishes and teachers' guidance taken into account.
2   School record prepared and sent to institutions to which applications have been made.
3   Entrance and joint achievement test administered for national and local public universities.
4   Entrance examination for junior colleges and private universities.

Fourth level   *Universities* Entry to postgraduate courses is based on qualifications and opinion of admitting universities.

Curricula

Pre-school Health, social life, nature, language, music and rhythm, art and craft. (220 days a year, 4 hours per day.)

First level *Elementary*

Stage 1 Japanese language, social studies, arithmetic, science, music, art and handicraft, homemaking, physical education, moral education, special activities. (Course of Study for Elementary School (1980)).

Stage 2 850 rising to 1,015 periods per year of 45 minutes' duration.

Second level *Lower and Upper Secondary Schools*

Stage 1 *Lower Secondary* Japanese language, social studies, mathematics, science, music, fine arts, health and physical education, industrial arts or homemaking, moral education, special activities, elective subjects (Course of Study for Lower Secondary School 1981)). 1,050 class hours each year, lasting 50 minutes.

Stage 2 *Upper Secondary* Japanese language (language, expression, modern classics), social studies (modern society, Japanese history, world history, geography, ethics, political science and economics), mathematics I and II (algebra and geometry, base analysis, differentiation and integration, probability and statistics), science I and II (physics, chemistry, biology, earth science), health and physical education, arts (music, fine arts, handicraft, calligraphy), foreign language (English), domestic arts (general homemaking) (Course of Study for Upper Secondary Schools, (1982)). 35 periods per week of 50 minutes' duration.

Third level

Stage 1 *Junior College, Technical College and Universities* General education, foreign languages and a range of professional subjects and electives.

Stage 2 *Universities* Longer overall course with some subjects.

Fourth level *Universities* 30 credit hours in professional subjects.

Teacher Education and Training

Type of Institution	Qualification awarded	Level of school in which teacher can teach
Upper secondary school	Upper secondary school diploma	Pre-school
Junior college	Kindergarten teacher certificate (temporary and second-class)	
University (depending on qualification sought)	Bachelor's degree (first-class certificate)	
Upper secondary school	Temporary certificate and upper secondary school diploma	Elementary
Junior college	Second-class certificate teaching and professional subjects First-class certificate	Elementary
College and university	Bachelor's degree First-class certificate	Elementary
Upper secondary school	Diploma Temporary certificate	
Junior college	2-year post-secondary-school course (second-class certificate) Teachers and professional studies	Lower secondary school
University	Bachelor's degree (first-class certificate) Teachers and professional subjects)	
University and teaching experience	Master's degree (first-class certificate) Teachers and professional studies	Upper secondary school

UNESCO Statistical Information: Japan

UNESCO date of entry: 2 July 1951
Surface area (km²): 372,313
Population 1980 (millions): 116·78
Persons/km² 1980: 314
Rural population (%) 1980: 21·8
Births per 1,000 pop. 1975–80: 15·1
Deaths per 1,000 pop. 1975–80: 6·3
Infant deaths per 1,000 live births 1977: 9
Life expect. at birth 1979: 76 years
Pop. growth rate (% p.a.) 1975–80: 0·9

Est. illiteracy rate 15+ (%) 1980
  M: 0·5 F: 0·5 MF: 0·5
National currency: yen
National currency per US $ 1980: 203·00
GNP per capita in US $ 1979: 8,810
GNP per capita real growth rate
  (% per annum) 1960–79: 9·4
% agriculture in GDP 1979: 5
% industry in GDP 1979: 42
of which manufacturing: 30

Data Series	1975	1977	1978	1979
Education				
Education Preceding First Level				
1 pupils enrolled	2,292,591	2,453,687	2,497,895	2,486,604
2 of which female (%)	49	49	49	49
3 teaching staff	93,853	102,587	106,332	109,328
4 of which female (%)	88	86	88	88
Education at First Level				
5 duration (years)	6		6	6
6 official age range	6–11	6–11	6–11	6–11
7 gross enrolment ratio (%)[a]	99	99	99	101
8 pupils enrolled[a]	10,280,642	10,735,927	11,065,096	11,629,110
9 of which female (%)[b]	49	49	49	49

continued

Data Series	1975	1977	1978	1979
10 teaching staff[a]	402,553	419,958	432,222	462,343
11 of which female (%)[b]	55	55	58	57
12 pupils repeaters (%)	—	—	—	—
13 pupil/teacher ratio[a]	26	26	26	25
Education at Second Level				
14 duration gen. educ. (years)[c]	6	6	6	6
15 official age range gen. educ.	12–17	12–17	12–17	12–17
16 gross enrolment ratio (%)[a,d]	91	93	91	90
17 pupils enrolled[a,d]	8,795,346	9,111,661	9,090,491	9,480,878
18 of which female (%)[b,d]	50	49	48	49
19 teaching staff[a]	502,946	520,342	529,162	541,374
20 of which female (%)	25	26	26	26
21 pupils repeaters gen. ed. (%)	—	—	—	—
Education at Third Level				
22 students per 100,000 inhabit.	2,017	2,150	2,129	2,091
23 students enrolled	2,248,903	2,436,862	2,432,052	2,422,915
24 of which female (%)	32	33	33	33
25 students scient./tech. fields (%)	28	—	27	27
26 foreign students	14,485	—	15,006	5,194
27 teaching staff	191,551	—	206,131	213,000
Public Expenditure on Education[f]				
28 total in nat. currency (000,000)	8,156,673	10,332,439	11,692,710	12,787,107
29 of which current expend. (000,000)	5,826,604	7,262,222	7,932,421	8,636,769
30 total as % of GNP	5·5	5·5	5·7	5·8

31 current expendit. as % current government expenditure	—	—	—	—
Science and Technology				
32 stock of university graduates per million inhabitants	36,991	—	—	—
33 stock of persons with complete second educ. per million inh.	147,058	—	—	—
34 scientists and engineers in R&D per million inh.g	3,548	3,576	3,548	3,608
35 technicians in R&D per million inh.g	825	771	734	719
36 expend. on R&D as % of GNPg	2·0	2·0	2·0	2·1
Culture and Communication				
37 book titles published	34,590	40,905	43,973	44,392
38 circulation daily newspapers per 1,000 inh.h	526	546	555	569
39 consumption (kg) newsprint per 1,000 inh.	18,670	20,353	21,277	21,824
40 consumption (kg) printing and writing paper per 1,000 inh.h	23,332	26,061	29,116	31,936
41 cinema seats per 1,000 inh.h	10·1	8·4	8·2	8·2
42 radio receivers per 1,000 inh.	520	571	775	777
43 TV receivers per 1,000 inh.i	237	242	242	245
44 volumes in public libraries per 1,000 inh.h	534	516	—	—

continued

252 *Equality and Freedom in Education*

Notes:
[a] Including special education in 1979.
[b] Including special education.
[c] The educational structure allows for another alternative.
[d] Including part-time education in 1979.
[e] Including correspondence courses.
[f] Not including public subsidies to private education.
[g] Not including social sciences and humanities in the productive sector.
[h] Data for 1975 refer to 1974.
[i] Licences.

Source: Statistical Digest 1981 (Paris: UNESCO, 1981).

Index